PENGUIN BUSINESS

Management Worldwide

David J. Hickson is Emeritus Professor of International Management and Organization at the Bradford University School of Management, England. He holds a Swedish Honorary Doctorate, is the first Honorary Fellow of the European Group for Organizational Studies, was a Fellow of the Netherlands Institute for Advanced Studies and was Founding Editor-in-Chief of the international research journal *Organization Studies*. He has lectured at leading business schools worldwide, and has published extensively.

Derek S. Pugh is Emeritus Professor of International Management at the Open University Business School. He is an Academician of the Academy of Learned Societies in the Social Sciences and an Honorary Fellow of University College, Northampton. Professor Pugh has published 15 books and over a hundred papers on management topics for both academic and management audiences, including *Organization Theory: Selected Readings* (fourth edition, 1997) for Penguin.

Pugh and Hickson also co-author the bestselling *Writers on Organizations* (first edition, 1964; current fifth edition, 1996).

Management Worldwide

Distinctive Styles Amid Globalization

NEW ENHANCED EDITION

David J. Hickson and Derek S. Pugh

PENGUIN BOOKS

PENGUIN BOOKS

Published by the Penguin Group
Penguin Books Ltd, 80 Strand, London WC2R 0RL, England
Penguin Putnam Inc., 375 Hudson Street, New York, New York 10014, USA
Penguin Books Australia Ltd, 250 Camberwell Road, Camberwell, Victoria 3124, Australia
Penguin Books Canada Ltd, 10 Alcorn Avenue, Toronto, Ontario, Canada M4V 3B2
Penguin Books India (P) Ltd, 11 Community Centre, Panchsheel Park, New Delhi – 110 017, India
Penguin Books (NZ) Ltd, Cnr Rosedale and Airborne Roads, Albany, Auckland, New Zealand
Penguin Books (South Africa) (Pty) Ltd, 24 Sturdee Avenue, Rosebank 2196, South Africa

Penguin Books Ltd, Registered Offices: 80 Strand, London WC2R 0RL, England

www.penguin.com

First published in 1995
Second Edition 2001
2

Set in ITC Officiana and Adobe Minion
Typeset by Rowland Phototypesetting Ltd, Bury St Edmunds, Suffolk
Printed in England by Clays Ltd, St Ives plc

This book has been written in the hope that it will, within its own field at least, aid its readers to better see others as those others see themselves, and to better see themselves as others see them. Especially we wish this for the youngest generation of our families, Benjamin, Christopher, Daniel, Danit, Gilad, Jessica, Joshua, Kezia, Nicholas and Philip, who will be among the future citizens of a shrinking world.

Contents

List of Box Illustrations

Preface to the Second Edition

This new edition of *Management Worldwide* has been updated, expanded and, we hope, clarified, with the benefit of fresh published research and writing. As before, chapters showing how contrasting cultures bear upon managing and organizing are followed by seven chapters which describe the approach to management in seven principal culture areas of the world. They give examples of countries with each culture, which should be read together with the general cultural description that begins the chapter. This second edition adds three more exemplifying countries, Hungary, Indonesia and South Korea.

A single book could not possibly include more than a selection from around the globe. If any readers do not find a portrayal of management features in a particular society in which they are interested, we hope the broad characterizations of management and organizations in different types of cultures will provide them with a starting point from which to search further. Indeed, the book as a whole should be regarded as a series of starting points from which to move on to greater depth.

The book germinated in the cross-fertilization of teaching and research. In research, it began many years ago when the results of our own comparisons of organizations between even such relatively similar societies as the American, British and Canadian demanded a cultural explanation. In teaching, it began when the discussion of management and organization with multinational, multi-ethnic groups of MBA students at Bradford Management Centre demanded ever more mutual awareness of cultures. It continued in the writing of learning material for management courses of the Open University.

We, its British authors, view the world from a grey-green island in one of its far northern corners. Strive though we may, we cannot eliminate any latent bias in our treatment of management worldwide which may arise from our cultural and geographical perspective; indeed, we are by definition unaware of it. We hope that those from cultures other than our own who read this book will forgive us our inadequacies. All readers should beware of adding their own biases to ours.

We owe a debt to all the authors from many lands on whose work we have drawn for this book. And to more besides, since we have listed only the most accessible material for further reading. The overwhelming bulk of relevant research is published in English, a language which gives the widest international accessibility. But, as with all languages, it carries its own subtle linguistic idiosyncrasies and variations of meaning in relation to others. Like other authors using sources in this field, we cannot avoid that limitation; we can only warn about it.

We owe thanks to numerous colleagues and friends worldwide who have personally helped us with advice, articles, examples or secretarial skills. They include: Saleh Alqahtani, Lamya Al-Zubaidi, Jonathan Ariel, Hamid Attiyah, Runo Axelsson, Koya Azumi,. Karoly Balaton, Chris Barkby, Peter Blunt, Richard Butler, Jack Butterworth, John Child, Hazel Crabb, Dagmar Ebster-Grosz, Anne-Wil Harzing, Sally Heavens, Adrian Hickson, Bob Hinings, Dezso Horvath, John Iredale, Arzu Iseri, Alfred Kieser, Witold Kiezun, Pat Knowles, John Konrad, Sarabajaya Kumar, Sunil Kumar, Ran Lachman, Cornelis Lammers, Chang-Won Lee, Philip Martin, Hafiz Mirza, Ashar Munander, Beto Oliveira, Taneji Sakai, Gill Sharpley, Oded Shenkar, Milo Shott, Paul Smith, Peter B. Smith, Monir Tayeb, Cas Vroom, Pam Waterhouse, Susan van der Werff, Gilbert Wong, Yoram Zeira, and Librarians at Bradford Management Centre – Jenny Finder, Michelle Phillips and Peter Newsome. To everyone else from whom we have learned or by whom we have been helped, we also say thank you. Where our book falls short of what might be, we are responsible.

Finally, in words we first wrote together many years ago, it is our wives, Marjorie and Natalie, who 'suffered most in the cause'. It is to their forbearance and support that we again owe most.

David Hickson
Derek Pugh
Summer 2001

| **Managing with Wide Horizons**

Box 1.1 Bookstall at Heathrow

They sat there, the three of them. They eyed each other occasionally, but they did not know each other. It was quite a time to their separate departures from Heathrow airport, and each was bored. She had allowed for the London traffic but it had not been too bad, so now she had time on her hands before the Stockholm flight. He had almost three hours between arriving from Frankfurt and leaving for Shanghai with his colleague from the London office, who had not yet arrived. The third traveller awaited her student friends. They were headed for what they anticipated as a wild fun week in sunny Spain to get over the exams. They were to meet two hours before the flight and she was there first.

Though Stockholm would be new to the first traveller, it had not occurred to her, or her Project Manager, that she might need preparation for Sweden. It wasn't far. It wasn't Asia. Browsing the bookstall while she bought a newspaper, she noticed a colourful cover with *Management Worldwide* on it. She flicked the pages and was surprised to see something on Sweden. Realizing that she knew nothing at all about the managers she would meet, she bought a copy. Its other contents were intriguing and would fill empty evenings.

The German traveller awaited his colleague joining him for the long flight to Shanghai with resignation. He knew it well. Maybe an English language novel would help, if his language was up to it. Alongside the fiction shelves he noticed a book on management. Yes, it was reasonably easy reading. More surprising, it had a section on management in China with historical and cultural background, which might help him understand better what was going on there. And also Japan, if he had to go on to their associated firm in Osaka. There was nothing equal to this published in German. He bought a copy.

Her fellow students had still not arrived. She bought a magazine. Her eye was caught by some business books. Now there was one she had seen on the reading list for next year's international business course. It was called *Management Worldwide*. It looked interesting and easy enough to dip into during the summer. She could buy her own copy at a Penguin book price, so she did.

One by one, the three copies took off worldwide.

The world is getting smaller, figuratively speaking, but horizons are getting wider, especially managerial horizons. The three travellers portrayed in Box 1.1 are typical. Managers at all levels in all countries have more and more contact with their counterparts elsewhere, and students of management must prepare for this. Managers travel to appraise new equipment, different management practices, potential investment opportunities. They may find themselves under foreign ownership, working in joint ventures with foreign companies, and spending portions of their careers as expatriate managers. They phone, fax or e-mail their counterparts in other lands, and receive visits from them.

Their personal experience is part of the enormous growth of international trade and finance in the twenty-first century. This has been facilitated by a non-economic factor, the emergence of a language that is the first to approach being a world language, English. It is used not only by those for whom it is a natural first language, but also by those who wish to communicate and do not know each other's languages yet who each speak English as a second language. For instance a Japanese management group visiting Argentina who do not speak Spanish but who can talk with their hosts in English. It is the language of air traffic control worldwide, and of international finance. Other languages are or have been spoken by large numbers of people as a consequence of differing forms of empire, including Latin (from the Roman empire), Mandarin (from the Han Chinese expansion across what is now the People's Republic), Arabic (from Islamic conquest of the Middle East and North Africa), Spanish (from colonization of South America), and Russian (from the dominance of surrounding peoples by both Tsarist and Communist Russia). None have attained the relative universality of usage brought to

English by the British empire's most vigorous offspring, the United States, having become the twentieth century's superpower just as that empire was fading away. Moreover, this was at the epoch of truly worldwide travel and communication. Inevitably, therefore, English was the first language in which this book is printed.

MANAGEMENT WORLDWIDE

Contemporary forms of organization and the problems of managing them are new in scale and detail, but not in kind. They have arisen before in the ancient civilizations. A time-honoured case of executive overload is described in Box 1.2. In long-ago China, India, Egypt, Israel, Greece and Rome, the dilemmas of governance, of commanding armies, of controlling religions and of administering commerce would be recognizable today in their fundamentals. To centralize or decentralize, to direct or delegate, to exclude or consult, to specialize or broaden, to formalize rules or leave to discretion, to reward or penalize ('stick or carrot'), to inform or keep one's own counsel, to accentuate or diminish hierarchy. And so on. These managerial dilemmas, and more, were all there for those in charge of building Egyptian pyramids, guiding Jewish tribes in search of a territory, regulating Greek city-states, resisting invading Mongol hordes, or constructing the administration of Christianity, which resulted in the world's largest and most long-standing organization, the Roman Catholic Church.

The greater prevalence of these dilemmas now is due to the **Industrial Revolution** more than to anything else, for, as it spread outwards from its origins in England and Western Europe, it spawned the enormous proliferation of organizations which cover the world today. Banks and builders, superstores and shipping, military and mosques, hotels and hospitals, farming and fruit, energy and education, organizations do everything that conceivably can be done by mobilizing the abilities and energies of numbers of people. They are now engulfed in a second revolution, the **Information Revolution**, whose electronic technologies are generating, storing and communicating vastly more information for them far faster than ever before.

Economic, political and social conditions must be propitious for industrialization, of course. Two cultural elements on opposite sides of the northern hemisphere have been singled out as giving it a particular impulse. First was what has been called the **Protestant Ethic** of north-western Europe. From the sixteenth century onwards, the churches here – furthest from Rome – 'protested' at and broke away from Roman Catholic dominion. They laid responsibility for conduct and for its rewards in any after-life more on the individual and less on the Church. The Christian believer was held to account directly to the Deity, and did not need the Catholic priestly hierarchy as an intermediary on his or her behalf. Nor could that hierarchy forgive transgressions and so 'wipe the slate clean' here on earth. This encouraged an abstemious, or at least not profligate, lifestyle, which demonstrated virtue by hard work and success in the hope of heavenly riches to come. The consequent worldly achievement accumulated savings, financial capital. Thus effort and wealth together spurred on capitalist industrialization.

This much-debated but broadly supported thesis is now paralleled by a very similar thesis about the societies of the western Pacific rim. Their equally spectacular success in industrializing manufacture during the second half of the twentieth century has been partly attributed to the residual latterday **Confucian Ethic**. The persisting influence on Asian outlook of the fifth-century BC Chinese sage, Confucius, who promulgated a way of life resting on mutual loyalties and duties in a stable social order, has been held to explain in some degree the social cohesion and thrift accompanying Asian economic prowess. This (also much-debated) thesis is examined more fully in Chapter 7.

After two revolutions and two ethics, finally two tensions must be singled out. Both recur throughout this book. First is the tension between **Private Interest** and **Public Interest**. How far should the owners and the managers of organizations be left free, within basic legal limits, to pursue what ends they will, and how far should they be constrained or directed by some wider public interest? Can private interest be more than self-interest? Does State planning and regulation, in what is conceived of as the public interest, unavoidably take decisions out of the hands of those directly responsible for management and, by taking away decision-making autonomy, remove also the essential initiative? How much of each? Different countries take different stances on such issues. Currently they are paramount issues in East-Central Europe and China especially, as comes through in Chapters 6 and 9.

Box 1.2 The Overloaded 'Executive'

Management processes basically have changed little over time, and this will remain so. They differ less from period to period than from part of the world to part of the world, and even from country to country . . . Because management is always about people, its essence is dealing with human nature. Since human nature seems to have been extremely stable over recorded history, the essence of management has been and will be equally stable over time.

So argues the Dutch researcher Hofstede who has exceptional experience of comparing management worldwide. He instances a widely known case:

A group of refugees, about ten thousand strong, follow their charismatic leader in search of a safe haven. A powerful friend sends a consultant to help them. The consultant notices that the leader tries to handle all problems and conflicts of people himself. People queue up before his office; because he is overworked, he cannot handle all the business. So the consultant has a private talk with the leader and tells him to structure his organization by delegating authority: to nominate able men as managers of thousands, hundreds, fifties, and tens. Candidates should be selected not only on their leadership abilities but also on their character: they should be law-abiding, truthful, not driven by material gain. The management structure should resolve all daily issues at the lowest possible level; only the big and difficult issues should be brought before the leader. He should focus on strategy – on dealing with the supreme authority, on establishing new rules and laws and teaching these to the people, on showing them the way to go and the work to be done. The case states that the leader listens to the consultant and carries out the re-organization which is a success, and the consultant returns home.

Asian readers think that this a is a reference to the Long March of Chairman Mao. The refugees in this case, however, were Israelites and their leader was Moses, and he led them from Egypt to Israel. The Supreme Authority was God, and the consultant, Jethro, was Moses' father-in-law – a fact which definitely helped in making Moses listen to him. The case is codified in the book Exodus of the Old Testament of the Bible (Exodus 18:13–27). It is one of the oldest source books of Western civilization, recognized by Judaism, Christianity, and Islam alike. The migration is supposed to have taken place in the 12th century BC, over 3,000 years ago . . . Many problems in modern management are not so modern at all; they are basic human dilemmas, and every generation anew has had to cope with them.

(from Hofstede 1999, pp. 34–5)

Second is the tension between relatively **Impersonal** and **Personalistic** modes of management. This is most pronounced in Africa, Arabia, India, Asia and South America, and therefore pervades Chapters 7, 8 and 9, and also 4. The 'Tale of Two Cultures' in Box 1.3 is a clash between the more impersonal, task-focused, Western approach and the more personal, relationship-focused, Middle Eastern approach. This shows in the world-wide struggle that can be seen in country after country to reconcile traditional features of life in developing economies with Western-derived models of management. Western models take for granted procedures in which appointments are made, authority is exercised, jobs are allocated, pay is arranged, and rules are applied, impersonally, at least in principle if not always in practice. That is, what you can do matters more than who you are. Everyone, every person, is to be treated the same way without special preference. The word 'impersonal' does not mean that everyone is aloof and unfriendly – though that may also be so, and it certainly appears so to some visitors from other societies – rather it means that the *system is run impersonally*, without favour.

Attempts to emulate this in developing, industrializing countries frequently run counter to existing more 'personalistic' ways of life. Here personal respect is due to each because of whom he or she is, inside work as well as outside. Friends and relatives matter, friends of relatives matter, and relatives of friends matter, as do those with the wisdom of age; and obligations to them do not cease at an organization's door-way. How could it be possible to separate off one section of daily life, working life, as if it had nothing to do with the rest? How could people with whom there were personal relationships one minute outside work be treated impersonally just like anyone else half an hour later? Must a helping hand to friends, family, ethnic group or tribe become nepotism? Must respect for seniors become hierarchical rigidity, must generosity become bribery? Have the Japanese or Chinese or other societies found an alternative way? Or is Western-style impersonalism in every aspect of management an unavoidable condition of effective modern organization?

Box 1.3 A Tale of Two Cultures

The British project manager waited in his office in the English Midlands for the arrival of his Egyptian counterpart, who had said he would make his own way from Heathrow airport. They were to finalize and sign a contract to instal control equipment in Egypt.

The Egyptian watched London slide by beneath him as the plane came in, anticipating an enjoyable trip to strengthen personal relationships and, moreover, see some of his family there. His deputy, a European, was in charge back home, as he was much of the time. His own role, as he saw it, was keeping contacts 'warm' in Egyptian circles as well as abroad. He had never been interested in the practicalities of engineering, ever since his family had despatched him to study for a foreign engineering qualification against his inclinations.

His relations ran a small hotel in central London, and he phoned from there to ask the British manager to pick him up. It puzzled him that the voice on the phone seemed surprised.

Indeed, the British owner of the voice was taken aback to be suddenly asked to drive so far. Why had his visitor not made full and firm travel arrangements beforehand?

Then the Egyptian did not want to go straight to the Midlands, but rather via a 300 mile excursion to another supplier's premises, where he shook hands and took a number of photographs of personalities and plant. Next day he did likewise at his host's Midlands location, and then flicked through the bulky contract documents before leaving.

After he had gone, his British host, tired from almost 600 miles' driving, frustrated by being unable to pin the talk down to engineering issues and get firm answers, was astounded to discover that there was no actual signature to the contract and, worse, that a series of clauses seemed to have been queried despite weeks of prior negotiations. This meant more delay. Thoroughly exasperated, he went to see his main board director.

As London slid away beneath the Egyptian visitor, he felt he had had a successful visit. Personal contacts had been renewed and he had photographs to prove it. He had put back the start of work sufficiently for his own staff – who were some months behind – to be ready for the British. He had managed to do this without any face-to-face argument or rudeness. This would also make it more likely that the money might be ready, despite a third of the credit having been switched last month to another project which fitted new priorities. His host had presented him with nothing more than a road map book, but that was the British for you.

As for that host, the final irritant had been seeing the visitor walk off with the map book from his company car, just as if it had been given to him.

(from the experience of a British business contact of the author's)

DISEMBODIED ORGANIZATION THEORY

Alongside the growing international and intercultural experience of managers themselves, the scholarly effort to describe, analyse and explain organizational behaviour is also coming to pay proper attention to the multitude of influences from societal culture. The worldwide tension between impersonal and personal approaches is just one consequence of cultural differences that is plain to see. There are many more.

One way to see the situation as it has been is shown in Box 1.4. This lists seventy-one 'writers on organizations' who have been included in successive editions of our book with that title since it was first published in 1964 to its fifth edition in 1996/97. The principal contribution of each is summarized in the book in a few pages. The book is a continual 'top of the pops' of authorities on organization and management, each edition bringing in the rising stars and dropping out those whose lustre is fading. It embodies a judgement of who has produced the most distinctive and widely used ideas, and has become the longest existing public record of 'writers on organizations', past and present. They personify this field of study as it is and as it has been for a century. Who are they?

The large majority, forty-eight, are Americans, with fifteen Britons, two Canadians, two Frenchmen, two Germans, one Dutchman and one Indian. The huge Anglo predominance of Americans, Canadians and Britons is no surprise since the study of management and organization accelerated first in these societies, even though its origin is attributed to Weber, one of the two Germans, and Fayol, one of the two Frenchmen. Nor is it surprising that all are from among the richer societies where research could be financed and freedom of ideas was encouraged. But for these reasons, all are Westerners even (in his academic persona) the sole Indian, Ghoshal, who works in Britain and the U.S. Vitally, almost all are unaware of their 'Western-ness'.

True, Weber did see in different societies and different historical periods the conditions from which impersonal (bureaucratic) organization was arising. True, Crozier took a step forward when he attributed his findings to peculiarly French cultural elements. True, Hickson in the Aston Group with Pugh began the attempt, with various colleagues, to explain what is and is not due to national cultures.

Box 1.4 'Great Writers on Organizations'

Argyris	Herzberg	Pugh (and the Aston
Bakke	Hofstede	Group)
Barnard	Jaques (and the	Schein
Bartlett & Ghoshal	Glacier	Schumacher
Blake & Mouton	Investigation)	Senge
Boulding	Kanter	Silverman
Braverman	Lawler	Simon
Brown	Lawrence & Lorsch	Sloan
Burnham	Likert & McGregor	Tannenbaum
Burns	Lindblom	Taylor
Chandler	March	Thompson
Crozier	Mayo	Trist (and the
DiMaggio & Powell	Michels	Tavistock Institute)
Drucker	Miles & Snow	Urwick & Brech
Etzioni	Mintzberg	Vickers
Fayol	Morgan	Vroom
Fiedler	Ouchi	Weber
Follett	Parkinson	Weick
Galbraith	Peter	Whyte
Gouldner	Peters & Waterman	Williamson
Handy	Pettigrew	Woodward
Hannan & Freeman	Pfeffer & Salancik	

Authorities included since 1964 in one or more of five editions of *Writers on Organizations*, by Pugh and Hickson (5th edition published in Britain by Penguin Books, 1996, and in the United States by Sage, 1997). All are collected in one volume, *Great Writers on Organizations: The Second Omnibus Edition*, published by Ashgate, 2000.

But only two out of the seventy-one writers fully consider how management is affected by the cultures of different countries. One is the Japanese-American, Ouchi, known for his comparison of management in the American and Japanese cultures. The other is the Dutchman, Hofstede, author of the most extensive study of 'culture's consequences' (the title of his major book) whose ideas figure prominently in our next chapter.

Apart from these, most of the others were apparently unaware of the extent to which their ideas might be culture-bound. Can it be accident that, working from within orderly German society, Weber espied orderly bureaucracy, that years of being a manager in hierarchical French society led Fayol to extol unity of command, that the Americans assume individualistic competition within impersonal systems? Hofstede, too, has asked these challenging questions.

The bulk of what has been written and taught about management has been and is from a Western, mainly Anglo, standpoint. Every reader of this book, from West or East, North or South, has to be aware of that, and to join the authors in trying to see beyond it.

THE THEME OF THIS BOOK

This book is about how far and in what respects the cultures of societies around the world play a part, together with other influences, in shaping how organizations are set up and run. What is the approach in southern (Latin) Europe, and why? Or in Asia or Africa or Arabia, and so on across the globe.

Culture, in the wide sense of the term that is intended here, shapes everything but does not determine everything. It is an insoluble conundrum how to disentangle its influence from that of other factors. Fundamentally this is an impossibility, since culture colours all that is done. Every manager is a person in a society, who has been formed by a society or societies, and so the processes of managing and organizing are ultimately not separable from societies and their cultures. Worse, it is difficult to say exactly what is meant by 'culture', to pin it down so as to examine it closely. Yet to learn to recognize it and its features in practice is a powerful aid to mutual understanding. Though indistinct, it forms a powerful means of explanation.

The next chapter, Chapter 2, considers management-relevant culture. It shows how five broad features of management – managing authority, managing others, managing oneself, managing uncertainty, and managing time – differ from society to society as basic cultural values differ. Primary characteristics of culture and management in many countries are compared.

Having thus begun with two general chapters, this and the next, the book ends with two more. Like the present chapter and Chapter 2, they are general in so far as they do not concentrate on particular societies but deal with issues common to all. Chapter 10, 'The Cross-Cultural

Manager', examines what faces the expatriate who moves from working in one society to work in another, probably in a multinational corporation: the problems of personal adjustment, the opportunity, and the chance of failure. The final chapter, Chapter 11, deals with the overriding question for both manager and scholar: which way are things moving? Are cultural differences being eroded, so that managing and organizing are becoming more and more the same everywhere (the convergence argument); or are cultural characteristics resisting this pressure?

The bulk of the book, Chapters 3 to 9, describes and analyses the characteristics of societies around the world. As far as possible, societies with cultural features in common are grouped together. These seven chapters cover the Anglos, the Latins, the Northern Europeans (and Israel), the East-Central Europeans, the Asians, the Arabs, and Developing Countries. Each begins with a short historical and socio-political introduction, because neither a culture nor an approach to management can be understood without some awareness of the nature of a society. Each then gives a general picture of the culture, and the managing and organizing typical of the peoples concerned, where possible following the framework given in Chapter 2: managing authority, managing others, managing oneself, managing uncertainty, and managing time. There follow portraits of the cultural and managerial characteristics of some typical countries, which illustrate both what is shared by all those covered in the chapter and aspects that are particular to themselves.

As in this chapter, evidence and examples are highlighted in Boxes, with the chapter number and consecutive numbering within each chapter for easy reference. Sources are listed in full at the end of each chapter.

The chapters vary in the depth to which they can go. On some areas of the world, some societies, some nations, material is abundant. On others, pertinent research is scanty and evidence is thin. Indeed, on very many nations of the world there is still no available direct information about their approach to management and organization which can be relied upon.

Despite that, it would have been possible to say much more in many of these chapters, sometimes very much more. The cost of attempting to come as near as possible to a world view in a single volume has been to risk superficiality. Further, any selection must be a bias, emphasizing what is selected and diminishing what is not. The danger is of stereotyping, especially where the available information is limited; that is, an over-simplified picture is drawn that verges on caricature. Hopefully that danger has been avoided; but if it has not, then it should always be kept in mind that, though any individual manager will have something of the characteristics described, no individual will have them all to the same degree. Within what makes people recognizable to others as culturally similar, all individuals are unique in themselves. So are organizations.

This book, then, takes the view that some knowledge is better than none when mutual understanding is the aim. It does so on condition that this knowledge is treated as *relative*, and that this book is read in that light. To avoid becoming wearisome the words 'comparatively' and 'relatively' are not repeated endlessly throughout the text, but they are always implicitly there. For it is possible to see how things are done in Society A only because by comparison they differ in Society B. Then the gain, even from a stereotype, is greater than the risk.

Further Reading

Adler, Nancy J. 1997. *International Dimensions of Organizational Behaviour*. 3rd edn. South-Western College Publishing.

Clegg, Stewart R. 1990. *Modern Organizations: Organization Studies in the Post-modern World*. Sage.

Hofstede, Geert. 2001, 2nd edn. *Culture's Consequences: Comparing Values, Behaviors, Institutions and Organizations Across Nations*. Sage.

—— 1994. *Cultures and Organizations: Software of the Mind*. HarperCollins.

—— 1999. 'Problems Remain, But Theories Will Change: The Universal and the Specific in 21st Century Global Management'. *Organizational Dynamics*, Summer edition, 34–44.

Pugh, Derek S. and David J. Hickson. 1989. *Writers on Organizations*. 4th edn. Penguin and Sage.

—— 2000. *Great Writers on Organizations: The Second Omnibus Edition*. Ashgate.

Wren, Daniel A. 1994. *The Evolution of Management Thought*. 4th edn. Wiley.

Other Sources

Clegg, Stewart R. and S. Gordon Redding (eds.), assisted by Monica Cartner. 1990. *Capitalism in Contrasting Cultures*. De Gruyter.

Hickson, David J. (ed.). 1993. *Management in Western Europe: Society, Culture, and Organization in Twelve Nations*. De Gruyter.

Osigweh, Yg., Chimeze A. B. (ed.). 1989. *Organizational Science Abroad: Constraints and Perspectives*. Plenum Press.

Ronen, Simcha. 1986. *Comparative and Multinational Management*. Wiley.

Weber, Max. 1984. *The Protestant Ethic and the Spirit of Capitalism*. Allen & Unwin, 1930; Peter Smith, 1984.

Managing and the Cultures of Societies

This chapter examines the notion of societal cultures that is basic to understanding how the differing cultures of differing societies shape the ways in which organizations in them are set up and run.

Where can culture be found? The simple answer to that is: everywhere, everywhere that people can be found. How can it be recognized? The answer to that is not so easy, for there is a sense in which the culture of a society cannot be pictured of itself, but only by comparison with other societies. Each of us is largely unaware of the culture in which we have been reared and educated and have gone on into adult life. We have been moulded by cultural socialization to be the kind of people we are: we eat certain things in certain ways; we regard our families in certain ways; we give instructions to others in certain ways, commandingly or permissively; we join in meetings with others in certain ways, punctually according to the clock or not so; we relate to others in certain ways, assertively or more considerately; and we rarely notice these and a myriad other culture-induced characteristics of what we do.

Not until we come up against what someone else does which is different. Box 2.1 tells of the discomfort of one of the authors in such a situation. Even then we are inclined to blame the peculiar ways of the other person, their odd culture, rather than our own! Yet it is in 'culture-shock' that we experience what the culture of a society has created, when we are not among our own kind and things happen differently. We go to work in another land for a while and things happen at unexpected times – unexpected to us, that is – or people treat casually what we regard as important, or show disrespect when we feel respect is due. At an extreme, it is possible for an 'expatriate' posted abroad to feel so disorientated, so confused, that the job cannot be finished satisfactorily and he or she has to give up and return home.

It is possible to feel this sense of strangeness in our own lands, too. Hardly any nations even approach cultural homogeneity. Each includes peoples with differing cultures. The minorities make this most obvious: French-Canadians in Canada; people of Puerto Rican or Italian or Mexican origin in the United States; or of Arab origin in France; or of Pakistani origin in Britain; or Basques in Spain, Kurds in Iraq, Tamils in Sri Lanka. Examples are endless.

Box 2.1 How to Get Fat on Business

The business lunch is commonplace in the Western world for those whose jobs take them to such tables. Indeed, mutual entertaining is a fundamental feature of building personal relationships in all societies, including working relationships. Even if a language barrier prevents conversation over a meal, the food can speak for itself.

One of the authors was being so entertained to a lavish meal by high-ranking officials. The table groaned, as the (Western) saying goes. No sooner was one dish consumed than another appeared. The cuisine was delicate and delightful. It was of a Northern Chinese variety, for this enchanting scene was in Beijing.

Happily our author munched his way through helping after helping. But there came a time when he was not so happy. His stomach was beginning to groan like the table. It was full. Yet the food continued to cascade upon his plate. Struggling clumsily with his chopsticks, he wondered with growing desperation what to do. How might he stop eating? Every time he finished a helping another was heaped upon his plate before he could stop it. Eventually he managed to convey somehow that enough was enough, politeness crumbling under necessity, and he stumbled away.

Only afterwards did this son of an English Protestant Christian home, where the proper thing to do is to eat every morsel on your plate and leave it clean, discover that to show appreciation in Beijing it is proper to leave a moderate pile of food on your plate to indicate that you have eaten well and can eat no more. Every time he had showed appreciation in *his* way by eating everything on his plate, his kindly hosts had felt obliged in *their* way to fill it again instantly, whatever his protestations. The process was virtually unstoppable unless the right signal was given.

Yet almost all nations have a predominant culture with which they are identified, and, so that this book can be straightforward enough to be a foundation from which readers can delve into the greater complexity, it deals only with these predominant cultures. With the effects, that is, of the encompassing Anglo cultures in, say, the United States and in Britain, of the French Latin culture in France, of the Portuguese Latin culture in Brazil, of the Han people's culture in China, and so on. Indeed, the information available that is relevant to management and organization is not yet enough to do more, even if that were feasible within the confines of a single book.

CULTURE AS CATCH-ALL

When comparing management and organization in different nations, it is all too easy to attribute too much to societal culture. Culture is a handy catch-all for explaining whatever is found. If commercial firms in Africa or in some parts of Asia do not plan and budget and market in accord with contemporary North American business school teachings, are they not held back by a restricted traditional outlook that hinders effective management? Possibly, but suppose that they are supplying local markets where they sell all they produce so that the cost of sophisticated techniques would be unjustified?

Again, is a highly personal, verbal practice of communication due to a culture that values person-to-person contact, or to illiteracy among employees who could not read written instructions? Is the speed of an investment decision in Brazil due to a culture which values fast action, or to hyperinflation which removes financial gains unless they are reaped quickly? Is the comparative centralization of management in Egyptian enterprises due to a culture where people wait for a lead from the top, or to those organizations being State-owned in a semi-planned economy in which the main decisions are therefore necessarily taken centrally?

It is not easy, it may be impossible, some would say futile, to try to disentangle what is due to a society's culture with any precision and clarity. In the last analysis, the illiteracy and the hyperinflation and the central planning may well be themselves the outcomes of cultures that foster them to some degree. What is due to what? Perhaps it helps most to see the world as multi-causal, with many factors acting and interacting simultaneously. Or perhaps it helps most to see the world rolling as an interwoven whole. Whatever one's view, a sensitivity to the part likely to be played by societal cultures does aid understanding. Difficult though it may be to say exactly what that part is, the notion of culture is persistently useful and its manifestations are persistently recognizable.

But, as has been said, it can be overdone as an explanation. As a corrective, there are some especially obvious alternative influences to watch out for to avoid the inclination to jump to the conclusion that every feature arises directly from culture. In any society, what might arise from societal culture might also arise from:

a) the **specialist jobs** people do, their **level in the hierarchy** and their **training**. Someone in a marketing job does not see things in the same way as someone in a finance job. A salesperson in marketing does not see things in the same way as a director or vice-president of marketing. Someone trained as an electronics engineer owes as much or more to that training when handling problems at work as to being Anglo or Latin in culture.

b) the **organizational culture**, which is another rather general notion but one that has grown in favour. Organizations all in the same nation and societal culture will differ in their own cultures (and sub-cultures within them again). Exactly how is not clear, but, before assuming that something is due to societal culture, it is as well to wonder how much it may be due to the ways of the particular organization or even of the industry.

c) the **operating field** or domain or market in which the organization functions. If supplies are precarious and orders hard to come by, a firm is likely to be more centralized and controlled than if the situation is easier, for example. It is argued that some organizations will be forced out of existence if the number in a given field becomes too great for the available resources.

d) the **scale of operation** or size of organization. A larger organization may construct formal control systems such as budgeting, regular written reports, detailed work-schedules and quality returns, because there are so many people to be controlled as much as because those people feel culturally comfortable with clear procedures and instructions.

e) the **institutional environment**, meaning here how organizations take shape under various ownerships and legal provisions. Americans and Britons, for instance, are inclined to take for granted the ownership of business corporations by impersonal shareholders, which leaves them open to sudden takeovers, in an environment of perpetually shifting who-owns-whom. But in other societies, organizations may not be constituted that way (see Box 2.3).

More than that, cultures everywhere have things in common. There is evidence, for example, that all of us worldwide, wherever we come from, admire the same qualities of leadership on the job. We respond to the same characteristics when these are shown by our superiors. In our view, an effective leader is trustworthy, and so can inspire us and give us a vision of what it is we should be aiming at. Such a leader is encouraging and positive, giving us confidence, communicates well, and is administratively competent.

So everyone who reads this, from East or West, North or South, around the globe, will feel 'Oh, yes, that is what I like about leadership.' No one will be surprised, everyone will think it obvious. In this, humankind is of one mind. We can take for granted that the more effective leaders among managers in any country tend to be like this, whatever the culture. This, too, cautions us from overestimating the effects of cultural differences. In some ways cultures are much the same.

And yet . . . This example is not the whole of leadership. There are other sides to leadership, and to the use of authority in management, which differ sharply between different peoples. Box 2.2 has some examples.

What then is culture?

WHAT IS CULTURE?

The concept of societal culture becomes useful only when there is some idea of what it means. Not a precisely defined idea – indeed a fuzzy idea may be more useful, for it is certainly a broad and rather abstract concept.

In this book it does not mean a knowledge of the arts such as music and sculpture, nor does it refer to social graces, both combined in the image, in Europe at least, of the culturally refined person. It does mean the shared values that typify a society and lie beneath its characteristic arts and architecture, clothes, food, ways of greeting and meeting, ways of working together, ways of communicating, and so on. It is the differences in these artefacts and behaviours, compared to those they are used to, that first strike any newcomers. The word 'culture' is often used to encompass all of these; to prevent it becoming unwieldy, its meaning here focuses on the *common values* from which these derive. The Dutch researcher Hofstede, whose work on culture which placed him among the 'great writers' listed in Box 1.4 has already been commented on, aptly called culture the 'software' or 'collective programming' of the mind, the programming of values being fundamental. People are programmed by a society to value the advice of older people rather than younger, to value looking forward rather than backwards, to value cultivating personal relationships rather than finishing a task, to value clear instructions rather than vague opportunities, or the other way round – and so on, depending on how society shapes their values and how they themselves take part in shaping society. And it is a short step from what is valued and desirable, or undesirable, to what is right or wrong for a particular society.

Box 2.2 Similar and Different Leadership

A very large research network, with members throughout the world, co-ordinated by an American, Robert House, obtained answers to questionnaires from 15,022 middle managers in the financial, food and telecommunications industries in 60 societies, and as many cultures and subcultures (e.g. both black and white in South Africa), in the mid-1990s.

They found that outstanding leadership was everywhere regarded as having the same primary qualities. In summary, it is trustworthy and honest, inspirational and visionary, encouraging, confidence-building, team-oriented, and administratively skilled.

On the other hand, their research also began to find 'distinctly different views' on other features of leadership. As they put it:

Consider the following statements taken from interviews with managers from various countries:

- Americans appreciate two kinds of leaders. They seek empowerment from leaders who grant autonomy and delegate authority to subordinates. They also respect the bold, forceful, confident and risk-taking leader, as personified by John Wayne;

- The Dutch place emphasis on egalitarianism and are sceptical about the value of leadership. Terms like *leader* and *manager* carry a stigma. If a father is employed as a manager, Dutch children will not admit it to their schoolmates;
- Arabs worship their leaders – *as long as they are in power!*
- Iranians seek power and strength in their leaders;
- Malaysians expect their leaders to behave in a manner that is humble, modest and dignified;
- The French expect leaders to be 'cultivated' – highly educated in the arts and mathematics.

(summarized and quoted from House *et al*, pp. 213 and 178)

Box 2.3 The *Kaisha*, the *Chaebol* and the Family Business

In Japan, the shareholders of the *kaisha* or big business corporations are not readily susceptible to hostile bids, thus leaving management relatively free of short-term capital market pressures. Though because they specialize in areas of business where their managements have skill and experience, sub-contracting other work to other firms, they are very interdependent with related firms as well as with agencies of government.

The *chaebol* of Korea are different again. They are often 'vertically integrated', owning their suppliers and customers in some degree. They are involved in a wider range of businesses and so are more self-sufficient than the Japanese. Though they do depend on support from the state and from banks, ownership is family dominated. A *chaebol* can be called a 'patrimonial bureaucracy'.

Whereas the businesses run by expatriate Chinese in Thailand, Indonesia, the Philippines, Malaysia, Hong Kong and Taiwan are typically smaller, though also family concerns. They rely even more on personal links with relatives and friends in other firms, spreading their owners' interests through such links whilst themselves remaining small and specialized.

(summarized from Whitley)

Yet even if values are taken as the focus of the concept of culture, that concept still remains hazy, since the word 'values' itself is another portmanteau term into which too much can be stuffed. Societal culture is a necessary concept none the less for, as has already been said, it does not need to be defined with clean precision in order for its consequences to be experienced.

Of course, not every member of a society shares that society's principal distinguishing values to the same degree. Every society experiences some strains between the values of the old and the young, for example, and one family differs from another. Yet values, and customs, are passed from generation to generation and are hard to change. There is a tendency for Westerners who come upon books on Japanese management, especially for Americans whose economic eminence has been challenged by Japanese success, to want to do things the Japanese way, as if to *become* Japanese. They cannot. They do not have Japanese values. They have to realize, when their first enthusiasm has died down, that the Japanese learned carefully from American management methods, adapting all they wanted without having to transform themselves into Americans, and it is such adaptation that is practicable, not personal metamorphosis.

Core values are particularly hard to change, such as respect for one's elders (see Box 2.4). These are central to the stability of a society, whereas other values seem to be comparatively *peripheral* and easier to change since they matter less, such as style of dress.

Box 2.4 Confucius and Mao

During the ten-year attempt at a Cultural Revolution from 1966 onwards in China, the enthusiasm of Maoist-style Communists for a more egalitarian society came up against longstanding core values. What they saw as excessive respect for the experience and social position of those older and senior both at home and at work stood in the way of change. So organizations were even turned upside down, managers and professors and surgeons being demoted to unskilled jobs or sent to till the fields whilst younger folk from lower in the hierarchy tried to take charge. But, a few years later, little lasting change seemed to have occurred. Core values dating back to the time of Confucius or beyond had substantially survived, and with them traditional acceptance of authority. There had been no 'revolution' in culture.

(Lachman, Nedd and Hinings; see also Chapter 7)

The persistence of cultures, come what may, needs no more demonstration than the survival of an identifiable Jewish people across the world, despite nineteen centuries without a Jewish State, or the survival of Romany Gypsy people across Europe striving to sustain vestiges of a nomadic life in settled urbanized States, or the Hinduism of the people of the small island of Bali when they are part of a State with the world's largest Islamic population, Indonesia.

FIVE PRIMARY MANAGEMENT-RELATED FEATURES

There is no such thing as an established list of elements of cultures most related to organizing and managing, a list that ends all discussion and can be learned by heart. What is needed is a feel for what is going on, rather than a pretence of exactitude. However, there are major elements that recur frequently. Five of them are the values put upon:

- authority
- other people
- oneself
- certainty
- time

They have to be handled – or, in the wide sense of the word, managed – by everyone, whether or not their job is managerial. Each will be looked at here in turn, beginning with managing authority.

Managing Authority

Culture reveals itself, more than anywhere, in the relationships between people. Superficially, in how to shake hands and what to talk about, more deeply in the view each individual holds of other individuals and, indeed, in how individually each is seen. Basic to organizing and managing is the view taken by subordinates of those superior to them and who have authority over them.

The authority of superiors in all organizations in all societies rests on some mix of position or status with personal competence. The mix varies. In some countries position matters more, in others competence matters more. As a generalization, the tendency is for position to matter more in economically less developed nations where family and seniority are accorded greater respect, and competence to matter more in economically developed nations where personal expertise in the work to be done counts for more. It is the contrast already drawn in the last chapter between *who someone is*, in terms of level of job and age and connections, and *what someone does*, in terms of knowledge and skill.

This influences who gets promoted to a position of authority, the criteria being biased one way or the other depending on the society in which an organization is located. It produces strains within multinational corporations, when advancement in one subsidiary rests comparatively more on standing in society, but in another subsidiary in another country it rests comparatively more upon demonstrated job performance irrespective of who the candidate for promotion may be in terms of class, caste, tribe or race. Westerners might jump to the conclusion that the latter is best, yet that is not necessarily so. If to command the respect due to authority a manager needs wider social standing, then to pass over such a person would be an affront felt by subordinates too, disturbing the working of the organization. In both situations the criteria are taken to be 'natural, right and proper'.

Whichever way people gain positions of managerial authority, how that authority is handled is vital to the running of an organization. Do subordinates look for directions from superiors, and usually accept those instructions without question, regarding an attempt to query them as disrespectful to a superior whose word is founded on higher status and greater experience of life than their own? Or do subordinates more readily doubt what they are told to do, initiate discussions with their superiors and even challenge what comes from above, feeling comparatively at ease with and close to their boss? The value given to authority is usually somewhere in between these extremes, of course, but the extremes indicate the dimension of 'power distance'.

Power distance shows how removed subordinates feel from superiors in a social meaning of the word 'distance'. In a high power-distance culture, inequality is accepted, 'a place for everyone and everyone in their place', and subordinates prefer managers who take decisions and do not offload the responsibility on to them. In a low power-distance culture, inequalities and overt status symbols are minimized and subordinates expect to be consulted and to share decisions with approachable managers.

Box 2.5 shows some results of remarkable work by Hofstede, who has been mentioned previously. It is research that is influential throughout this book because of its scale and the strength of the findings.

Whilst employed by the giant American multinational computer corporation, IBM, Hofstede had been responsible, with a team of colleagues, for questionnaire surveys of IBM employees in countries worldwide. They amassed over 116,000 questionnaires, of which 72,000 were used to compare countries, by far the largest study of organizations and their personnel ever carried out. Upon leaving IBM, Hofstede obtained

---

Box 2.5 Power Distance

High Power Distance

Malaysia	104	South Korea	60
Guatemala	95	Iran	58
Panama	95	Taiwan	58
Philippines	94	Spain	57
Mexico	81	Pakistan	55
Venezuela	81	Japan	54
Arab countries	80	Italy	50
Ecuador	78	Argentina	49
Indonesia	78	South Africa	49
India	77	Jamaica	45
West Africa	77	USA	40
Yugoslavia	76	Canada	39
Singapore	74	Netherlands	38
Brazil	69	Australia	36
France	68	Costa Rica	35
Hong Kong	68	Germany (West)	35
Colombia	67	Great Britain	35
Salvador	66	Switzerland	34
Turkey	66	Finland	33
Belgium	65	Norway	31
East Africa	64	Sweden	31
Peru	64	Ireland	28
Thailand	64	New Zealand	22
Chile	63	Denmark	18
Portugal	63	Israel	13
Uruguay	61	Austria	11
Greece	60	**Low Power Distance**	

Scores on a PD Index composed from answers to three survey questions by IBM employees in seven occupations in 1967/69 and 1971/73.

(from Hofstede, 1991 and 2001)

permission to analyse the data further. Box 2.5 shows the differences he found in what he came to call power distance.

Nations are ranged from high to low on a PD index calculated from their average answers to three questions about how often subordinates feel afraid to disagree with their superiors, how far they would prefer a superior who makes decisions in a manner which is directive, as opposed to consultative, and how far their own superior is in their eyes directive as against consultative. Whilst managements near the top of the range tend towards being autocratic or paternalistic, and those towards the bottom to being comparatively participative, it is crucial to grasp that the subordinates of both find this quite acceptable. There can be no chant of 'High scores are bad, low scores are good.' That would be a culture-bound assumption. When people change jobs between high PD and low PD nations, the frustration of those who have transferred 'up' from the low end at the confines put upon them by higher authority is matched by the bewilderment of those who have transferred 'down' at the failure of those in authority to display a grip on things.

There is no point in debating whether any particular nation ought to have scored a little more or a little less, or be a few places higher or lower; this kind of data does not have that degree of precision. But the broad contrast between higher and lower PD is corroborated by many studies in greater detail of organizations in smaller numbers of nations.

Among forty nations from which the highest numbers of completed questionnaires were received, some Asian former colonies (the Philippines, India, Singapore and Hong Kong) stand high in PD, all apparently affected by being subjected to imperial hierarchy, since other Asian nations (Thailand, Taiwan and Japan) are more middling. Latin American nations are mostly higher PD, and so are most Latin European nations. Coming down towards lower PD, the Anglo and the Germanic nations appear (such as the USA, Australia and Britain, with Germany and Switzerland and Austria). The clusterings of the Latins and also of the Anglos are the transcontinental legacy of empires past, the Roman long ago and the British not so long ago. Distinctively low are the Israelis and the Scandinavians, who seem to share a non-aristocratic tradition among geographically isolated peoples in northern lands.

Subsequently, scores were published for ten additional nations and three groups of nations from which, despite their having a weaker basis in smaller numbers of questionnaires, meaningful results appeared under further scrutiny. Of the ten additional nations, six are in Latin America, three in Asia, and one in the Caribbean. In Latin America, Ecuador, Guatemala, Panama, Salvador and Uruguay score high PD in line with the other Central and South Americans in Box 2.5. Costa Rica appears lower, reflecting the particular history of this nation. Indonesia and Malaysia come very high. Korea is in a middling position; and Jamaica, the only Caribbean inclusion, is in the lower-middle range.

Putting together small numbers of questionnaires from Africa and the Middle East added three groupings of similar nations on which there was not enough data to treat each separately. Data from seven Arabic-speaking countries (Egypt, Lebanon, Libya, Kuwait, Iraq, Saudi Arabia and the United Arab Emirates) suggests high power distance for Arabia generally, and so too for West Africa (represented by questionnaires from Ghana, Nigeria and Sierra Leone). East Africa (Kenya, Ethiopia, Tanzania and Zambia) seems to be middling by comparison.

As the questionnaires which yielded these results were filled in as long ago as 1967/69 and 1971/73, it may be asked whether they still hold good. That is a matter of judgement, but it was emphasized earlier how cultural values are slow to change, especially core values on basic elements such as authority. Whilst power distance may well be changing, it is likely to be doing so only slowly. Even if power distance generally is decreasing under the influence of Western-dominated mass media and of economic development, it is likely that the nations are all moving downwards together, so maintaining much the same positions relative to one another.

The comparison is limited to those nations which at the time were economically at a stage where they could provide a market for IBM equipment and so would have an IBM branch, so it excludes most less-developed nations. It also excludes nations which at the time had communist governments that did not admit American multinationals. And since it is of the personnel in the branch or branches of a single corporation in each nation, it is not a full representation of the variety within each nation.

Nevertheless, it does give a broad *comparative positioning* of each relative to the others, for it has the great strength that it compares like with like with a stringency rarely achieved. In each nation, the personnel were in the same managerial, technical, sales and clerical occupations, selling and servicing the same equipment, under the same head office and ownership. That it was an American ownership, intent on training everyone to a high level in the same way and thus inculcating an American-style organizational culture, makes the findings even stronger since, given such pressures to uniformity, the distinctiveness in values is the more startling. Despite IBM, in the way authority is handled, Mexicans remain Mexican, Turks remain Turkish, Finns remain Finnish.

The ramifications of this finding for organizing and managing are examined in the chapters which follow, especially in the chapters on the principal world cultures.

A word of caution here. When gross comparisons of societies are made in this way, it is too easy to begin to forget the wide range of differences between individuals in any one of them. To say that Sweden has comparatively low power distance, for example, means that Swedes generally show a tendency that way, on average. Likewise for the French high power distance. But since the Swedes are different as between themselves, and so are the French, it is entirely possible that some Swedish individuals are personally higher in power distance than some among the French who are on the low side. Yet the broad Swedish and French averages as societies differ markedly.

The wielding of authority and the regard for authority should not be seen in isolation. Due consideration has to be given to other associated elements of societal culture. In Japan, for instance, hierarchical relationships have rested on comparatively greater trust of those in authority, and greater obligation and interdependence, than is characteristic of the more brittle relationships in Latin America. So in Japan authority has been used more effectively to direct economic growth.

Trust concerns relationships generally between people, a second primary management-related element in culture which is considered next.

Managing Relationships

The use of authority is one particular aspect of relationships among people. Cultures also differ in values put upon relationships more generally.

The first people most of us know after we are born are our family, either mainly a 'nuclear' one, which means our parents and any brothers or sisters we may have, or maybe an 'extended' one, within which our nuclear family is absorbed into a welter of cousins, uncles, aunts and grandparents whom we know just as well. It depends on the kind of society into which we are born. So we grow either to concentrate highly felt emotions on to a few others, a small group focused around our own individuality, or to disperse our feelings away from ourselves through a larger collectivity.

This is not so remote from the subject of this book as it might at first seem. It is the origin of contrasting approaches to organizing and managing, especially marked between East and West.

In societies which emphasize bonds with the extended family, feelings of loyalty, though spread wide, do not spread infinitely. There tends to be strong identification with that family and less concern for those outside it, **familism** as this is sometimes called. By comparison, in societies where the nuclear family is emphasized, loyalties and concerns can more readily be sustained far beyond the confines of the small family in a less personalistic, more *impersonal* way. People do much less to help families and friends, but respond to appeals for funds to help people in other lands whom they will never see.

It was stated in Chapter 1 that, although family businesses continue to be the most numerous in all economies, industrialization sees the growth of impersonal (bureaucratized) organizations from which family loyalties are, in principle, excluded and so, too, are any other personal friendships. In banks, factories, hospitals, universities in so-called Western societies, appointments and who-gets-to-do-what and discussions in meetings are not supposed to be influenced by personal relationships. People try to avoid having relatives coming to work in the same place and are embarrassed by the appointment of a friend. There are constant tensions in family firms between the family's wish to bring in sons or daughters over the heads of others and the resentment this causes among people who see more impersonal and 'fair' systems in other organizations round about.

Whereas in a society with stronger familism, this tension occurs far less. Organizations work best when family and organization coincide. It is honourable loyally to fulfil obligations to family members and to other people who are personally known, not only in family firms but in other organizations as well, including government administration. It is honourable to share the benefits of one's employment by helping family members to obtain jobs. If the manager's brother-in-law walks into the office, it is honourable to welcome him and entertain him, even if colleagues or subordinates or customers have to wait – they will understand. To people in a more impersonal society, such conduct would be shocking, just as their cold ignoring of such personal bonds is shocking, seen from the other point of view.

A struggle between the two approaches can be seen in more recently established organizations in many kinship-orientated economies in Africa and Asia, and sometimes, too, in Latin nations. Set up, frequently by the State, under the influence of (impersonal) Western management principles, the organizations do not function as imagined on the organizational drawing-board. They can be made to work only through an accepted network of family and other connections. For example, neither of the authors of this book would ever contemplate having a brother-in-law or sister-in-law as his research assistant, but such a link is quite acceptable among our South American colleagues.

Furthermore, in impersonal organizations in the West it is taken for granted that people in the various departments or at different levels in the hierarchy are likely to have different points of view, probably arising from differing interests. Much of Western management literature is given to counteracting this, trying to widen participation in decisions and improve communication. Yet in societies where organizations have more of an image as pseudo families, the starting assumption is that harmony will prevail. Especially this is so in Japan, and also in China (see Box 2.6). However, should disagreement be too great to be contained and open conflict break through, it can be the more bitter because personal relationships break down, compared to the effect when relationships are more distantly impersonal.

Box 2.6 Don't Say That, It's Disharmonious

The overfed joint author of this book, on the same trip to Beijing (see Box 2.1), was giving a talk to the assembled staff of the mining institute. It was about managerial decision-making, based on research in Britain. He had been startled to realize just minutes before that a talk was expected, so it had to be the only one he could give from instant recall; he had no time to re-think it. On his feet, he foresaw that a tricky moment was approaching. Frantically trying to think how to avoid it, whilst keeping talking, he could do no better when the moment came than to say, as gently as the English language allowed: 'There are many contributors and, er, participants in decision making.' The translators hesitated, but continued. He was relieved. At least he had avoided aggressive Anglo-Saxon words about decision making, such as there being 'interests' or, worse still, 'divergent interests'. But the logic of his talk brought him to the same point again, a few minutes later. 'There are,' he said (shrinking from saying 'differing opinions'), 'various points of view ...' The translation came to a stop. The translators conferred. One who had spent a period in the United States and who knew the problem, turned to him to apologize: 'Sorry,' said she, 'but we don't see things that way here.'

Trust in others differs between societies, only the other way around, so to speak. Where there is high familism, full trust is concentrated within family relationships and runs beyond them only where personal relationships have been built up, face to face. Hence the greater time and trouble expended upon entertaining and on lengthy getting-to-know-you conversations, preliminary to business talks in Arabia and Asia, than in the West. Though, even in the West, the dilatory niceties in Britain or in France may frustrate an American who wants to get down to business faster still. Personal confidence has to be created within which written agreements or instructions can be put into place.

By contrast, in societies with wider-spread trust, impersonal contacts can be relied upon more. Officials and bosses and subordinates are regarded as more or less trustworthy even if not known personally. There is less need for managers to ensure close supervision of those below. Decentralization is easier. Very broadly, among European and European-derived cultures, trust generally seems higher in the Anglo, Germanic and Nordic cultures than in the Latin.

These kinds of differences are summed up in the idea of **individualism** versus **collectivism**. Hofstede finds this contrast in his analysis of IBM questionnaires. He sees individualistic cultures reflected in a stronger desire for challenging work and freedom in doing it, yet having time left for a private life beyond the purview of one's employer, and collectivist cultures reflected in a relatively stronger value given to the provision for everyone of training and good working conditions. In individualistic cultures the emphasis is on getting ahead and the ideal is to be a good leader, whereas in collectivistic cultures the emphasis is on belonging and the ideal is to be a good member.

Box 2.7 shows the comparatively individualistic nations towards the top and the more family-orientated, collectivist nations lower down. It is apparent that the ordering is similar to that on power distance (Box 2.5), *but* the other way up. That is, the extremely individualistic Anglo and quite individualistic Scandinavian and Germanic nations towards the top here are towards the bottom on power distance, whilst the more collectivistic Latin and Chinese nations are towards the top on power distance. In brief, Anglos, Nordics and Germanics are inclined to be individualistic and less authority-conscious, whilst Latins and Chinese are inclined to be collectivistic and authority-conscious. Japan is middling once more.

Among the interesting changes in positioning are those of Israel, which though very low in PD is not very individualistic, even somewhat collectivistic, and of France, which has a distinctive combination of high individualism *and* high power distance – in other words, an apparently contradictory assertion of the individual combined with a need for strong authority.

Of the additional nations included later, the other Latin Americans all appear collectivistic, as would be expected, and so do Indonesia and Malaysia. Korea again fits alongside Taiwan. Both groups of African nations, East and West Africa, are collectivistic. But the Arabic group is in a relatively middling position, much more collectivistic than the highly individualistic Anglo nations, for example, but not so strongly collectivistic as the Chinese or Thais. Jamaica is similar.

Difficulties in **communication** across cultures occur not only when individualist meets collectivist, experiencing each other respectively as evasively time-wasting or assertively rude, but in the means of communication itself. Translation between one language and another is fraught enough, but over and above that is the difficulty of comprehension between what has been called **low-context** *and* **high-context languages** (see Box 2.8). In low-context communication, as among Anglos, Germanics and Scandinavians, a great deal depends on what is said or written, on the words explicitly used. Things have to be fully, though concisely, spelled out. But in high-context communication among, for example, Arabs or Japanese, more information is already 'in the person' and in implicit assumptions, so that more of what is communicated passes by *who* is speaking or writing, by 'body language', by nuance. People who are closely in touch informally with what is going on do not need it baldly stated. Hence arises what seems to the Japanese to be the blunt

Box 2.7 Individualism *versus* Collectivism

Individualistic

USA	91	Turkey	37
Australia	90	Uruguay	36
Great Britain	89	Greece	35
Canada	80	Philippines	32
Netherlands	80	Mexico	30
New Zealand	79	East Africa	27
Italy	76	Portugal	27
Belgium	75	Yugoslavia	27
Denmark	74	Malaysia	26
Sweden	71	Hong Kong	25
France	71	Chile	23
Ireland	70	Singapore	20
Norway	69	Thailand	20
Switzerland	68	West Africa	20
Germany (West)	67	Salvador	19
South Africa	65	South Korea	18
Finland	63	Taiwan	17
Austria	55	Peru	16
Israel	54	Costa Rica	15
Spain	51	Indonesia	14
India	48	Pakistan	14
Japan	46	Colombia	13
Argentina	46	Venezuela	12
Iran	41	Panama	11
Jamaica	39	Ecuador	8
Brazil	38	Guatemala	6
Arab countries	38	**Collectivistic**	

Scores on an Individualism Index calculated from answers to nine questions.

(from Hofstede, 1991 and 2001)

offensiveness of some Westerners and the baffled suspicions of those Westerners when complete information is so difficult to obtain from the Japanese.

Box 2.8 Talking High and Low

Anthropologists Edward and Mildred Hall contrast what they call high-context and low-context communication. *A high-context communication or message is one in which most of the information is already in the person, while very little is in the coded, explicit, transmitted part of the message. A low-context communication is just the opposite, i.e. the mass of information is vested in the explicit code. Twins who have grown up together can and do communicate more economically (high context) than two lawyers in a courtroom during a trial (low context) . . .*

(Hall and Hall, p. 6)

Managing Oneself

Organizing and managing is shaped by more than the use of authority and personal relationships. It is shaped too by how people see themselves and their prospects, particularly by the value they place upon certain aspirations rather than others. Is it more important to gain achievements, or to develop oneself in ways not aimed at accomplishment but rather at expressing personal qualities and ensuring social acceptability? In other words, is the emphasis upon *doing* or upon *being*? Is it upon achieving in life, or upon experiencing life? If it is upon achieving, then organizations offer explicitly achievement-linked rewards like bonuses, pay rises and promotions, as in North America. If it is upon experiencing life and oneself, then pleasure in the colleagues and tasks of the moment is more important, as in some Asian societies.

From this it would be easy to argue that, to accomplish economic development, a people must have a strong need for personal achievement, such as is visible among the Anglo-Saxons (the word 'achievement' itself is a very Anglo-Saxon one, a component of the English language that is less commonplace or has no counterpart in other languages). However, clear evidence for this argument is lacking, as will be seen.

The results of Hofstede's study both support and challenge it. He draws a contrast between **masculinity** and **femininity**. These are rather provoking words and might seem unduly loaded. Certainly they do not mean that some nations are all men and others all women! Nevertheless, the distinction they make is a useful one. They signify what might be called a harder versus a softer dimension in work-related culture, an emphasis on 'assertiveness' as compared to 'nurturance'. In higher masculinity cultures, advancement (promotion), challenging work, the chance of high earnings, and individual recognition are the aims, whereas in high femininity societies, working with cooperative colleagues and having a good relationship with your manager, secure employment and being able to reside in a desirable area are relatively more important (as indicated by the answers to questions on those topics which yield the comparison in Box 2.9). In the former, performance counts, money matters, ambition is the driving force. In the latter, quality of life matters, people and environment are to be considered, and to be of service is praiseworthy.

In higher masculinity cultures, men should be assertive and dominating, women should be caring. In higher femininity cultures, the view taken of the sexes is not so sharply differentiated. The roles of each are more flexible and there is a stronger belief in gender equality.

The masculinity of Japan is the most striking feature of Box 2.9. It again raises the question of what is needed for economic success. Is an assertive drive plus respect for authority (Box 2.5) and loyal cohesiveness (Box 2.7) the cultural recipe for success? In all conditions, or just when world conditions are right? However, Hong Kong, Singapore and Taiwan also have been economically successful in recent times, and these Chinese peoples (like the Indian peoples and the Thais) show much greater femininity. So this cultural distinction within Asia indicates that economic growth requires more than achievement-orientated masculinity, and so does the marked femininity of the prosperous Scandinavian nations and the Dutch. Indeed, the masculine Japanese have struggled as economic conditions changed. So conditions other than culture would seem to be critical.

Among Latin nations, Portugal looks somewhat higher in femininity than Spain, and this corresponds with its one-time colony, Brazil, showing greater femininity than most former Spanish colonies, though Spain itself is towards the 'feminine' end. Canada stands out as least 'masculine' of the high masculinity Anglo nations.

The other Latin nations which Hofstede later included are moderately masculine, with Costa Rica giving evidence of femininity. Once more Korea resembles Taiwan. Jamaica is highly 'masculine'. Indonesia and Malaysia are middling, as are the East and West African groups and the Arab group.

Box 2.9 Masculinity *versus* Femininity

Masculinity

Japan	95	Singapore	48
Austria	79	Israel	47
Venezuela	73	Indonesia	46
Italy	70	West Africa	46
Switzerland	70	Turkey	45
Mexico	69	Taiwan	45
Ireland	68	Panama	44
Jamaica	68	France	43
Great Britain	66	Iran	43
Germany (West)	66	Spain	42
Philippines	64	Peru	42
Colombia	64	East Africa	41
Ecuador	63	Salvador	40
South Africa	63	South Korea	39
USA	62	Uruguay	38
Australia	61	Guatemala	37
New Zealand	58	Thailand	34
Greece	57	Portugal	31
Hong Kong	57	Chile	28
Argentina	56	Finland	26
India	56	Costa Rica	21
Belgium	54	Yugoslavia	21
Arab countries	53	Denmark	16
Canada	52	Netherlands	14
Malaysia	50	Norway	8
Pakistan	50	Sweden	5
Brazil	49	**Femininity**	

Scores on a Masculinity Index calculated from answers to eight questions.

(from Hofstede, 1991 and 2001)

Managing Uncertainty

It is a truism that life is uncertain. That truism troubles some individuals more than others, and some societies more than others. People in some cultures just live with it, while those in other cultures make more effort to try to fend it off, or to push it away. They value certainty and avoid uncertainty.

So **uncertainty avoidance** is the fourth cultural dimension found by Hofstede to separate IBM subsidiaries in different nations. The same nations are ordered in Box 2.10 from most uncertainty-avoiding to least uncertainty-avoiding, as indicated by answers to three questions on how

Box 2.10 Uncertainty Avoidance

Uncertainty Avoiding

Greece	112	Ecuador	67
Portugal	104	Germany (West)	65
Guatemala	101	Thailand	64
Uruguay	100	Iran	59
Belgium	94	Finland	59
Salvador	94	Switzerland	58
Japan	92	West Africa	54
Yugoslavia	88	Netherlands	53
Peru	87	East Africa	52
Argentina	86	Australia	51
Chile	86	Norway	50
Costa Rica	86	South Africa	49
France	86	New Zealand	49
Panama	86	Canada	48
Spain	86	Indonesia	48
South Korea	85	USA	46
Turkey	85	Philippines	44
Mexico	82	India	40
Israel	81	Malaysia	36
Colombia	80	Great Britain	35
Venezuela	76	Ireland	35
Brazil	76	Hong Kong	29
Italy	75	Sweden	29
Pakistan	70	Denmark	23
Austria	70	Jamaica	13
Taiwan	69	Singapore	8
Arab countries	68	**Uncertainty Tolerating**	

Scores on a UA Index calculated from answers to three questions.

(from Hofstede, 1991 and 2001)

readily company rules should be broken, how long the person responding is likely to stay with the company and how often he or she feels nervous or tense at work. People in uncertainty-avoiding cultures, as Hofstede sees it, are more often nervous about what may happen and do not want to make their situation yet more uncertain by breaking rules (even if it is 'in the company's best interests to do so'), let alone by leaving the security of their job.

Nations such as Greece, at the top of the list, and Japan, seventh from the top, are strongly inclined this way. So are the Latin European and Central and South American Latin nations, all of which are highly uncertainty-avoiding, as is every one of the six Latin American nations counted in later (Costa Rica, Ecuador, Guatemala, Panama, Salvador and Uruguay).

Low in the list, where the events of life are taken more easily as they come and uncertainties are treated more casually, are the Scandinavian nations, the Anglo-Saxons, India and the two mainly Chinese islands, Hong Kong and Singapore. When Indonesia and Malaysia were included, they, too, appeared as low uncertainty-avoiding, though perhaps significantly Korea came nearer to Japan.

The groups of African and Arab nations referred to before are all in middling positions.

If not masculinity alone, then could high uncertainty avoidance be the vital spur to economic performance, stirring people to assure a secure future by hard work? Some evidence for this is summarized in Box 2.11, evidence from data very different from that used by Hofstede. Health statistics are compared, statistics which, although they have a degree of unreliability since they may be counted up in slightly different ways in different countries, do not depend on how people feel about answering questionnaires. If these statistics do indicate *anxiety*, as is claimed, then clearly being a high anxiety culture and a high uncertainty-avoiding culture is much the same. Anxious people avoid uncertainty.

And the higher anxiety nations do appear to have done well economically at the time the study was carried out – though, as the statistics are from the 1960s, it is an open question whether cultures have materially changed since then in this respect.

Most obviously, Japan's combination of high anxiety (high uncertainty avoidance) with masculinity has been successful in the circumstances of the twentieth century. On the other hand, Britain and the

United States both prevailed economically in their day, with typical Anglo mixtures of *low* anxiety (*low* uncertainty avoidance) and masculinity. If culture is a key to economic performance, then it is not the same culture in all circumstances. It is a culture that happens to be appropriate to getting the most from the political-economic conditions of the times.

Another way of fending off uncertainty, as well as by working hard, is through orderliness. This can be created by having a framework of rules and regulations in organizations within which people can work with some sense of certainty. They can feel confident that the organization is functioning as it should. This depends upon how the rules are treated, of course. In Germany, for example, the rules tend to be abided by and things work as intended, whereas in another fairly uncertainty-avoiding country, Brazil, the rules tend to be treated lightly. Indeed, across the Latin cultures generally, there is a tension between a demand for elaborate rules to make things appear to be under control and an inclination to get around them in practice. In northern Europe, Anglo-Saxons and Scandinavians tend to treat rules in a relatively pragmatic way, accepting the need for them up to a point but bending them where justified. The wide similarity of cultural features between the British and the Germans is broken here by their difference in uncertainty avoidance, the 'disorderly British' (as Hofstede has called them) being much more tolerant of uncertainty. Fewer and more ambiguous rules on the job, a more casual attitude towards them and less concern when things do not work as they should characterize the relatively easy-going British approach to management.

People in contrasting cultures also think differently about the uncertainties of life. They focus on differing information and put it together in different ways. They tend towards **abstractive** or towards **associative thinking**. In abstractive-inclined cultures, thinking is more analytic, more based on logical principles applied to any situation, more scientistical, more general. Links are seen between (uncertain) events, which lead logically to what should be done. In associative-inclined cultures, on the other hand, communication is more often face to face and people readily associate what they are saying with what is around them, and with shared memories and images, in an accustomed pattern of mental associations. They seem illogical to an abstractive thinker, who seems to them limited and given overmuch to fine distinctions. Generally speaking,

Box 2.11 Successful Anxiety

Alcoholism (deaths from cirrhosis of the liver), suicides, mental illness (patients in hospital) and overeating (daily calories intake), proportionate to population, have shown a surprising pattern across eighteen nations:

Japan, Germanic nations and Latin Europeans } have more *alcoholism and suicides*

Anglo-Saxons and Scandinavians } have more *mental illness and calorie intake*

Do differing responses to anxiety show differing amounts of anxiety? Is *higher anxiety* revealed by more alcoholism and suicides in response to the stresses of life, a *lower underlying anxiety* by mental breakdown and high calorie eating in response?

If this should be so, as the researcher suggests, then when this pattern is compared with economic growth, the highest-anxiety nations among those included, namely:

Japan, Germany, Austria, France and Italy

did very much better economically than the lowest-anxiety nations:

Britain, Ireland and New Zealand

(This analysis is by Lynn: a general review of possible links between psychological factors and economic growth is given by Triandis)

economically more developed nations tend to be more abstractive, the less developed more associative. It is a difference close to that between low-context and high-context communication described earlier in this chapter.

Managing Time

No more common thread binds humanity than the passing of time. Yet it is experienced differently and valued differently.

In some cultures there is relatively more concern with *time past*, in others with *time present* or with *time future*. A greater concern with time as it runs back into the historical past underlies **traditional** values. Long-standing customs are still followed, and in business deals it is usual to review what has happened beforehand to lead up to where things are now. Older societies, such as the British, the Indian and the Chinese, are past-orientated and have tended to be conservative in management and slow to change. British gradualism is well known; it frustrates managers from Brazil, for example, who want quicker, more decisive action in business matters (to the British they appear impatient, of course). But despite reverence for tradition, the Japanese, ancient in origin, seem to have surmounted it by a deliberate effort to look ahead and modernize.

Time present is the primary concern of comparatively **immediatist** cultures. Latin Americans, in particular, see the past as having gone and the future as uncertain, and so want results here and now, preferring short-term benefits. They do not have the British patience, which rests also on trusting that people tomorrow will carry out what is understood today.

In a **future-orientated** culture there is comparative optimism that things can be changed for the better. Americans have long been held up as the prime example of this, being more forward-looking than any of the European or African nations from which they originate. Their view of organizing and managing as an active, challenging, get-ahead process fits their 'get up and go' stereotype.

Interwoven with time past, present and future is a second major cultural time dimension, the tendency to feel time as *finite* or *infinite*. If it is experienced as finite, then it is in short supply and every minute counts. It is flashing by in a linear form, so managers must save time and must prevent their subordinates wasting it. Measured by constant glances at watches and clocks, it has to be fully used, so punctuality is important. A manager must neither be kept waiting nor keep others waiting. Again, Americans value time especially highly and are said to want an answer before their French opposite numbers have finished considering the question. 'Time is money.'

In the more clock-conscious Westernized cultures, the first to be affected by the Industrial Revolution which brought people into a clock-watching factory regime, the careful use of time requires planning ahead. Lead times are long in managerial schedules. In contrast, phoning senior Brazilian executives three weeks in advance to make an appointment can be greeted with cheerful laughter: 'Oh, phone me again a couple of days before.'

The Western one-track notion of time contrasts with a perception in which it is experienced rather as multi-track and infinite. Time is an endless rolling cycle in which many things can be done at once. There is no need to hold on to it, or to try to plan and control it. Queues can wait patiently in the offices of officials in, say, India or Turkey, and at the end of the day can be told to come back tomorrow. Time can be taken to get to know business visitors and create trust (see the section on 'Managing Relationships', above).

Points in time matter only in the context of other priorities, so the clock-conscious idea of punctuality is less to the fore. Arriving at a set time on a clock matters less than finishing the social proprieties of the previous business engagement properly, in Latin America for instance. In some situations it is of little consequence which side of the appointed time something occurs (see Box 2.12). Nor does time everywhere flow away irretrievably into a history that is lost; in Islamic cultures, history carries forward constantly with the present, both encumbering those who have to manage affairs now while at the same time giving them perspective.

Box 2.12 Rubber Time

It was a bright blue sunny morning, not too hot, near Kuala Lumpur, the capital of Malaysia. One of the authors of this book was lazily getting up, watching the lizards scurry across the bedroom wall. However could they be so flat as to get in and out of such tiny cracks? To his English mind there was plenty of time, for the car to take him to a meeting was not due until ten o'clock. He munched a treasured English biscuit he had with him as a prelude to breakfast and had a leisurely shower. He was just pulling on his trousers when there was a knock at the door. Hastily finishing dressing, he opened it.

'Shall we get going?' said the driver. It was just half-past eight.

'But weren't we starting at, er, ten?'

'Yes, but it's a lovely morning!'

Malayan 'rubber time' (so-called from the rubber tree plantations introduced under the British Empire) can start before the appointed time as easily as after it.

CULTURE IN SLICES

Each society has its own particular combination of the five features of culture given prominence in this chapter. Its cultural combination has evolved in the context of its own geography, political institutions, economic wealth, social structure and religious beliefs. To understand a culture, a knowledge is therefore needed of the history of a society in these terms.

To begin with, what is a society's **geography**? For instance, is it an island, like the world's two most influential island states, Britain and Japan, or a continental land mass, like the United States or the Russian Federation? Would an element of interpersonal insularity in both the British and Japanese cultures, and the reserve which foreigners find in each, be explained by island isolation, whereas the multilingual familiarity with all-comers shown by the Dutch stems from their living in a small land constantly traversed by other peoples in conquest and, nowadays, on holiday? Could the openness and urgency of Americans and Brazilians be explained by their living in a New World of opportunities, whereas the greater caution of Europeans comes from their inhabiting an Old World long explored and exploited?

The consequences of empires have been commented on already in this chapter. **Political institutions** often show their imprint. Latin cultures in Europe show where the influence of the Roman empire was longest and greatest; the British empire scattered Anglo cultures across the globe; and the USSR, the Union of Soviet Socialist Republics ruled by the Communist Party (or the Russian empire, as it largely was), left common administrative institutions as all empires do. Such empires account for the origins of many States, most obviously in Africa, where the European empires left behind more or less arbitrary borders, and in South America, where the same happened rather earlier. So who has controlled a society in the past? Further, is a culture evolving in the boundaries of a very recent State, such as Namibia, or in one that has a longer history, such as France? Is a culture the outcome of an unbroken ancient civilization, as in China or India, or of a more recent civilization, such as the European?

Differences in the **wealth** of societies are plain to see and may well shape their cultures. It is apparent that most of the wealthier nations are lower in power distance (Box 2.5) and higher in individualism (Box 2.7). Even within the same kind of culture, wealth may make a difference, for the richer Latin European States are more individualistic than the poorer Latin American States. Whilst it is not at all clear how far economic growth can be attributed to culture, as was said earlier, it can be argued the other way around, that greater wealth allows a more democratic and individualistic way of life. As nations become wealthier people become less dependent upon superiors and upon their extended families for their own survival.

Differences in **social structure** may not be quite so obvious to the casual observer as are differences in wealth, but they are not hard to find. Is a society partly tribal in form, like much of Africa and the less settled Bedouin people of Arabia, or has this been obliterated by urbanization? Indeed, how far is a society substantially rural, as is China, or urban, as are the largely Chinese city-states of Hong Kong and Singapore? Does it have a social class stratification, as in Europe, or a more rigid caste-type of form, as in India? Is it comparatively homogeneous ethnically (as are, say, Japan or Norway) or extremely heterogeneous (as for example is Malaysia, with Malay, Chinese and Indian populations that give it not one but three principal cultures)? Of course, the majority of nation-states have some degree of ethnic heterogeneity since even where there is a single ethnic majority there are differing minorities. This diversity is linked to diversity in languages, as are the empires of the past. As the previous chapter has already mentioned, Arabic spread across North Africa with Muslim conquerors from Arabia, Spanish came to South America with Spanish conquest, and English to North America with the British. In central and southern Africa, many nations have not only local languages but also English or French as the national administrative and external language, depending on whether it was Britain or France which conquered their lands.

Mention of the Muslim faith is a reminder, if reminder were needed, of the great importance to culture of **religion**. Religion is about values as well as faith, and values are the basis of culture. How much did the Protestant Christianity that was commented on in Chapter 1 contribute to Western individualism? In Islam, how far is a historical emphasis on respect for the will of Allah responsible for comparatively less interest in planning among Arab managers? Have they an unspoken sense that all is planned anyway, whereas – equally unawares – managers in a Christian tradition are impelled to control and plan in order to succeed in life? How far is the very low power distance of Israel (Box 2.5) due to a historical emphasis in Judaism on a contract with Jehovah that is open to renewal, interpretation and discussion? Even the Almighty can be negotiable. How far does the hierarchical form of the pantheon of gods in Hinduism likewise link with India's very high power distance? But does the element of reincarnation in Hindu belief allow a more relaxed view of personal success than that in Christian-dominated cultures, where this life is seen as the one and only chance? Does the family orientation of Chinese peoples in business ensue from a mixture of Buddhist and Confucian philosophies, both of which stress respect for one's family and ancestors?

Evolving, as each culture does, in a particular geographical, political, economic, social and religious context, it nevertheless shares features with other cultures in other societies. Whilst each culture is distinctive, it is more like some cultures than it is like others. Therefore societies can be grouped according to their cultural similarities or dissimilarities.

Box 2.13 shows seven groupings of nations in the slices of a 'world culture cake' diagram. In broad terms, those with relatively lower power distance and individualistic cultures are on the left of the diagram: the Nordic and Germanic and Anglo groupings. On the right are the relatively higher power distance and collectivistic slices: the Arabs and Asians, together with a general category of Developing Countries. Straddling the bottom are the Latins, the Europeans among them rather more to the left and the South Americans rather more collectivistically towards the right; whilst the very mixed East-Central Europeans come together in the slice at the top.

Shared religious traditions show clearly. All four slices at the top, left and bottom of the diagram have a dominant Christian tradition, whereas Islam dominates the Arab slice and runs through the Developing Countries (parts of Africa) and the Asians (Malaysia and Indonesia). These last two slices have much more besides Islam, of course, including the Buddhism of most of Asia and the Hinduism of India. Perhaps because of this, India did not readily fit the classification in which the culture cake originated; nor did Japan and Israel, both of which also have distinctive national religions, namely Shinto and Judaism.

Common languages characterize the Germanic societies and the Anglo, Latin American (Spanish-speaking) and Arab groupings, though in the

Box 2.13 A World Culture Cake

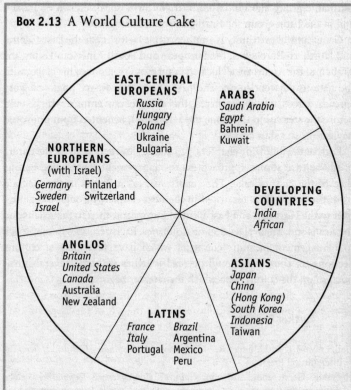

EAST-CENTRAL EUROPEANS
Russia
Hungary
Poland
Ukraine
Bulgaria

ARABS
Saudi Arabia
Egypt
Bahrein
Kuwait

NORTHERN EUROPEANS
(with Israel)
Germany Finland
Sweden Switzerland
Israel

DEVELOPING COUNTRIES
India
African

ANGLOS
Britain
United States
Canada
Australia
New Zealand

ASIANS
Japan
China
(Hong Kong)
South Korea
Indonesia
Taiwan

LATINS
France *Brazil*
Italy Argentina
Portugal Mexico
Peru

This diagram is derived from one by Ronen and Shenkar. These authors synthesized eight questionnaire studies by different researchers published between 1966 and 1980, chosen because each compared societies on job orientation and values. The most extensive was that by Hofstede described in this chapter. Ronen and Shenkar grouped nations by the cultural affinities they found in the research results. Two 'slices' have been added. East-Central Europeans and Developing Countries, for, although these do not have the same kind of internal cultural affinity as is apparent in the other slices, they complete the diagram so far as each slice is a chapter in this book.

The nations shown are self-evidently not complete listings. They exemplify the coverage of each of the Chapters 3 to 9. Those described in greater detail in each chapter as illustrative examples are italicized.

Germanic group substantial numbers of Swiss speak French or Italian, and in the Latin group the Brazilians speak Portuguese.

Geographical proximity is another major factor, since the East-Central and Northern Europeans, the European and South American Latins, the Arabs and the Asians are all located in their own regions of the globe, with the nations adjacent to one another. The extraordinary Anglo category spreads across the hemispheres, the effect of an empire which, even before the steamship (let alone the aeroplane), benefited from improved navigation and ship design.

Each of the following chapters, 3 to 9, describes and analyses the nature of the culture(s) and approach(es) to management represented by one slice of the culture cake. The chapters work outwards in the diagram from the Anglo slice, discussed in the next chapter, through the Latins, over to the Northern and East-Central Europeans, then to the Asians and the Arabs and, finally, Developing Countries. Each describes the approach to management in some countries which have that kind of culture. Sections on countries should be read together with the general introduction on the culture with which the chapter begins.

Further Reading

Hall, Edward T. and Mildred Reed Hall. 1990. *Understanding Cultural Differences*. Intercultural Press.

Hofstede, Geert. 2001, 2nd edn. *Culture's Consequences: Comparing Values, Behaviors, Institutions and Organizations Across Nations*. Sage (summarized in D. S. Pugh and D. J. Hickson, *Writers on Organizations*. 1996. 5th edn. Penguin and Sage).

—— 1991. *Cultures and Organizations: Software of the Mind*. McGraw-Hill.

Lewis, Richard. 1996. *When Cultures Collide: Managing Successfully Across Cultures*. Nicholas Brealey Publishing.

Schneider, Susan C. and Jean-Louis Barsoux. 1997. *Managing Across Cultures*. Prentice Hall.

Trompenaars, Fons. 1993. *Riding the Waves of Culture: Understanding Cultural Diversity in Business*. Economist Books, and Irwin.

Other Sources

Au, Kevin. 1997. 'Another Consequence of Culture: Intra-Cultural Variation'. *International Journal of Human Resource Management*, 8, 5, 743–54.

House, Robert J., Paul J. Hanges, S. Antonio Ruiz-Quintanilla, Peter W. Dorfman, Mansour Javidan, Marcus Dickson, Vipin Gupta and Associates. 1999. 'Cultural Influences on Leadership and Organisations: Project Globe', in *Advances in Global Leadership*. JAI Press.

Den Hartog, Deanne N., Robert J. House, Paul J. Hanges, S. Antonio Ruiz-Quintanilla, Peter W. Dorfman and Associates. 1999. 'Culture Specific and Cross-Culturally Generalizable Implicit Leadership Theories: Are Attributes of Charismatic/Transformational Leadership Universally Endorsed?' *Leadership Quarterly*, 10, 2, 219–56.

Lachman, Ran, Albert Nedd and Bob Hinings. 1994. 'Analyzing Cross-National Management and Organizations: A Theoretical Framework'. *Management Science*, 40, 1, 40–55.

Lynn, R. 1971. *Personality and National Character*. Pergamon.

Newman, Karen L. and Stanley D. Nollen. 1996. 'Culture and Congruence: The Fit Between Management Practices and National Culture'. *Journal of International Business Studies*, 27, 4, 753–79.

Ronen, Simcha and Oded Shenkar. 1985. 'Clustering Countries on Attitudinal Dimensions: A Review and Synthesis'. *Academy of Management Review*, 10/3: 435–54.

Triandis, Harry C. 1982/83. 'Dimensions of Cultural Variation as Parameters of Organizational Theories'. *International Studies of Management and Organization*, Winter 1982/83, 139–69.

—— 1984. 'Toward a Psychological Theory of Economic Growth'. *International Journal of Psychology*, 19, 79–95.

Whitley, Richard D. 1992. *Business Systems in East Asia*. Sage.

The Anglos across the Continents

The Anglo nations are one of the distinctive groups of societies in the Culture Cake at the end of the last chapter. They differ between 'Old World' and 'New World', between those in the 'old' British Isles and those in the 'new' Americas and Australasia.

Because of the British empire, they are a geographical curiosity, unique among cultural groupings in not being in one area of the planet's surface, as are the Northern Europeans or the Asians or Arab nations, for example. They are spread across its surface on islands (Britain and New Zealand) and land masses (Canada and the United States) and what might be called an island land mass (Australia). They were parts of the most far-flung and largest empire the world has yet known, encompassing more than a quarter of the human race. In the case of the British, they were its origin. Numerically the 272 million Americans overwhelm the 59 million British (including here their not-so-Anglo Scots, Welsh and Irish minorities), 30 million Canadians (including here French-Canadians), 19 million Australians, and only 4 million New Zealanders.

The Anglo colonies of the British empire were indeed new, inasmuch as they populated huge lands only sparsely inhabited by the tribes already there, who quickly were reduced to small minorities. This contrasted with the incorporation of India into the empire, for that was the inclusion of a far older, very different, and already populous civilization. In the Anglo colonies, not only were the previous peoples overwhelmed, but often other Europeans who had got there first were ousted, usually the Dutch and the French. New York began as New Amsterdam. New Orleans still retains its French connection.

The explorers, treasure-hunters and settlers carried with them a 'low-context' language. This needs most of what is to be communicated to be stated explicitly. It depends less on 'body language', social situations and implication than do 'high-context' languages (see Chapter 2). So English was appropriate to becoming the world's most international language, for it did not require the slow intuitive learning of an undue profusion of accompanying subtleties. And, as Chapter 1 has explained, no sooner did the British empire fade than the pre-eminence of its most precocious colony, the United States of America, reinforced the prevalence of English in international converse. Not that English is exactly the same everywhere. It has been and is being adapted by different societies. George Bernard Shaw, an Irishman, remarked that 'Britain and America are two nations divided by a common language', and it is not only these two nations which have mutual problems. Canada and Britain also do, for example (see Box 3.1).

Together with the English language went Christianity. Since the English monarchs had broken away from Papal allegiance to head their own Church of England, a compromise between Catholic and Protestant practice, it was the Protestant version of Christianity that prevailed in the new lands, though they all have strong Catholic churches. It still does so, in contrast to the Latin societies.

Box 3.1 Getting Edgy at the Margin

The Canadian lecturer told the class to 'compute it in the margin'. Baffled by familiar words in an unfamiliar combination at an unexpected moment, as well as by the accent in which they were spoken, the British newcomer to the class just did not know what to do. What should be written, and where should it be written? She would have responded easily and readily to a less snappy, more long-winded, British-style suggestion: 'Why not work it out on the edge of the page.'

(from the authors' personal experience)

THE ANGLO WAY

The individualistic Anglos contrast with the Latins in their more relaxed, less personal **managing of authority and of uncertainty**. They live more easily with both. Once the early days of personal entrepreneurship, and patronage, in and from Britain were over, the vehicle of British economic success in the nineteenth century and of American in the twentieth century was impersonal organization. Whilst the ancient Chinese devised bureaucracy, and the Germans made it work efficiently and recognized it for what it was, the Anglos made it the prevailing form of organization, the instrument of the modern economy. Here the term 'bureaucracy' is not used in a pejorative sense. It means just an organization in which who does what, specialization, is demarcated; who is over whom, hierarchy, is defined; and what should be done, rules and procedures, is laid down. Of course, this is a matter of degree, for some organizations have more of these features and some have less, and the organizations in some societies have more than do those in other societies. In German and Japanese businesses, for example, there is less of the Anglo-French view of management as a distinctly defined activity, something to be done by entirely separate people who specialize in doing only that. More managers are technically qualified and get directly involved in production problems or design or maintenance engineering.

Nevertheless, the Anglos spread impersonal organization in which, more or less and in differing degrees in practice, the organization outlasts individuals and forms a stable institution to support economic growth. Characteristically, they balance its potential rigidities by day-to-day pragmatism, working things out as they go along, rather than taking bureaucratic prescription too far. They do not try to manage uncertainty by issuing regulations and declarations, of which they are sceptical. Hence it has been said that the British see an organization as a 'market' in which people negotiate what has to be done, and that an American organization is a 'negotiated order' (Box 3.2). This is not an order that always works well, of course. Mistakes are made, and Anglo management books constantly preach against faulty communication and excessive conflict.

Being the world's most individualistic societies (see Box 2.7) probably exacerbates these problems. This feature of **managing relationships** which is common to the Anglos distinguishes them sharply from all other societies. It is this that enables them to run things impersonally. Since personal obligations and personal relationships matter less than in more collectivistic societies, favouritism and giving family responsibilities priority over company responsibilities are less likely. People can be expected to get on with the job unemotionally. Trust extends more readily beyond friends and family, as explained in Chapter 2, so contacts and contracts with people about whom nothing is known personally can be relied on. It is a commonplace remark that 'we worked in the same office for twenty years but I never knew anything about his private life'. Privacy is valued, and, unless someone volunteers information about where they live or their family, it is improper to ask. The job should be done separately from external circumstances, impersonally. Life is to be compartmentalized, its parts put into separate mental slots that rarely overlap. So Western kinds of organization, which usually means just the Anglo form, are managed very differently when other societies use them. Anglo management forms may be transferable, but their management practice may not be.

Box 3.2   Flying Implicitly

Planes fly the world over, using the same technology controlled in much the same way everywhere. The bulk of the larger airliners are of a single brand from one manufacturer, the Boeing Corporation of the United States. Any more uniform international activity could hardly be imagined. Yet airlines are not run in the same ways. In a study of thirty-one airlines, there were 'autocracies' (e.g. Hong Kong, Indian and Indonesian airlines), 'traditional bureaucracies' (e.g. Argentinian, Pakistani and Spanish airlines), and 'modern bureaucracies' (e.g. French, German and Italian airlines). So where were the Anglos? All five that were included – Australian, British, Canadian, New Zealand and (in so far as it is Anglo influenced) South African – turned up in a category with implicit structure, where more administration was left to intuitive judgement.

(from Wong-Rieger and Rieger in Osigweh, ed.)

Nor may the Anglo way of **managing authority**. As has been said, this is comparatively relaxed, inasmuch as superiors tend to be approachable and their subordinates are more willing to risk questioning what they are told or what the rules say than they might be if they were within a different culture. It is easier for managers to delegate and decentralize than it might be elsewhere. They see themselves as undertaking responsibilities as much as exercising authority.

Even so, organizations typically have a unitary apex to the hierarchy. In other words, they are headed by a single board of directors on which sit the chief executive and heads of principal functions such as (in manufacturing) production, sales, finance and planning, usually with part-time external directors. Lower employees are not represented. This contrasts with the two-tier German structure in which a 'Supervisory Board' of employees and external representatives oversees – nominally, at least – the management board below it.

However, although they have so much broadly in common, the Anglos are no more alike in every respect than are, say, the Latins. Whilst it can be said that they are all relatively assertive and competitive peoples, in **managing oneself** (as it was termed in Chapter 2) some are more stridently masculine than others in this way (Box 2.9). Perhaps Britain and Ireland – so far as the latter can be mentioned here, for the Irish, although not Anglo at heart, live in the British Isles – are most so inclined. Certainly Canadians are least so, being concerned with quality of life and service as much as with ambitious drive and monetary rewards.

Probably a greater division is the Old World/New World difference in **managing time**. At one extreme among Anglos, the Old World British have by far the oldest society, the deepest traditions and the greatest concern with the past. At the other extreme are the New World Americans, optimistically future-orientated, to whom anything may be possible. It is an orientation that, together with their assertiveness, makes them an achieving people, always setting goals to accomplish. Corporations plan sales targets, tourists count their miles flown or the number of nations they have visited.

Even so, all Anglos are inclined to put financial performance first when assessing achievement. Firms have relatively high proportions of accountants in senior positions, in Britain especially. The annual financial results are crucial, and often this is said to encourage 'short-termism', that is, an over-concern with immediate financial returns and financial indices, as compared to the longer view typical among Asian and Continental European managements, who are held to be more concerned with quality products and services which give long-term pay-off. In business, the Anglo countries are conspicuous for bouts of takeovers and mergers based entirely on financial considerations, to an extent unheard of anywhere else.

The three largest Anglo nations best portray these general characteristics in greater detail, namely:

Britain

the USA

and Canada.

ENGLISH CULTURE AND MANAGEMENT

We switch from generalities about the British to the English because it is the English who are at the origin of what it is to be Anglo. Britain is a 'United Kingdom' of three societies, English, Scottish and Welsh (and also Northern Irish), which had various degrees of separate nationhood before they came together under one monarch. All speak English, all are Anglo-influenced, but it is the English people who are most thoroughly Anglo. Therefore it is England which we will focus on here; but England is not synonymous with Britain. This has to be said, since the rest of the world often confuses the two (Box 3.3), though the English do predominate, being 49 million out of a total population of 59 million. Theirs is one of the most densely populated lands on earth, and by far the most densely populated Anglo country.

Although England was itself within the Roman empire for four centuries, and though the Romans pushed many of the earlier Iberian and Celtic population into Wales and the westernmost extremities of England, the imprint of Roman occupation was comparatively light. The English, and the Anglos generally, take these labels by which they are known now from the Angles and the Saxons who came in the fifth and sixth centuries from what is now western and northern Germany and Denmark. They were followed by Vikings from Scandinavia and then, in 1066, by England's last invaders, who believed that they had a rightful title to the country, the Normans from what is now northern France. The feudal system they imposed is the origin of the pronounced social class structure today.

Box 3.3 Belgian Blunders

One of the authors (both of whom are English) was enjoying a guided coach tour of Brussels. 'And 'ere, if you look on the left, we 'ave the English embassy,' said the Belgian guide. Oh no, oh dear, England does not have any embassies, only Britain does, thought our author. Worse was to come. The coach rounded the corner, into a square. 'Over on the other side,' said the misguided guide, 'you can see the statue of General Montgomery, who in World War II led the victorious English army.' Oh no, oh dear, England does not have an army, thought our author: how many of those British troops were Scots or Welsh or Irish? Shaking the guide's hand at the end of the tour he said: 'You should be careful. One day you will have a large irritated Scotsman or Welshman or Irishman on this coach!' The smiling Belgian did not get the point.

In the twentieth century people emigrated from central Europe and, most recently, from the countries of the one-time overseas empire. But long before that, the earlier peoples had blended together to form the English who, as islanders, are oddities among the otherwise predominantly continental Europeans. The British, not just the English, are (with the Irish) the only Europeans to drive on the left, to have a non-proportional voting system and an uncodified piecemeal national constitution, with police unarmed for daily duties, and to speak of 'going to Europe' on their travels! It was all the British, and by no means just the English, who, being maritime, created that vast empire based on small sailing ships. And from its exploitation, together with coal and iron at home, sprang the extraordinary industrial revolution in which the British were prime movers in the eighteenth and nineteenth centuries. Britain produced more coal and iron, and had more shipping, than the rest of the world put together, and the pound sterling was the world's international currency.

But during the twentieth century the empire dissolved, and Britain dropped down the Western European economic league table. Its manufacturing industries and coal-mining contracted. There was something of a revival from the 1980s onwards in the thriving service sector, especially financial services concentrated in the City of London. Though ownership of firms became more and more international, less and less British.

Their long past as an identifiable and free nation leaves the English both liberal and proud of their traditions. Longstanding social class differences are marked, and people are implicitly aware of fine gradations. They are deferential in the sense that they accept the authority of their 'betters', though this is held to be fading away. Change comes slowly, for the English are gradualists. A researcher, who is herself Iranian by origin, summed them up as in Box 3.4.

Box 3.4 What the English Are Like

From a remarkable amalgam of English history and literature, contemporary mass-media features, and the answers to one hundred questionnaires about culture given to English people at random, Tayeb saw them as:

- less emotional
- respectful of people in positions of power
- less obedient to seniors
- less dependent on others
- less fatalist
- aggressive
- less open to bribery
- more able to cope with new and uncertain situations
- more concerned for others outside own community
- accepting responsibility more
- more disciplined
- more arrogant
- more reserved
- more individualistic
- class conscious
- bending the law if necessary
- opposed to change
- more self-controlled
- more trustworthy
- less friendly
- more tenacious
- less clan orientated
- more willing to take account of other people's views

It must be stressed that this characterization comes from research comparing the English with the Indians. It is stated comparatively, *relative to Indian characteristics* (which are listed in Box 9.14).

Box 3.5 Paper-weight

One of the authors was talking to the Managing Director, or Chief Executive, of an engineering factory. It stood in an English industrial city that had been built almost entirely in the boom times of the Industrial Revolution, beside the railway where factories were situated before road transport took over, though now it had modern premises. Even so, in the executive suite the hum of machinery could still be heard and the odour of machine oil could still be smelt.

The company which owned the factory was now a subsidiary of one in New York. 'I'll tell you how I spend my time, too much of it,' said the MD. He jerked open a drawer in his desk, heaved out a wadge of papers many centimetres thick, and banged it on the desktop. 'All this Head Office bumpf to be completed. Every month.' Whilst that sort of thing is an everyday irritant to the Chief Executives of subsidiaries the world over, this was a very American-sized paper pile.

English traditionalism shows in the lingering notion of the 'gifted amateur' as manager, the man without formal qualifications whose social standing equips him to command (a notion which pre-dated the advent of women managers). Its effects can still be seen in the much lower proportion of English managers with higher educational qualifications than in other advanced, industrialized nations.

It also shows in comparisons with American management, in which the English – indeed, the British – persistently manage with lower formalization. This means that they have less formal documentation, both fewer documents and less pages and detail per document (see Box 3.5). In particular, there are fewer kinds of working instructions, job descriptions, manuals of procedures, and schedules, which tell employees what to do or which are a point of reference if they disagree about what to do. It can be argued that this is because in a society with longer traditions, more can be left to implicit mutual understanding. While the larger international British corporations are not so different from their American equivalents in this respect, the average is lower across organizations as a whole. In a word, they are less 'bureaucratized'.

This is but one of many indications of a comparatively casual attitude which shrinks from too great a precision or supposing too great a certainty (Box 3.6, and also Box 2.10). It is an attitude which shows in how the

English language itself is used (Box 3.7). Industrial relations between employers and unions are conducted with less voluminous regulation than in the other main Western European nations, resting more upon negotiation and compromise in the workplace itself. This is a continual point of difficulty when trying to frame European Union rules to cover everyone. Further, as in all the individualistic Anglo societies, bosses do not take personal responsibility for helping with problems in their subordinates' 'private lives' to the extent that occurs in more collectivistic cultures, for this would be an 'invasion of privacy'. Nor do English bosses seek more information and greater control over what goes on down below. There are fewer reports and less data in them than is usual in France or Germany. Authority is dispersed, and in commerce and industry the loosely controlled holding company is typical, owning majority shareholdings in subsidiaries and monitoring their reported financial performance but otherwise allowing them to work as they please. Individuals prefer work which allows them autonomy and scope to learn, comparatively speaking, and they see what they do in less routine terms than do, say, German employees. Yet their trustworthiness (Box 3.4) might also mean conformity. The trust placed by a superior in subordinates means relying on them to do as he or she would wish without detailed 'bossing about', which the English resent. It assumes compliance with implicitly understood requirements, rather than with explicit American-style procedural control, and in American eyes this can appear too conformist.

Box 3.6 Grey British

In the answers to questionnaires on probability and uncertainty given to Asian and British managers, civil servants and students, Wright and his colleagues noticed that the British were different. They were 'better calibrated in their assessments', they were 'expressing a finer differentiation of numerical uncertainty', they used 'many more different probability words'. That is, their view of life had more degrees of uncertainty and was more grey than black or white, compared to Hong Kongese, Indonesians and Malaysians, who tended to respond either/or, black or white, with greater certainty and less probabilistic thinking.

(from Wright, pp. 74–7)

Box 3.7 Speaking Uncertainly

Being comfortable with uncertainty is inherent in how the English language itself is used by all the British:

One might note that this tolerance for ambiguity is well served by the English language, as used by the British rather than by others of Anglo-Saxon origin. Consider that in this native usage:

- *precision is not a virtue as in French,*
- *explicitness is not a virtue as in German, a language that lends itself marvellously to heavy exegesis,*
- *directness is not a virtue as in American.*

English is the language of irony and understatement, of allusion and metaphor, of the rendering of pastel shades of meaning, the language of 'fudging'. One can fudge a lot better in English than in French.

(Lawrence and Edwards, p. 202)

When faced with a problem, the English tend to turn to a committee, usually a continuing or 'standing' one, such as a monthly executive meeting, a financial sub-committee, or a technical advisory group; but also committees set up for the purpose, such as special planning groups or design working parties. This, too, diffuses control and responsibility, more than is customary in Latin organizations, for example. Furthermore, greater delegation and trust than, for example, in French organizations means that there are proportionately fewer supervisors and staff sections to watch over the work of lower employees, even though somewhat more than the Germans need.

In such a decentralized system, the competitive conflict to be expected in an assertive Anglo culture is restrained by a willingness to listen to others (Box 3.4) and a sense of 'fair play'. Those in authority are approachable, relatively speaking; whilst on one hand historically there has been an adversarial view of management–worker relationships and the status symbols of a class-conscious society are everywhere, with larger offices and larger cars and separate higher-quality dining-rooms up the hierarchy, on the other hand pay differentials have been less than in Latin countries or the USA (though wider than in Scandinavia).

Anglo assertiveness is also balanced, in the case of the English by the conservatism inherent in a traditionalistic society. Their conservative nature can be exaggerated by constant comparison with the Americans rather than with the rest of the world. They are, for instance, an inventive people, and did lead the world on indices of new patents per head. Yet they are relatively slow to put new ideas into practice. In contemporary new technologies, such as the application of microelectronics and robotics, their main industrial competitors are often ahead of them. The English want to be more sure that something will work before leaping into it, American-style. They are wary of the future, more able patiently to let things work out (again compared to the typical American approach), and so are less concerned with long-range planning, which seems to them illusory. They take longer to arrive at more cautious decisions, and this makes Brazilians, especially, impatient. But then Brazilians, like Americans, are from the New World (Box 3.8).

Box 3.8 Get a Move on!

When asked about their English counterparts, Brazilian managers living and working in London emphasized their own frustration. Themselves used to getting on with decisions and taking risks (see Chapter 4), they found the English procrastinating. To them, whenever a decision was near, the English asked for more information or for more time to consider it. They were over-cautious and lacked the Brazilian sense of urgency.

(Oliveira)

So major changes are more often brought about by changing top managers, more often than in the relatively stable, commercial and industrial scene on the European continent, or in collectivistic societies where individualistic 'head-hunting' is not so acceptable. The deliberate appointing of a new chief executive with the intention of forcing change through, perhaps as part of a financially motivated takeover, is a common tactic.

The strains of change, the difficulties of relationships with colleagues or superiors, the daily greetings in office or workshop, are eased by humour. The visitor from another land is struck by the constant quips – or witty remarks, the subtle puns made easy by a flexible language, the jokes about the organization itself, which lighten the stress of managing.

AMERICAN CULTURE AND MANAGEMENT

First and greatest of the colonies to break away from Britain was what constituted itself as the United States of America. For it was not one colony then but thirteen, strung unevenly down the Atlantic coastline of North America, which as separate States came together to begin the United States. Their Declaration of Independence in 1776 followed a successful revolutionary war which forced crown and government in London to relinquish control. Founded in what was to Europeans a New World, where the domination of Old World aristocratic classes was weakened or non-existent, and brought together by thrusting off the monarchy, the new States drafted themselves an egalitarian constitution; it enshrined the liberties of a self-reliant people, and eventually led to the liberation of the enslaved population of African origin. Since it did not evolve slowly but had to be discussed and agreed as the legal starting point, it was written and explicit. It has stood for over two centuries, surviving constant litigation to affirm the rights given in it.

Between the eighteenth and nineteenth centuries the European-derived population spread westwards, often in conflict with the earlier Indian inhabitants. The legendary Wild West 'cowboy and Indians' stories were born, as mineral-prospecting and animal-trapping gave way to cattle-ranching and farming in order to feed the rapidly growing population of the east. The American population increased by around a third each decade throughout the nineteenth century, an astonishing phenomenon due to the birth rate in a young population and to waves of immigration from Europe. Its population now numbers over 270 million.

This expansion eventually multiplied the number of States that are federally United from thirteen to fifty, including two overseas: Alaska and Hawaii. It created the population for vigorous industrialization in quickly growing cities in the east. The New York skyscraper came to symbolize modern America. This industrial capacity produced unimagined quantities of weapons, planes, vehicles and ships in the Second World War, and clearly placed the US as the world's leading economy afterwards. In the 'Cold War', or stand-off confrontation with the Soviet Union, it was again successful.

It is difficult to speak of the characteristics of management in a land that spans a continent, coast to coast. These characteristics must differ in degree from north to south, from east to west, and around a 'melting-pot' – as it was once called – of races and nationalities . . . though they never melted away: they remained identifiable. Even so, an original Anglo (Yankee) culture predominates, the 'Anglo Way' described at the start of this chapter though shaped by the spacious opportunities of a new society in vast territories.

Box 3.9 Book Tokens

Some titles of books on management by prominent authors:

In Search of Excellence (Peters and Waterman)
Business @ the Speed of Thought (Bill Gates)
The One Minute Manager (Blanchard and Johnson)
Competing for the Future (Hamel and Prahalad)
The Dance of Change: Challenges of Sustaining Momentum in Learning Organizations (Senge and colleagues)
Driving Change (Wind and Main)
Frontiers of Management (Kanter)
Executive Achievement: Making it at the Top (Blake and Mouton)

What other society could produce such an array of goal-setting, achieving, fast-paced book titles on management? They are unmistakably American.

It gives to all a vigorous, forward-looking style, a sense that time is to be seized upon to advantage (Box 3.9). 'Time is money', as the saying goes. Time is not to pass idly by, but to be controlled and exploited. Time is seen in a linear way, extending into the future; a resource to be made use of, rather than a history to be treasured, which it tends to be to the English. Managerially, therefore, time can be scheduled in detail. There must be clear, written plans, proposals and estimates. Since there is no time to waste in ambiguity, clarity should come from research, numerical modelling and calculable data. Quantification makes things seem more real. This data should be produced by trained specialists who concentrate on financial analysis or market research or quality control, and so on. There is no 'gifted amateur' tradition here, but rather an analytical approach. It is no accident that in the first half of the twentieth century this culture gave rise to the high point of 'scientific management', linked with the name of F. W. Taylor, by which time and effort were to be saved by giving employees precise instructions on what to do, how to do it, and precisely when to do it. From this comes the image of the worker on the assembly line, endlessly screwing the same bolts into the same holes in the same way as the half-assembled product passes by.

So the typical American manager's reaction to a suggestion is: 'Let me look at my schedule.' When can something be fitted in? He or she goes straight into negotiations, openly and candidly and perhaps simplistically (compare Box 4.3), seeking a conclusion to discussion as soon as possible. Time-consuming socializing, entertaining and 'getting to know you' niceties are frustrating. The friendly, informal, direct (low-context) American style, quickly on first-name terms, has no need of such social paraphernalia. It is American conferences which begin with business sessions over breakfast.

A future-orientated view of time is a hopeful view. Maybe things can be changed in future; maybe things can get better. So change in an organization is to be welcomed. Whilst it carries the risk that your job or career may be adversely affected, it brings the chance of improvements and a 'lucky break' with brighter prospects. New ideas are to be tried in case they do work, rather than regarded sceptically because there is no evidence that they will work, which is the English inclination.

This is proactive managing which has a go to see what will happen rather than a 'wait and see' approach – which more than anyone else does see's problems as opportunities to do something, to learn, rather than difficulties to be overcome. Try now the new computer-controlled equipment, try now selling 'someplace else', and see if it succeeds. It might.

It has been said earlier of the English that they manage with less formalization. Putting that the other way around, American management and American society generally tend to have rather more, as any immigrant who has tackled United States tax returns for the first time, even with the aid of the almost unavoidable accountant, will despairingly confirm: they are startlingly bulky and detailed. So, too, are documents concerning the job. There are likely to be more – and more bulky – job descriptions, written instructions, manuals of procedures, work schedules, and the like. This is not to say that organizations in Britain do not have a lot; the bigger the organization the more so, as is the case the world over. It is to say that American managements generate noticeably more. Perhaps this is because, just as a society which lacks the unifying customs of an older nation such as Britain needs a fully codified constitution, so employees need more explicit guidance and control at work (Box 3.10). This American/English difference is relative of course, within the tendency of the Anglos to be somewhat casual about rules and regulations and to avoid them overmuch in management.

The American desire to have contracts cut and dried and complete can be offensive to those who place more reliance on establishing personal trust, such as many Arabs and Asians. The Americans can separate the matter in hand from the personalities concerned more than they do.

The strong and individualist (Protestant) work ethic of the first settlers still lies behind the urgent drive for achievement (Box 3.11). The high masculinity, as it has been called (Box 2.9), of Americans shows most

---

Box 3.10 Formalized Informality

How top managers take decisions was being compared in companies in Britain. The researchers noticed that among them were two subsidiaries of American corporations. So they compared these two, manufacturers of chemicals and paint and of tools and components, with two British-owned subsidiaries, manufacturers of automotive friction products and of contractors' equipment. There were no American managers in any of the companies, not even in the two that were under American ownership.

In the two that were American subsidiaries it was found that when making major decisions, such as expanding the factory or adding departments, top managers (a) used more informal, temporary, working groups (whereas the British-owned firms used more formal standing committees such as boards, management meetings, and finance committees); (b) reached a conclusion faster (averaging around seven months compared to fourteen). Thus distinctly American characteristics showed up even in British managers when they were affected by American ownership.

Bearing in mind the American propensity for greater formalized documentation, the researchers concluded that American management is *'informal within a formalized frame'*, whereas British management is *'formal within a non-formalized customary pattern'*.

(Mallory *et al.*)

Box 3.11 Achieving the Best Hamburger

In Search of Excellence was, and is, the most famous management book of all time. It has been read throughout the world. Yet it was written by two *American* consultants, Peters and Waterman, from a study of forty-three of the largest *American* companies selected because of their consistent above-average performance. These included such leading names as Boeing, Hewlett-Packard, IBM, Johnson & Johnson, McDonald's, Proctor & Gamble and 3M.

The suggested recipe for success in business, distilled from the experience of these companies is:

1 *A bias for action*
2 *Being close to the customer*
3 *Autonomy and entrepreneurship*
4 *Productivity through people*
5 *Hands-on, value driven*
6 *Stick to the knitting*
7 *Simple form, lean staff*
8 *Simultaneous loose–tight properties*

(Peters and Waterman)

The *assertive, competitive* (masculine) American drive for achievement is instantly recognizable. There is a bias for action (1) in forward-looking entrepreneurial innovation (3), with high expectations of productive performance (4), aiming to be the best (5: value driven). Though group effort is extolled, the emphasis is on *individualistic* autonomous, personal initiative, and personal rewards for achievement (3, 4).

Decentralized authority goes with a *toleration for the uncertainty* inherent in 'loose' elements in structure that allow individuals freedom to get on with the job (8).

The right practices in sales (2), production (6) and organization structure (7) carry this culture-shaped approach into effect.

A different culture in a different economy would have produced a recipe which was different in the degree both to which these items were emphasized and to which others were included.

clearly here. The drive for success and high regard for those who succeed colours management discussions and policies to a degree that is unusual elsewhere. Personally managers see themselves in a win–lose competition for raises and advancement (or, as the English would say, rises and promotion). Openness of information does not include salaries, which are individually negotiated, differential and confidential. Managers are concerned with their personal career and departmental position as much as with the organization which they manage. In an individualistic and assertive society they hire and fire, and are themselves hired and fired. Job mobility is not so restrained by social class considerations as it is in Europe – and, indeed, in most of the rest of the world.

Just as the newcomer to the USA is struck by the service without servility in diners and stores, so authority is handled without deference. Low power distance means that subordinates can speak readily and directly with those above them in the hierarchy. When an American says briskly, 'Yessir', he or she does not say 'sir' with the deferential meaning that it and equivalent terms carry in the rest of the world.

Not surprisingly, Management by Objectives (MbO) started in the USA and has had most success there. It requires superior and subordinate to work out together the objectives the subordinate is to aim at. So it implicitly assumes that the subordinate feels sufficiently independent to be able to discuss freely his or her future with the boss. But in France, a high power distance society (Box 2.5), where superiors and subordinates find it more difficult to talk personally in such an open, easy-going manner, MbO does not work (see Box 11.13).

Box 3.12 Organizations Afloat

Richardson, an American, worked on both American and British merchant ships for nine years, and later (as a researcher) interviewed seamen from both, as well as again himself working on two ships. He found that the Americans worked under clear and formalized rules; they played down status distinctions, and knew their rights to 'due process' of appeal if an officer overstepped the mark. The British were more aware of customary fine status distinctions, which they did not challenge, taking authority for granted and protesting against its misuse in a more *ad hoc*, personal way.

On American ships, a grievance would be handled by an elected union delegate, discussion centring on the interpretation of a written union contract which described in great detail the rules and conditions of work. On British ships, a complaint, for example that the ship's mate had not fully recorded all the overtime worked, would be made personally to the mate or bos'un. Anyone aggrieved might be accompanied by a delegation of his shipmates to give him support in the presence of authority, and might be spoken for by an informally emerging spokesman among them who could talk and think fast. Whilst it would be understood that the complaint should be taken step by step up the hierarchy, there was no explicit written procedure.

Although this contrast was drawn quite a few years ago, and British practice will have become more formalized since then, the relative difference persists.

(Richardson)

The American way of handling authority, on the other hand, is not only to delegate but to restrain authority by defining its limits and prescribing 'due process' of appeal if those limits are exceeded. Unlike the English, Americans do not trust those in authority to act within the customary bounds of what is proper and acceptable. Job descriptions state more fully who has authority for what, and rule books spell out how to appeal against the misuse of authority (Box 3.12). Given this, there is less suspicion of the powerful than in France and less inclination to politicize an organization by constantly seeing everyone as manoeuvring for position (compare Box 4.5).

CANADIAN CULTURE AND MANAGEMENT

This curious nation is much smaller in population than either Britain or the United States with only 30 million people, but larger even than the USA in territory. Indeed, territorially it is the second largest nation on earth (after Russia), its realm stretching towards the North Pole in colossal areas of tundra and ice-covered surface. Its people, however, mainly inhabit a comparatively narrow strip close to the US border – narrow, perhaps, but no less than 4,000 miles long, the width of Canada from Atlantic to Pacific.

Canada's interest lies in its unique composition, geographically and culturally, combining something of both the Americans and the British yet at the same time contrasting Anglo and Latin in the same State.

Its earliest peoples were Indians and Inuit (or Eskimos, as they were once called) further north. From Europe the French were the first to explore what became Canada. Gradually a thinly scattered network of trappers and trading posts began to hunt for fur, mainly beaver pelts, in and around the seemingly endless rivers and lakes. Slowly control came into British hands during the seventeenth and eighteenth centuries, either piecemeal by settlement or wrested from France by conquest or cession. Britain relinquished colonial sovereignty in 1867 when independent nationhood began.

The earliest farming and townships being towards the east, around the St Lawrence river, with easiest access to France and Britain, the population and principal cities have continued to be concentrated there. But they are divided between the Anglo-dominated province of Ontario, centred on the city of Toronto, and French-dominated Quebec, centred on Montréal. The sparseness of population elsewhere is revealed by eleven million being in Ontario and seven million in Quebec out of the total nationally of 30 million.

Canadians often feel their nation has too much of a 'branch plant economy', too much of its commerce and industry being conducted by subsidiaries of US corporations. Certainly it has with its economically giant neighbour the largest one-to-one proportionate trading relationship in the world. Internally, the Québécois, the people of Quebec province, feel somewhat the same about business in their province having been mainly Anglo-Canadian controlled.

Despite the Anglo-Canadians being the most considerate and temperate and the least driving (relatively feminine, Box 2.9) of the Anglo peoples, and the French culture being even more so, the juxtapositioning of Anglophones and Francophones in one nation is uncomfortable. Whereas England and France are separated by a strip of water (though even this symbolizes the contrast between them, as they insist on calling it respectively the English Channel and La Manche), there is no such watery buffer between Anglo and French Canadians. Whether they can continue as one nation is constantly in question.

Managerially, Anglophones and Francophones differ exactly as would be expected, in the directions of their parent cultures. The Latin in the Francophones shows in their less competitive and focused approach to management. Comparatively speaking, a job is a means to a full life around family and friends, not just an end in itself. Time is not so urgent, punctuality not so vital. Management meetings tend to meander and may neither start nor finish on schedule. Yet regulations are necessary to ensure order. So when a Francophone moves into Anglo-Canada as a chief executive (a rare event), he ruffles the feelings of his (never her) fellow managers. Suddenly an increased stream of memoranda and policy statements issues from the chief executive's office. Anglos who previously did without the paperwork, and who are time-conscious, become irritated. What they want are fair opportunities to pursue their careers untrammelled, whereas their Francophone equivalents would accept a more formal exercise of authority, provided their benefits and futures were assured (Box 3.13).

Box 3.13 Dual Aspirations

A comparison of Francophone employees in a Francophone organization (French in a French setting) with Anglophone employees in an Anglophone organization (Anglos in an Anglo setting), and of both with Francophones in the same Anglophone organization (French in Anglo), all in the French-Canadian city of Montreal, showed that: (a) *French in French* put greatest value on security, fringe benefits, and promotion to higher status; (b) *Anglos in Anglo* put greater value on personal achievement and fair pay. They were less satisfied with their situation since they were always seeking to better it; (c) *French in Anglo* came in between. The comparison was of employees in two large service organizations, respectively 187, 115 and 82 employees in the above categories.

(Kanungo *et al.*)

Box 3.14 Conserving Jobs

Comparing seventeen American and seventeen Canadian construction companies, banking institutions and loan companies, Carroll found that, though the Canadian managements were responsive to change, they were conservative in protecting the administrative fabric of their organizations. They held on to staffing levels and levels of general administrative expenditure more than the Americans did.

(Carroll)

Box 3.15 The Cash Cost of Culture

Noticing that a high proportion of successful Canadian retailers failed when they opened branches over the border in the United States, Canadian researchers tried to find out why this was. Talking with executives of ten Canadian firms which had ventured into the US, eight of them unsuccessfully, they found that although Americans were so near, and the USA loomed so large in Canadian eyes, there was more 'cultural distance' than was recognized. The higher 'masculinity' American culture showed in more assertive and more competitive behaviour. As the researchers put it:

Canadian executives made the erroneous assumption that 'the United States is just like Canada, only larger'. Learning begins with the ability to see differences, and this projected similarity interfered with executives' ability to learn about the markets, the regions, the consumers and the competition. It was often believed that Americans were just like Canadians, sharing a similar language, culture, values, tastes and business practices. Notably, it was precisely the fact that these two countries probably are more similar than any other two that masked some fundamental differences in values and attitudes. Consumers were different; they were more competitive and they reacted differently than in Canada.

Compared to Canadians, American consumers were more price-conscious and more aware of their buying power, so they demanded to be 'treated with importance' when they shopped. Store employees complemented this by working harder and expecting pay to match.

(from O'Grady and Lane, p. 325)

Anglo-Canada might be better termed 'non-French Canada', for it has a high proportion of peoples of Continental European and, most recently, Asian origin. Not everyone is an Anglo. But the language is English, the institutions are British derived, and the prevailing ways are Anglo in character. Although so near to and affected by the United States, management differs from the American pattern. There is less written formalization of the kinds described earlier in American organizations, but more than in English organizations. Management is less overtly competitive in manner and, in an English direction, more conservative and perhaps considerate (Box 3.14). This may not be recognized by either, most likely not by the more numerous Americans. Yet the Canadians, too, can see Americans as just Canadians with a difference, to their cost as Box 3.15

shows. Differences in culture should not be overlooked even between nations which are close culturally, geographically and economically. The difficulty for Canadians is that they are in between these American, British and French influences upon them, not knowing quite how to behave, whether it is beha*viour* or beh*avior*.

* * *

The far-spread Anglos, then, have many similarities in their approach to management, which help them to work together when occasion arises. Generally speaking, they understand each other's individual competitiveness and impersonal but not overly bureaucratic view of organization. Their common language-base is a tie between them. Yet they see neither authority, nor openness in relationships and communication, nor the value of time in the same way at all. American management and British management, the 'New World' and the 'Old', make the contrast here.

The Anglos appear as a left-hand slice of the 'culture-cake' diagram (Box 2.13), on the broadly lower power distance and individualistic side. The next chapter is about the Latins of both Europe and South America, who straddle the bottom of the diagram and so widen the picture.

Further Reading

ENGLAND

Dubin, Robert. 1970. 'Management in Britain: Observations of a Visiting Professor'. *Journal of Management Studies*, 7/2, 183–98.

Lane, Christel. 1989. *Management and Labour in Europe*. Edward Elgar.

Lawrence, Peter and Vincent Edwards. 2000. *Management in Western Europe*. (Chapter 12: Britain). Macmillan.

Tayeb, Monir. 1987. 'Contingency Theory and Culture: A Study of Matched English and Indian Manufacturing Firms'. *Organization Studies*, 8/3, 241–62.

1989. *Organizations and National Culture: A Comparative Analysis*. Sage.

UNITED STATES

Alston, Jon P. 1986. *The American Samurai*.* De Gruyter.

Dubin, Robert. 1970. 'Management in Britain: Observations of a Visiting Professor'.* *Journal of Management Studies*, 7/2, 183–98.

* describes Americans by comparison

Hall, Edward T. and Mildred Reed Hall. 1990. *Understanding Cultural Differences: Germans, French and Americans*. Intercultural Press.

Harris, Philip R. and Robert T. Moran. 1991. *Managing Cultural Differences* (3rd edn, Ch. 13). Gulf Publishing.

Lawrence, Peter. 1996. *Management in the USA*. Sage.

Moran, Robert T. 1985. *Getting Your Yen's Worth*.* Gulf Publishing.

CANADA

Carroll, Barbara Wake. 1990. 'Systemic Conservatism in North American Organizations'. *Organization Studies*, 11/3, 413–34.

Kanungo, Rabindra N., Gerald J. Gorn and Henry J. Dauderis. 1977. 'Motivational Orientation of Canadian Anglophone and Francophone Managers', in H. C. Jain and R. N. Kanungo (eds.), *Behavioural Issues in Management: The Canadian Context*. McGraw-Hill Ryerson.

Lipset, Seymour Martin. 1986. 'Historical Traditions and National Characteristics: a Comparative Analysis of Canada and the United States'. *Canadian Journal of Sociology*, 11, 113–55.

Other Sources

ENGLAND

McMillan, Charles J., David J. Hickson. C. R. Hinings and R. E. Schneck. 1981. 'The Structure of Work Organizations Across Societies', in David J. Hickson and Charles J. McMillan (eds.), *Organization and Nation*. Gower.

Maurice, Marc, Arndt Sorge and Malcolm Warner. 1980. 'Societal Differences in Organizing Manufacturing Units: A Comparison of France, West Germany and Great Britain'. *Organization Studies*, 1/1, 59–86.

Tayeb, Monir. 1993. 'English Culture and Business Organizations', in David J. Hickson (ed.), *Management in Western Europe: Society, Culture and Organization in Twelve Nations*. De Gruyter.

Wright, George. 1984. *Behavioural Decision Theory*. Penguin.

UNITED STATES

Kanter, Rosabeth Moss. 1997. *Frontiers of Management*. Harvard Business School Press.

Mallory, Geoffrey R., Richard J. Butler, David Cray, David J. Hickson and David

* describes Americans by comparison (especially Chapter 2)

C. Wilson. 1983. 'Implanted Decision-Making: American Owned Firms in Britain'. *Journal of Management Studies*, 20/2, 191–211.

Peters, Thomas J. and Robert H. Waterman Jr. 1982. *In Search of Excellence: Lessons from America's Best-Run Companies*. Harper & Row.

Richardson, S. A. 1956. 'Organizational Contrasts on British and American Ships'. *Administrative Science Quarterly*, 1, 189–207.

CANADA

O'Grady, Shawna, and Henry W. Lane. 1996. 'The Psychic Distance Paradox'. *Journal of International Business Studies*, 27, 309–33.

ANGLOS IN GENERAL

Wong-Rieger, Durhane and Fritz Rieger. 1989. 'The Influence of Societal Culture on Corporate Culture, Business Strategy and Performance in the International Airline Industry', in Chimezie A. B. Osigweh, Yg (ed.), *Organizational Science Abroad*. Plenum Press.

4

The Latins – Southern Europe and South America

Highlighting:
France
Italy
Brazil

ORIGINS

Two groups of Latin nations are brought together in the same slice of the culture-cake diagram (Box 2.13) because of their predominantly Latin characteristics, even though they differ between the 'Old World' of Europe and the 'New World' of the Americas, just as the Anglos do in the previous chapter.

Also like the Anglos, those in the 'New World' far outnumber the Europeans. Whilst there are something over 160 million people in Latin Europe (59 million French, 58 million Italian, 39 million Spanish, and 10 million Portuguese), the number in Central and South America is expanding towards twice that number. Central America is dominated by around 100 million Mexicans, and South America by the geographical bulk and perhaps 170 million population of Brazil. Otherwise piecemeal conquest left a bespattering of smaller, often tiny, States, though Argentina exceeds 37 million people.

The pronounced Latin nature of these nations – and indeed the use of the word 'Latin' to describe them – arises from successive empires. The first of these was the Roman empire which spread across Europe, the second the more or less contemporaneous Spanish and Portuguese empires which reached across the Atlantic Ocean.

As the Roman legions pushed Roman rule outwards in the last centuries before Christ, so that a small town on the River Tiber in what is now central Italy became the largest city on earth, at the hub of the largest empire then known, so they carried with them a civilization which is still the most marked feature of western Europe. Roman rule was longest and tightest south of the River Rhine, which cuts in a crooked diagonal across from the North Sea to the Alps, and it is the nations south of it which are now indelibly Latin. How organizations today are managed still shows the influence of the vast hierarchic order, topped by a strong dictator or an emperor, which held sway, ruling through a common codified legal system and a common language, a version of Latin being spoken everywhere in the Roman-built towns. The Romance languages (French, Italian, Spanish and Portuguese) carry this inheritance today. Eventually a common Christian religion was also proclaimed, leading to a Catholic church which is still based in the city of Rome and is strongest in Latin lands where professed moral standards are still inclined to be stricter compared to those elsewhere in Europe.

From the end of the fifteenth century, adventurers from Spain and Portugal, the two Latin nations which faced the ocean, carried Latin rule to Central and South America. Overwhelming the inhabitants, richer civilizations in Central America and to the west and sparser tribes in the south, they turned to the Church to settle which of them should rule what. The pope drew a line on the map which confirmed present-day Brazil as Portuguese-speaking and all the rest as Spanish-speaking.

THE LATIN TOUCH

Very broadly, in the Latin lands there is a comparatively personal approach to managing and organizing; personal authority counts and personal relationships matter. The personal touch makes organizations work, despite many-layered hierarchies and bureaucratized procedures, often by overriding or circumventing the rules.

The Latin lands are most alike in **managing uncertainty** (they can all be found at the top of the list of nations in Box 2.10). Their managers tend to want to do something to reduce uncertainty, rather than just to live with it. Since all forms of organization – companies, hospitals, universities, professional firms or whatever – are beset by changes which can heighten uncertainty over what may be happening, this is a constant pressure which arouses anxiety. The anxiety is fuelled by a relatively political view of organizations, which readily leads to suspicions about what may be going on and whether others can be trusted. The authority, rules and routines that make organizations what they are, are both the means of management and also the means of dealing with this uncertainty and exerting control. Clearly laid-down authority, rules and routines give a pseudo-certainty that someone is in control and that things are being done as they should be done. Doubts may persist as to whether that is so, but at least people know where they are and what should be. Ambiguity over who is supposed to be responsible is minimized.

Yet a relatively bureaucratic form of organization, for this is what it may become, can be inflexible. If so, then it can be made to work by the use and, sometimes, abuse of personal power, and by the personal touch in getting around the rules. And that can succeed, as the comparative economic success of France and (northern) Italy implies (Box 2.11). It can do so despite this strain between the need for clear and complete rules and the need to get around them. For the strain results in generally lower satisfaction on the job, relative to the northern European nations at least, especially if exacerbated by officious officialdom.

The last may well be more likely because of the other feature which is similar across the Latin world, namely the way of **managing authority**. There is a tendency to be authority conscious, for those above to wield their authority and for those below to look for a strong lead. This reinforces the centralized hierarchies. It also brings an inclination to pin responsibility for what happens on particular individuals, to find scapegoats from above or below.

However, alike though they are as a group compared to the rest of the world, the Latin countries show sharp differences among themselves. Most pronounced are the big differences in assertiveness or, as it has been called, masculinity. In this aspect of **managing oneself**, a competitive striving to achieve and to dominate, the Italians stand out among the Europeans for their 'macho' tendency, and it looks as if the Venezuelans and Mexicans lead the South Americans in this respect (see Box 2.9). At the other extreme, the Portuguese are the least 'macho' of the European Latins, more nurturing and considerate, and so are the Chileans and Costa Ricans in Latin America.

This difference is one which cuts across the southern Europeans and the Latin Americans, but they are divided from one another as between Old World and New World by their approaches to **managing relation-ships** and to **managing time**. The New World Latins are more collectivistic than their Old World kindred, even more involved in family and even more inclined to overlap family and organization. They more often retain family control of management, put family members in senior positions, and circumvent the rules for the benefit of their families as much as for themselves personally. Management is not coolly impersonal – though this, as everything in this book, is *relative*, for the Latin Europeans are themselves more inclined this way than the highly individualistic northern Europeans, if the two are compared within Europe.

Latin Americans are not only more collectivist but are probably generally more immediatist than the Latin Europeans, though the latter can surprise Europeans from further north by their flexibility, leaving arrangements to the last minute and changing long-agreed plans. But Latin Americans tend to be inclined even further that way. To them, time is seen as in the present and the future, more than it is in the past; so managerial action and results should be immediate, without delay, taking a comparatively optimistic view of the future, whereas the Europeans with a longer history behind them can be more patient in awaiting results.

From among the Latin nations, we have chosen the three largest to exemplify these generalities, namely:

France
Italy
and Brazil

FRENCH CULTURE AND MANAGEMENT

France is a nation similar in numbers to Britain and Italy, about 59 million people, geographically the largest in western Europe, situated at the centre of the European Union. Its early conquest by the Romans laid the basis for the longest existing unified State in western Europe, notwithstanding later periods of feudal warfare and dismemberment by the Norman-led English who once ruled much of the north and the west. The legacy of many centuries of dominance by the Roman Catholic Church still frames attitudes, even though active involvement in the Church has declined.

From glittering monarchs to revolutions, the French have long looked for strong leadership, most obviously in their great military leaders.

Napoleon at the end of the eighteenth and beginning of the nineteenth century and De Gaulle in the Second World War of the twentieth century. The term *les cadres*, for what in English are called managers, is of military origin.

This history is embodied in Paris, the capital of a comparatively centralized state. From Paris, standard systems of governance, law and education have been prescribed, the last an elitist system in a class-conscious society. From Paris, the State has reached out to become heavily involved in business, stimulating, protecting and owning it. There is a record of well-known successes in what might loosely be called 'prestige transport' – the high-speed train, the Concorde supersonic plane and the Airbus plane manufacturer, and the Ariane rocket (all but the train having other European contributions). Even privatization – following the British example – leaves government influential and often financially involved.

Yet the French revolution of 1789, which stands with the Russian revolution of 1917 as one of the two most influential revolutions in world history, was fought for ideals of individual freedom against central authority, the elusive *Liberté, Egalité, Fraternité*. And this contradictory combination of authority and freedom did not prevent – and may have fostered – notable economic growth in the second half of the twentieth century.

It is a contradiction that pervades the French approach to managing and organizing. Culturally, the French approach is distinctive, indeed unique, in the tension it embodies between looking for and responding to a strong, authoritative lead, while individualistically resisting the encroachment of authority (see both high power distance and high individualism in Boxes 2.5 and 2.7). No other Latin nation has this tension to this degree.

That authoritative lead begins at the top, represented in business organizations by the characteristically French figure of the PDG, the *Président Directeur-Général*. He – and it is, of course, he and not she – often represents the controlling family, for a high proportion of even large organizations continue to be family-owned. Public companies are legally required to have employee representatives on their boards, but they can do little to constrain the power of top management since they are non-voting, and since the board ratifies rather than takes decisions. The PGD is its head rather than merely its chair. Like the heads of other organizations, he works with a comparatively absolutist view of formal authority, an authority which he exercises in a personal and idiosyncratic manner. A tall hierarchy with many levels and big pay and status differentials, each level 'policing' those below, signifies this authority. There is not so much a 'negotiated order', as it has been termed in Anglo organizations, in which things are worked out piecemeal in discussion and argument around and across the levels; rather there is a pyramid, down which the instructions flow.

Decisions can be taken quickly in such a system, perhaps with the rational logic that the French admire. If decisions catch the imagination of those below and give scope for their capabilities, they can be implemented with *élan*, verve and inspiration (Box 4.1). If not, things may not go well. Box 4.2 quotes the view of two British authors.

When superiors and subordinates feel personally distant from one another, such top-down communication tends to be written as much as verbal, and is less casual than in Anglo organizations. There is a greater gulf between those who are above and those who are below, a lack of trust, which may underlie the nationwide mass strike waves that have occasionally swept across France.

Box 4.1 Deciding Rapidly, Starting Slowly

In decision-making, the French are able to move more rapidly than the Germans because they have a highly centralized authority structure. French executives can and do make independent decisions and don't have to go through the long, time-consuming process of lateral clearances or wade through several levels in the hierarchy for decisions, as is common in Germany.

The tempo of the business day is also different in the two countries. As one German executive described it. *The French start slowly and build; they peak at late afternoon and continue going strong far into the evening. The Germans start right out in the early morning and maintain a steady work pace with a slowdown at the end of the day. They are much more apt to have a short lunch hour and leave at 5:00 p.m.*

(Hall and Hall, p. 90)

When meetings do occur, whether among managers or between managers and lower-level employees, they are inclined to discuss more than to decide. Decisions are for those in authority, to be taken by them outside meetings. Moreover, intelligent discussion of the issue is valued for its own sake, not least because of the high proportion of managers who are well educated. In larger organizations most of them will have arrived via an exacting *grande école* or higher college, more appropriate to governance and harder to get into than a university. So management is regarded more as an intellectual challenge with less of the driving commercialism as in the American image. So there is a taste for argument, and as much merit seen in defining the question as in giving an answer. The French have been schooled to think around the question, its thesis and antithesis, point and counterpoint, and can even be said to think in circles (Box 4.3)! Yet they communicate in a high-context way (see Chapter 2) compared to the Anglos, Germanics and Nordics, leaving something to the imagination, something to be understood implicitly from the context in which it is referred to.

Box 4.2 Top and Bottom in France

French companies tend to do big things well and small things badly, because all the brains are concentrated at the top, the 'lower downs' are more alienated than their counterparts in other countries and are not going to 'buy into' the system.

(Lawrence and Edwards, p. 44)

Box 4.3 Thinking Around

Whereas the American tries to think in a straight line, the Frenchman insists on thinking in a circle. The American mistrusts complexities and tends to over-simplify. The Frenchman, by inclination and education, mistrusts simple things and tends to over-complicate ... By French standards, no American speaker can give a full, sophisticated answer. A Frenchman tries to define the question; the American tries to answer it.

All this might be summed up in a hypothetical translation of Hamlet's soliloquy. In American business jargon, the soliloquy would probably come out: 'To be or not to be? Fine. Let's take a vote.' A Frenchman would say, 'Etre ou ne pas être. C'est là la question. Mais la question est mal posée.' [In other words, 'To be or not to be? That is the question. But the question is badly put ...']

(Eggers, E. Russell, p. 139, in T. Weinshall, ed.)

In common with other Latin nations, the French act in such a way as to reduce or avoid uncertainty, as was said earlier. Thus the organizational pyramid both symbolizes authority and gives pseudo-certainty that things are in order and under control. It is wrapped in compendious rules and instructions detailing what is to be done, issued and administered not only by layers of supervisory echelons but also by numerous departments and sections. It exemplifies what has been called full bureaucracy or classic bureaucracy.

This administrative edifice is not treated with awesome respect, either by those within it or by those who have to deal with it (Box 4.4). As has been said, it can be manipulated to defend the individual against the encroachment of authority. Rules can be ignored. Rules can be broken.

Box 4.4 Umbrellas and the Law

Procedures are taken less seriously in France than in Germany or the United States. If a rule or regulation gets in the way of achieving a goal, the French will try to find some way to circumvent it. This is in direct contrast to Germans, who are meticulous in following procedures. Procedures bore the French: they think they inhibit their creativity and impinge on their individuality. They tend to be disrespectful of the law. We once observed a Frenchman walking against the light in Paris traffic, wading out into midstream and jabbing his umbrella at the cars. When his companion reprimanded him for not waiting for the traffic light, he replied, 'No machine knows better than I when it's safe to cross.'

(Hall and Hall, p. 106)

And they can be used to protect the independence of underlings. Undue interference from above can be held in check by demanding that authority itself shall stay within the rules. This reveals the ultimate tension between the need for authority and freedom for the individual. It has been suggested that this creates a 'vicious circle', higher authority continually imposing and attempting to enforce rules which lower employees continually stultify (Box 4.5 describes an example on the factory floor), and that it takes a leader of 'Napoleonic' proportions to break through the impasse by compelling an upheaval of change, after which the stalemate resumes. This very view is itself an example of a politicized Latin interpretation of what is going on, and contrasts with Anglo Saxon 'gradualism'.

Box 4.5 The Bureaucratic Vicious Circle

Cigarette manufacture in France was State-owned, and was dispersed around the country in small regional factories. Twenty-three of these factories were studied by the French researcher, Crozier, and his colleagues. They found simple, indeed deceivingly obvious, situations. But the similarity of what they found, repeated again and again around the regions, drove home the point.

The bulk of the several hundred employees in each plant were female production operatives, working on semi-automatic machines, with male maintenance mechanics setting and repairing the machines. In such a State-owned monopoly, administration was centralized in Paris. Raw material supplies, production quantities, prices, appointments to jobs, and pay, were all decreed from there. The same national system of bureaucratic instructions and regulations enveloped each factory.

Yet within each factory there was one eventuality that Paris could not control: the machines broke down. Only the mechanics could get them going again. Ultimately, therefore, the entire structure depended on the personal know-how of these mechanics. Their implicit but very real power rested on their ability to cope with this uncontrollable uncertainty, and they displayed it and protected it by aggressiveness towards plant supervisors and managers, and by a domineering attitude towards the production operatives.

Had Paris been able to impose regular preventive maintenance to minimize breakdowns, then the power position of the mechanics would have been undermined. No breakdowns to cope with, no dependence on the mechanics to get work restarted, so no power for mechanics. But Paris could do no such thing – the mechanics saw to that.

Thus the struggle by authority for greater control, through bureaucratic procedures, and by those lower down to resist, through thwarting such procedures, continued in an unending 'vicious circle', not just in these factories but in organizations throughout France.

(from Crozier; elaborated by Hickson *et al.*)

ITALIAN CULTURE AND MANAGEMENT

Italy, a new State with an ancient history, contains the origin of this whole chapter. Its capital city envelops the ruins of ancient Rome, whose language, arts and early struggles with the management of a far-flung empire make it possible today to speak of Latin lands with Latin cultures. It always has been and still is the seat of the largest and longest surviving international organization humankind has ever known: the Roman Catholic Church, governed from the autonomous Vatican enclave in central Rome.

Present-day Italy is equal in population to Europe's other major predominantly Latin nation, France, but it is of much more recent creation. To become what it is today it had to go through an agonizing history. Even before the collapse of the Roman empire in the west in the fifth century, successive consuls and emperors fought for control of a realm where manly prowess was esteemed; their severely masculine, sculpted features are still with us in the art galleries. After the empire, conquest and reconquest swayed to and fro within what is now Italy, in the Middle Ages increasingly involving the papacy as a temporal power. At various times different portions of the country were ruled from Constantinople (which became Istanbul), from France, Spain and what are now Germany and Austria. Final unification did not begin to take shape until 1861, and Rome did not become Italy's capital until 1870.

Italy's economy has a curious preponderance in the number of small firms, and in famous large firms, and is comparatively lacking in the medium-size band. There are proportionately more small firms than in any of the other major Western economies. Usually they are family owned, reflecting in the managerial context the importance of the family to life in general. This family influence is also pronounced among large firms which have household names, such as Benetton or Olivetti or Fiat, the latter competing with Volkswagen to be Europe's largest car manufacturer.

The other large organizations are mainly State-owned. Indeed, whilst the economy is distinctive in its numbers of small firms, at the other end of the scale it is also distinctive in the extent of involvement by the State, including direct ownership. Most remarkable is IRI, the Istituto per la Ricostruzione Industriale, a state conglomerate holding numerous subsidiaries in banking, manufacturing and services, including the national airline, Alitalia, and the national broadcasting corporation.

This peculiarly shaped economy has yielded conspicuous stability and prosperity within the European Union, to northern Italy at least where all the large firms are based. The south has long lagged behind, its population migrating northwards to escape lower incomes and higher unemployment.

A peculiarly shaped economy is paralleled by a peculiarly shaped culture which has the general 'Latin Touch' described earlier but combines individualism with extreme 'macho' assertiveness. This may well be behind the well-known tendency to 'cock a snook' at the system. There is achievement to be shown in cheating the system, as well as in bossing it. Rules can be dodged and taxes avoided. This can escalate into corruption. And from the same characteristics might well come the Italian flair for design and style, from clothes to cars, which demands a sense of proud display.

This flair blends into a management style that has been said to be entrepreneurial more than managerial. It goes with an assertive masculinity which prefers to act, and is expected to act, decisively, even autocratically. The captains of industry are powerful, privileged individualists, whose reputations colour their organizations (see Box 4.6). They rule in a highly personal manner, concentrating on those aspects of the business which interest them and which they judge to be important, and leaving the rest to others.

Box 4.6 Colourful Captains

Consider the archetypal Italian industrialist, Fiat's Giovanni Agnelli. He was Europe's most powerful businessman. Like Henry Ford in his time, Agnelli lives in a country that places few limits on corporate power. Along with a number of Italy's leading corporate lights, Agnelli has a nickname, 'l'Avvocato' (the lawyer) – some of the others include Olivetti's Carlo de Benedetti, who was known as 'l'Ingegnere' (the engineer); Silvio Berlusconi, owner of the TV-to-supermarkets conglomerate [and since a prime minister], who was 'Sua Emittentza' (his emittence – pun on a cardinal's honorific); and Ferruzzi-Montedison's Rual Gardini, who was 'il Contadino' (the farmer). This profusion of sobriquets (shades of Mussolini's 'il Duce') reflects a very personalized view of management. Italian business is marked by the cult of personality and the accompanying penchant for flair and charisma. Could this be why the Italian economy encompasses so many small businesses – each one headed by an aspiring Agnelli?

(Calori and Lawrence, p. 202)

Those at the top see their organizations in personalized terms, less as administrative structures than as political networks of those they know and on whom they can rely. The first function of a hierarchy is to show who has authority over whom. Organizations are not impersonal fabrications, detached from the personalities who run them (see Box 4.7). Conversely, subordinates become dependent upon personal relationships with those above. So organizations work with an element of patronage, even paternalism, through mutual obligations or '*clientelismo*'. Though individualist societies tend to be less family-focused than do collectivist societies, the unusual pride in family among the individualistic Italians is such that this '*clientelismo*' is often family-linked. A managerial crisis

Box 4.7 The Personal Touch

One of the authors once edited an English-language international research journal. Getting an article published in it was highly competitive, for only a minority of those considered were accepted. Articles were assessed and commented on dispassionately by independent reviewers who were not told the name(s) of the author(s). Usually articles from Anglo or Germanic or Scandinavian authors arrived impersonally in the mail, with a terse single-sentence note hoping that the manuscript would be found suitable.

Italian authors, on the other hand, were more likely to seek out the editor in person at a conference, introduce themselves, and respectfully ask whether their work might be appropriate and what helpful advice the editor could give them. To Anglos and Germanics this would have been 'not done', a veiled attempt to slip through the procedures via personal favouritism. To Italians, however, the personal touch was the right one, and any other approach would feel clumsy, even rude. For them, too, the subsequent impersonal procedures of assessing manuscripts for such a journal, taken for granted in the Anglo world, could come as a brutal affront. Criticisms of their manuscripts, intended to improve them, were often taken personally as a hurtful attack upon the author's ego.

evokes the exclamation, 'Mamma mia!'. Bosses have more than their responsibilities for their subordinates on-the-job; they have obligations to help family members and others whom they know, even those who are officially not employees but with whom they are linked in a personal network. If strangers may not be reliable, then getting things done through those you know, and doing things for them, makes practical sense. As Italian managers are less mobile than their Anglo contemporaries, usually pursuing their careers within one firm, there is a stable, reliable middle management layer.

At the same time, there is not an overly deferential regard for authority. Low Italian 'power distance', the lowest among European Latin nations and low among all Latin nations (Box 2.5), and loyalty in personal relationships soften both authority and bureaucracy. Further, Italian management meetings do not always show the restraint (is it suppression?) that characterizes such situations in Northern Europe. Soft politeness is punctuated by emotionality.

BRAZILIAN CULTURE AND MANAGEMENT

The famous sunny beaches of Rio, and its annual carnival extravaganza, all beneath the outstretched arms of the Christ statue on its Corcovado pinnacle – these are the pictures in the brochures and in the memories of tourists. But there is another and far bigger picture of Brazil. By itself almost half of South America, it is still largely a developing country. A quarter of its perhaps 170 million people are unschooled and illiterate; many live in poverty in areas far from the comparatively prosperous south-east, or live in this region's shanty towns. So when we write of management in Brazil, we have foremost in mind the successfully employed citizens of this south-east, mainly in the São Paulo, Rio de Janeiro and Belo Horizonte triangle, and the territory running southwards from it. They have benefited most from the economic growth of the latter part of the twentieth century.

To rub in the obvious, this is not Europe. Nor is it just another – though bigger – nation of South America. Half the population are of Portuguese origin, all are Portuguese-speaking, and there is a prevailing Portuguese-derived culture, which makes Brazil distinctive among the

Spanish-speaking South Americans in the 'culture cake' diagram in Box 2.13. There has also been substantial immigration from Italy.

Brazil's story is quite unlike the two-thousand-year history of violent turbulence which lies behind present-day Italy. Rather it is a story of phases of economic dependence and of erratic development. The Portuguese colonizers in the sixteenth century searched for and found gold and other precious metals; but, more significantly, they brought with them ideas about cultivating land and about God (from the Roman Catholic Church). A plantation economy grew up, producing most memorably the sugar and coffee for which Brazil became famed, based on slave labour from Africa, as were plantations in North America.

Independence from Portugal came in 1822, leaving the economy open to incursion from an industrializing maritime Britain, which led trade and investment throughout the nineteenth century. When British power waned in the twentieth century, the United States took over foreign economic leadership, and the multi-national corporations moved in. Brazilian industry itself enjoyed sporadic booms behind protective tariffs and regulations.

But poverty and hyperinflation were incessant. Brazilians looked upwards and outwards for solutions: upwards to a variety of military regimes or populist regimes acceptable to the military, outwards to their idealized images, first of the British and latterly of the Americans.

Always hoping for a new dawn under a new leadership, the outlook of the Brazilians in this has a lot in common with that of the French. Looking for a lead from remote leaders is a characteristic which comes from the European 'Latin Touch' described before, transmitted through the early patriarchal plantation and farming families. So managerial decisions are often taken centrally, and are taken decisively. They can be very much one-man decisions. At the extreme, when senior managers meet in conclave with an organization's president, and a decisive moment arrives, the president has been known to leave the meeting and go for a walk alone, whilst the others chat over coffee and await his return to announce his decision. This manner of exercising authority is emphasized by two authors, one of whom is French and the other Brazilian, whose summarized main conclusions are in Box 4.8.

Yet this is not the macho-inspired leadership of Italy. As was mentioned before, the Portuguese are the least macho-orientated of the European Latins, and Brazil has a political history extraordinarily free of wars, civil wars and violent solutions, which seems to match this. Its managers today are inclined to avoid confrontation, to side-step conflict, and to be receptive to others rather than to be assertive. Perhaps it is this characteristic that makes those above considerate, and their decision-making style tolerable, without upheaval below.

Box 4.8 Salient Features of Brazilian Management

Prominent Brazilian management consultants, speaking to executives from their client companies, are reported to have said that:

- *Brazilian managerial performance is characterized by an immediatist view, directed towards short-term results with an emphasis on crisis solutions.*
- *There is a lack of strategic planning and/or a gap in planning between the tactical and the operational management levels.*
- *Decisions are centralized at superior hierarchical levels, with clear incompatibility between responsibility and authority.*
- *Organizational structure is excessively hierarchical, and the inner subsystems are excessively segmented, without integration.*

(Amado and Vinagre Brasil, p. 40)

Moreover, *jeitinho*, the Brazilian 'little way around', also helps. Brazilian managements share the general Latin propensity for formalization. They strive to define clearly what has to be done, to issue detailed policy statements, to give full instructions. There are volumes of words, just as there is a superabundance of laws and regulations from governments. But just as Brazilian governments found that inflation cannot be abolished by decree, so Brazilian managers find that by adroit *jeitinho* their subordinates can dodge what has been laid down – though it has to be said that the same managers, unawares, may depend on that adroitness and adaptability to make some of their decisions work at all.

Personalism, too (see Box 4.9), both hinders and helps. To Brazilians, good personal relationships are of primary importance, in life generally as well as at work. Getting to know the person you are dealing with is part of every business deal, and personal links – including family ties – cut across the formal departmental divides of organizations. The challenge, 'Do you know to whom you are talking!', when faced with threatening officialdom, brings personal connections into play. The exuberance

Box 4.9 Personalism and Cordiality

Research on how decisions were made in twenty Brazilian business corporations and public services showed how they were shaped by personalism. For example, the president of a security firm, storing and transporting valuables, spent more than a year getting on easy personal terms with the president of an equivalent Argentinian company before incipient collaboration began to turn into a proposal to overlap ownership in a joint holding company. As he put it, 'We have to eat from the same dish,' before any business deal can take place. And once the personal relationship was firm enough, the written contract did not need any detail for, between friends, 'One hair from your moustache is enough.'

So Brazilian personalism puts knowing someone before whatever (impersonal) position or office they may hold. There are extensive networks of who knows whom. An attractive feature of this is the Brazilian's well-known cordiality, and this too was found by the same research. Whilst both Brazilian managers and their English counterparts with whom they were compared made a lot of personal contacts during the working day, it was the Brazilians who saw each other much more, not only in breaks during the day but in chatting after working hours. Indeed, they even described their managerial meetings during working hours as frequently 'meandering' in a companionable way.

(Oliveira; and Oliveira and Hickson)

of family life in a culture more collectivistic than the European Latins, with the door ever open to brothers, nieces, cousins or whomever to drop in for a chat, has its equivalent in gatherings of managers at the end of the day. Not for them the solitary late hours over a desk, the last light still on, typical of American (and British) managers. This is an American habit that is not aped; rather, there is sociable converse around the coffee pot.

This unwinds the tensions built up during the day, for Brazilian managers do suffer more than most from stress. They often feel that they cannot rely as much as they should on their subordinates, as they struggle against pressure of time. For with characteristic Brazilian immediatism, their way of avoiding uncertainty is not only to issue wordy edicts but to get on with the job fast. They feel under pressure for quick action and results. They make major decisions much faster than the British do, for example. They find the British excruciatingly slow and cautious, as Box 3.8 in the last chapter has already instanced. Brazilians adjust flexibly to things of the moment – which can include adjusting time-schedules. Clocks tell the time, but they need not control it, so punctuality by the clock may take second place to overriding business or social obligations. A Brazilian researcher describes this in Box 4.10.

Box 4.10 Whose Is the Time?

To a foreigner, the pace of events and action in Brazil may seem chaotic and contradictory. Personal contacts have priority over work; family, friends and powerful people (those of high status, the rich and people in authority) come first . . . Time is perceived by Brazilians as being elastic. The rational sequence of planning in advance and then implementing is not part of the culture. Planning one year in advance seems like looking too far ahead. Everything is left until the last minute and management by crisis is a commonplace. Problems are given attention as they happen, or when it is impossible for them to be postponed . . . Present time is much more important than the past or the future. 'The future belongs to God', say the Brazilians . . . People are usually late for meetings, conferences and other occasions. Executives as well as employees are versatile in doing different things at the same time. Attention is given to problems and people as they come and go. It is common to find a Brazilian executive answering the telephone, signing a cheque and being interrupted to solve a routine problem while talking to a client.

(Rodrigues pp. 317 and 318)

---

*　　*　　*

Like the Anglos, the Latins are literally oceans apart. Yet the approach to management in southern Europe and in Central and South America has broad common features. Compared to the Anglos, there is inclined to be a more politicized view of the nature of organizations. Formalized bureaucratization can be made to work by relatively top-down authority, itself countered by circumventing the rules and by personalized relationships. Whilst the Latin Americans fit this simplification to some extent, they depart from it in being rather more attentive to personal links in a collectivistic way, and are more eager for quick results. For them, time will not wait.

The chapter which follows switches north into Nordic and Germanic

Europe, in the very different top-left segment of the 'culture cake' diagram.

Further Reading

FRANCE

Barsoux, Jean-Louis and Peter Lawrence. 1991. *French Management: Elitism in Action*. Cassell.

Hall, Edward T. and Mildred Reed Hall. 1990. *Understanding Cultural Differences: Germans, French and Americans*. Intercultural Press.

Lawrence, Peter, and Vincent Edwards. 2000. *Management in Western Europe* (Chapter 3: France). Macmillan.

Sorge, Arndt. 1993. 'Management in France', in David J. Hickson (ed.), *Management in Western Europe: Society, Culture and Organization in Twelve Nations*. De Gruyter.

ITALY

Gagliardi, Pasquale and Barry Turner. 1993. 'Aspects of Italian Management', in David J. Hickson (ed.), *Management in Western Europe: Society, Culture and Organization in Twelve Nations*. De Gruyter.

Lawrence, Peter, and Vincent Edwards. 2000. *Management in Western Europe* (Chapter 4: Italy). Macmillan.

Randlesome, Collin and William Brierley, Kevin Bruton, Colin Gordon, Peter King. 1990. *Business Cultures in Europe*. Heinemann.

BRAZIL

Amado, Gilles and Haroldo Vinagre Brasil. 1991. 'Organizational Behaviors and Cultural Context: The Brazilian "Jeitinho"'. *International Studies of Management and Organization*, 21, 3, 38–61.

Kemp, Tom. 1983. *Industrialization in the Non-Western World*. Longman.

Rodrigues, Suzana Braga. 2000. 'Management in Brazil', in Malcolm Warner (ed.), *Regional Encyclopedia of Business and Management: Management in the Americas*. Thomson.

Rodrigues, S. B. and D. Collinson. 1995. 'Having Fun? Humour and Resistance in a Brazilian Telecommunications Company'. *Organization Studies*, 16, 5, 739–68.

CENTRAL AND SOUTH AMERICA GENERALLY

Harris, Philip R. and Robert T. Moran. 1991. *Managing Cultural Differences* (3rd edn, Ch. 14). Gulf Publishing.

Other Sources

FRANCE

Crozier, Michel. 1964. *The Bureaucratic Phenomenon*. Tavistock.

Eggers, E. Russell. 1993. 'How to do business with a Frenchman', in T. Weinshall (ed.), *Societal Culture and Management*. De Gruyter.

Gordon, Colin. 1996. *The Business Culture in France*. Butterworth–Heinemann.

Hickson, D. J., C. R. Hinings, C. A. Lee, R. E. Schneck, and J. M. Pennings. 1971. 'A Strategic Contingencies Theory of Intraorganizational Power'. *Administrative Science Quarterly*, 16, 2, 216–29.

Lane, Christel. 1989. *Management and Labour in Europe: The Industrial Enterprise in Germany, Britain and France*. Edward Elgar Publishing.

Moran, Robert T. 1991. *Cultural Guide to Doing Business in Europe*. Butterworth–Heinemann.

Szarka, Joseph. 2000. 'Management in France', in Malcolm Warner (ed.), *Regional Encyclopedia of Business and Management: Management in Europe*. Thomson.

Weinshall, Theodore D. (ed.). 1993. *Societal Culture and Management*. De Gruyter.

ITALY

Barsoux, Jean-Louis and Peter Lawrence. 1991. 'Countries, Cultures and Constraints', in Roland Calori and Peter Lawrence (eds.), *The Business of Europe: Managing Change*. Sage

Calori, Roland and Peter Lawrence (eds). 1991. *The Business of Europe: Managing Change*. Sage.

Knights, David, Glenn Morgan and Fergus Murray. 1992. 'Business Systems, Consumption and Change: Personal Financial Services in Italy', in Richard Whitley (ed.), *European Business Systems*. Sage.

Laurent, André. 1983. 'The Cultural Diversity of Western Conceptions of Management'. *International Studies of Management and Organization*, XIII, 1–2, 75–96.

Moran, Robert T. 1991. *Cultural Guide to Doing Business in Europe*. Butterworth–Heinemann.

BRAZIL

Oliveira, Beto and David J. Hickson. 1991. 'Cultural Bases of Strategic Decision Making: a Brazilian and English Comparison'. Paper presented at *10th Colloquium of the European Group for Organizational Studies*, Vienna.

Oliveira, Beto. 1992. 'Societal Culture and Managerial Decision Making: the Brazilians and the English'. *PhD Thesis*, University of Bradford Management Centre.

5

The Northern Europeans, and Israel

Highlighting:
Germany
Sweden
Israel

The north European nations of Scandinavia and the Germanic countries are placed in the same slice of the culture cake shown in Chapter 2. The Scandinavian nations (Denmark, Finland, Norway and Sweden) and the Germanic ones (Austria, Germany, the Netherlands and Switzerland) owe some of their similarity to the impact of two of the greatest events in the history of Europe: the Roman empire (into which they were not taken) and the sixteenth-century Reformation of the Roman Catholic Church (at which they became predominantly Protestant).

As described in Chapter 4, the Roman empire at its maximum extent in the third century AD covered all of western Europe, but stopped at the Danube and the Rhine. The empire worked to stabilize these frontiers by punitive wars but did not extend its dominion. To the north and the east were the 'barbarians' (or babblers) – a xenophobic Roman term of abuse that has come down to modern times. These were the Germanic tribes who were '*Deutsche*' – now the German word for Germans, but originally derived from the word for 'local' or 'popular'. It referred to those tribes who 'babbled' in their own language as distinct from Latinized tribes, such as the Gauls. The barbarians included Huns, Vandals, Goths, Visigoths; their names strike fear into the hearts of those using Latin languages, since they were the instigators of the decline and fall of the Roman empire.

From the Roman point of view, they were barbarians because they did not have formal legal and administrative systems derived from established authority. They never looked upwards to an awesome faraway capital city with an emperor at the helm. They were not dominated from on high, but were preoccupied with their own local concerns.

Being almost completely illiterate, written laws did not have much impact. Issues were decided by the outcome of trials of strength, blood feuds and battles. They operated on a much smaller scale than Rome. Families, tribes, clans were very committed to one another and followed their leader to the death – *if* he could inspire them that his cause was right. If not, other leaders would spring up. Rivalries between brothers who fought for the allegiance of their tribe were an occupational hazard for the chiefs – and a considerable contribution to Rome's ability to maintain stable frontiers. Retaining the loyalty of his people, and therefore reflecting their wants, was an important task of an effective leader.

Further north in Scandinavia a similar pattern emerged. A considerable number of small kingdoms, the peoples of which later came to be called collectively the Vikings, were constantly fighting with one another and occasionally combining together long enough to wage war on a grander scale with an external enemy. Successful warriors were given honours. A really inspired warrior would cast off his tunic (called a *serk*) and fight bare-breasted, armed only with a club – the original meaning of 'going berserk'. If he was victorious, he could then join the top table. Over time this meant that top tables became rather large, and many could join in the arguments over what to do. So there existed what might be thought of as an ancient, rough-and-ready kind of democracy in the north European lands which the Roman empire did not affect.

Over a thousand years later, this may well have coloured the outcome of the Reformation. By the sixteenth century, most of the Germanic lands were part of a confederation (confusingly called, since they were not the Latin countries, the Holy Roman Empire) with, further north and in Scandinavia, a very strong maritime and commercial organization, the Hanseatic League, exercising economic dominance. When Martin Luther launched the Reformation by attacking the beliefs and practices of the Pope and the Roman Catholic Church, he split European Christendom. The Protestants, so called because they protested at an edict of the Pope that no changes were permissible, emphasized the personal nature of spiritual experience and that salvation came from an individual's faith and not through the ministrations of the Church and its priests. This led, as we saw in Chapter 1, to the development of an approach to conduct which emphasized individual virtue and hard work in what later came to be called 'the Protestant Ethic'. In Scandinavia the new beliefs were readily accepted. In the German-speaking lands there was a great divide and considerable conflict. The Habsburg monarchy in Austria to the east maintained the Roman faith, as did Bavaria in the south, and this may have been partly because the influence of the Roman empire was greater in these parts all those centuries before. But the majority, including the Netherlands'and Switzerland, became predominantly Protestant. So a belief in individual responsibility for one's own conduct may be said to characterize much of this area.

Also included in this slice of the culture cake is Israel – a country very far from northern Europe. But modern Israel is a very unusual country whose nature reflects its history rather than its geographical position. After about fifteen hundred years of independent existence, as described in the Old Testament of the Bible, the country was conquered in the first century BC and incorporated into the Roman empire as the province of Judea. About two hundred years later, after a failed rebellion, the Jews were dispersed and the Romans renamed the country after their neigh-bouring enemy, calling it Palestine, the 'land of the Philistines'.

Thus began nearly two thousand years of the Jewish diaspora, in which only a very small number of Jews lived in Palestine, and the vast majority lived anywhere in the world except Palestine. In spite of the dispersion, the longing to return was kept alive by the Jewish religion and, from the late nineteenth century onwards, Jews began to return in larger numbers to create a modern Jewish State. Most of these settlers came from Europe: in the beginning from Tsarist Russia; in the 1920s from Poland; later, with the rise of Hitler, from Germany; and, at the end of the Second World War, from the Nazi concentration camps. A mandate to rule Palestine on behalf of the then League of Nations had been allocated to Britain after the First World War, and a steady trickle of British and South African Jews went there. These immigrants created (with others from Romania, France and elsewhere) over a period of almost a century the full panoply of the institutions of a European State set in the Middle East. Israel, unlike its surrounding Arab neighbours, is a multiparty parliamentary democracy whose government changes hands as a result of regular elections based on universal suffrage. It has compulsory edu-cation, and a school and university system of European scope. This European culture still predominates, even though the establishment of the State of Israel in 1948 led to a large influx of Jews from Arab lands. Thus the nature of its culture leads to Israel being placed in this slice of the cake.

NORTHERN APPROACHES

The nations of this area are among the best established economically, with some of the highest standards of living in the world. Are there any aspects of their cultures which might be relevant to this achievement? A most distinctive aspect is the attitude to **managing authority**. They are all at the low power distance end of the scale in Box 2.5. Employees do not regard people in authority as remote beings whose word ought to be accepted without question; they expect to be consulted about possible decisions which affect them *before* they are made. They are not afraid to express disagreement with their managers if they think that this is justified, and they are more likely than in many other cultures to be technically or managerially qualified to do so. Indeed they consider that the key attributes of those in authority are greater experience, greater technical knowledge and greater competence. They themselves aspire to attain these characteristics in due course, and therefore to move up the hierarchy. This means that the 'social distance' between levels of authority in an organization is smaller than, for example, in the Latin culture of Chapter 4 or the Asian culture of Chapter 7, and is comparable with the Anglo culture described in Chapter 3. Those in charge see the need to explain and justify their decisions. They will often encourage contributions from those at lower levels who may have experience, knowledge and skills different from their own. Box 5.1 gives an illustration of these differences in attitudes. The Northern Europeans, and the Anglos, find it acceptable for a manager to be a facilitator as well as personally capable, able to ask whoever is appropriate, rather than needing to have the answers personally in order to sustain standing and authority.

Box 5.1 What Does a Manager Need to Know?

Laurent, a French researcher, questioned 817 managers from different countries attending executive training courses at INSEAD, the international business school in Fontainebleau, France. They were asked to agree or disagree with a number of statements, including the following:

'It is important for a manager to have at hand precise answers to most of the questions that his subordinates may raise about their work.'

	Percentages agreeing	Number of managers surveyed
Italy	66	32
France	53	219
Germany	46	72
Belgium	44	45
Switzerland	38	63
Great Britain	27	190
Denmark	23	54
USA	18	50
Netherlands	17	42
Sweden	10	50

Cultures where managing authority is through a high power distance approach are at the top of the list, a majority of their managers agreeing that they must have the answers to command authority. In low power distance cultures at the bottom of the list, managerial questions are more likely to be regarded as technical or system issues. In these cultures most managers feel that they can work together with subordinates to solve the problems, going elsewhere for information as required. This has the advantage that it helps to develop the subordinate's capability.

(from Laurent)

In terms of **managing relationships**, most countries in this group are firmly at the individual end of the scale in Box 2.7. In this they are similar to the Anglos of Chapter 3 and the European Latins of Chapter 4. Employees see their part in an organization as one bounded by their tasks and the expertise required in their jobs. They wish to keep their personal and family life private, and they require that their work be designed to allow this. The ambitious look to improve their skills by education and training; this is not only to make them more promotable within their present organization: they also wish to improve their ability to obtain jobs in other organizations when a suitable position arises. They have no pronounced loyalty to the impersonal organization. For reasons that we shall discuss later, the values in Israel are the most collective of this group but much less so than those of, say, the Arabs of Chapter 8.

Major differences arise among these societies, however, in regard to

managing uncertainty. Managements in Germany, Austria and Israel are likely to take a longer-term orientation in their strategic decisions, working towards a more stable level of economic activity. They are found towards the higher end of the scale of uncertainty avoidance in Box 2.10, though they do not show the degree of concern that characterizes the Latin nations. The economic traumas which Germany and Austria have gone through because of the First and Second World Wars may well have encouraged giving a high value to stability. Those in the Scandinavian countries, on the other hand, seem prepared to live with a greater degree of uncertainty, expecting changes to take place both for themselves and for their organizations. This same division occurs with regard to the values concerned with **managing oneself**. The Germanic nations put the emphasis on doing, on the achievement of the task. Their values are very much those labelled 'masculine' in Box 2.9. In the Scandinavian countries, much more concern is expressed about the impact of jobs and organizations on the individual, the family, the work group and the environment, and they are very much at the 'feminine' end of the scale. Indeed they are much the most caring of the individualist cultures. Israeli values are poised in between.

There are clearly ways in which the countries grouped in this slice of the culture cake are similar, but others in which they are very different. We shall now look more closely at three countries in the group to exemplify this. We have chosen the largest of the Germanic countries, the largest of the Scandinavian countries and an unusually distinctive one, namely:

Germany
Sweden
and Israel.

GERMAN CULTURE AND MANAGEMENT

In population Germany is the largest country of Western, Central and Northern Europe, with over 80 million people. It has had one of the most chequered political histories of Europe in the last two centuries, although economically it has always found the capacity to perform strongly.

After the dissolution of the Holy Roman Empire, a German confederation and later a customs union were established in the early nineteenth century. During the course of that century, the Kingdom of Prussia to the north rose in importance, finally throwing off Austrian influence, defeating France and encompassing the remaining German States to create, in 1871, a German empire. So was formed a comparatively new nation-state, occupying the central landmass of Europe but almost land-locked. The empire left many German-speaking peoples in the surround-ing countries outside its domains, thus giving continual pressure for nationalistic expansion. In the twentieth century, these pressures led to the First World War, in which Germany and its allies were defeated. Then followed the rise of Hitler and the Nazis and defeat in the Second World War. After that war the country was divided for over forty years into a capitalist West Germany and a communist East Germany, the latter developing the characteristics of communist states described in Chapter 6. With the collapse of the communist system in the last decade of the twentieth century, the country was reunified into a Western capitalist democracy.

Despite these political and military setbacks, Germany has been called the economic engine-room of Europe, and the *Deutschmark* was the lead-ing currency in the European Union prior to the Euro. Historically this is a development that has been going on for well over a century under varying political regimes. After each defeat, German economic achieve-ments have been considerable; for example, just before the 1990 uni-fication, not only was West Germany economically the leading State in Western Europe and the largest exporter in the world, but East Germany (although far behind West Germany, producing only 40 per cent of the output per worker) was the most efficient of the Soviet satellites and was being held up by hard-line leaders in the Soviet Union as an example of how communism could work if people were sufficiently disciplined. Are there any cultural characteristics which can be linked to this per-formance?

Box 5.2 Conference about a Conference

A group of European business school professors, including one of the authors, was planning a conference. Or, rather, they were attempting to plan a conference, because after an hour's uncomfortable discussion they had not been able to agree on how to run it.

'What we should do is to limit the scope to national business competitiveness,' said one. 'Then we can set the programme around two or three
lectures by experts in that field.'

Every time this was repeated, there was an awkward silence, centring on
the second professor. Persistently, he kept pointing out that this way of
going about it would limit in advance what people might want to do. 'It is
only going to be a small meeting,' he would say. 'So why not advertise it in
very general terms, see who applies to come, then group them according to
their interests. Let them discuss what they wish, without prearranged
speakers.' At one stage, agreement did seem near.

A third professor then intervened. 'If this is going to be about national
business systems,' he said, 'then what do you mean by business system? This
may have any of several possible meanings. For myself, I think business
systems are . . .'

The first professor, who preferred to have the procedure clear beforehand,
was German. The second, whose approach was gradualist and pragmatic
and who avoided clarity, was English (see Chapter 3 for these English
characteristics). The third, who wanted to examine the philosophical basis
of what was under discussion, was French (see Chapter 4 for this French
characteristic).

One of the most characteristic aspects of the German culture, which
certainly strikes an outsider, is their way of **managing uncertainty**
through an emphasis on planning and orderliness. The German professor
of Box 5.2 characteristically wanted to set some parameters and plan for
a more efficient operation. This is an individual example of what in the
whole of German society is the considerable commitment to long-term
stable goals. The German double experience of the pains of inflation in
this century, after both world wars, has led to the establishment of a
central bank, independent of the government or political pressures, which
is legally required to maintain a stable currency. Business, too, looks
for long-term stability and growth, as Box 5.3 shows. This long-term
orientation has ramifications throughout the managerial process. A German company will be bank-financed to a much greater degree than being
financed by the stock market – and German banks also take a long-term
view. So the emphasis on a yearly profit and its effects on the share price,
and thus on the market value of the company, is much less than in, for
example, the Anglo economies. Takeovers are much less likely anyway,
as the managerial emphasis on continuity favours organic growth of the

company. This means that there are far larger numbers of middle-sized firms, most still family-owned or controlled, than, for example, in Britain. There, is now, though, an increasing incidence of takeover of foreign companies by German corporations in order to gain position in world markets.

Box 5.3 German Business Goals

In 1999 the percentages of the adult population owning shares, either directly or through managed funds and pension schemes, were:

	%
Australia	54
Canada	52
USA	48
United Kingdom	40
Germany	25

(source Virginia Marsh, *Financial Times*, 9 February 2000)

German companies are much less pressured by the short-term financial goals of shareholders than are companies in the Anglo countries.

The belief in planning is another manifestation of higher uncertainty avoidance values. Formal structures of companies also favour commitment and continuity. For companies of 500 employees and over, the executive board of top managers has above it a supervisory board, elected for five years, on which are represented many stakeholders in the company, such as banks, suppliers, customers and the employees. In addition, the system of works councils in partnership with trade unions reinforces the long-term view, since managers would be loath to jeopardize well-established relationships based on negotiated consensus for possible short-term gain. Both the employers and the trade unions refer to each other as 'social partners' in the enterprise, and accept the 'co-determination' stemming from the employee representation on the board. The needs of the environment and the firm's responsibilities to society will also be considered; Box 11.4 gives an illustration from the automobile industry. This degree of management–employee co-operation also reflects the German lower power distance **management of authority** (see Box 2.5), expressed here in formal structures of a kind that the Anglos avoid.

This approach leads to a managerial view of business which is 'structured' rather than 'liberal' (see Box 5.4). Activities are product-led, with an emphasis on competition through product appropriateness and quality, rather than market-led, with an emphasis on competition through price. This can lead to 'over-engineering' when only products which are 'better' but more expensive are offered to the market. The impact of marketing has usually been limited to advertising and selling the good product or service (including after-sales service) for the long term, rather than in determining how to satisfy the consumers' immediate needs at a lower price. And, of course, the German market expects this. Thus the regular complaint of German exporters to Britain, for example, is of the difficulty of selling in markets where the customer, even when that customer is an industrial purchasing department, takes a competitor's cheaper product although it is obviously inferior in technical performance.

Box 5.4 is a reminder of how everything in this book is relative. Whilst American (Chapter 3) and Brazilian (Chapter 4) managers find their British equivalents relatively slow in taking decisions, the British are found here to be faster than their German equivalents.

Germany has a high-wage economy, but the involvement of staff in the technical development of both the product and the process has enabled productivity to rise along with wages. This builds on a long tradition of technical education and training, stretching back well into the last century. In Germany there is a very strong emphasis on vocational education and training. Technical universities of equal status to traditional universities were established in the nineteenth century, and their graduates go in large numbers into business management. Apprenticeships are pervasive at all levels, including those for engineering graduates, clerical staff and so on, with examinations to be passed and certificates to be gained. Both the workers and the management hierarchy are thus much more technically trained than in most other countries.

For example, a key role in German factories is that of the *Meister*; traditionally male, he is the first-line full-time supervisor. On the one hand a *Meister* differs from, say, a typical Anglo-American foreman or superintendent by virtue of the formal technical qualifications he has obtained. On the other hand, he differs from the Anglo-American professional engineer in having had a shop-floor apprenticeship and experience. He thus has a much wider role, building on his experience and knowledge, which combines both technical and supervisory tasks. This is

Box 5.4 German 'Structure' and British 'Liberality' in Management

One of the present authors was a member of a team of researchers from Britain and Germany carrying out a study of the different characteristics of German and British managements. They interviewed forty-six chief executives of German subsidiary companies in Britain and forty-five chief executives of British subsidiaries in Germany, asking such questions as, What issues tend to arise in co-operating with your German/British partner? In which areas do the Germans and the British have most difficulty in working together? What took you longest to get used to when you became involved in Anglo-German business collaboration?

Some of the differences regularly raised were:

	German	British
1. *The financial system favours*	long-termism	short-termism
2. *The marketing function emphasizes*	sales and financial analysis	marketing and market response
3. *Consumers look for*	high-quality performance	value for money and economy
4. *Advertising is*	more explicit and technical	more implicit and humorous
5. *Vocational qualifications of staff*	comprehensive system	middle level missing
6. *Top management qualifications*	highly technical, less work experience	general, more work experience
7. *Work attitudes of staff*	adherence to procedure	personal initiative
8. *Decision-making style*	risks calculated, decisions slower	risks uncalculated, decisions faster
9. *Management emphasis on*	reliability	flexibility
10. *Managements value*	efficient operations	strategic awareness

The researchers characterized the German management approach as 'structured' and the British one as 'liberal', and suggested that each is more effective in particular markets. For example, a 'structured' approach to the established machine-tool market would be appropriate, whereas a 'liberal' approach to the fast-changing consumer-electronics market is required.

(adapted from Ebster-Grosz and Pugh)

true at all levels, from the shop-floor worker upwards, and stems from high qualifications. For example, the distinction between maintenance workers and production workers (a very strong difference in Britain and France, jealously preserved, see Box 4.5) is weak and blurred in Germany, as is the distinction between technical staff and supervisory staff. This allows the firm to be managed with substantially lower overall indirect staffing levels compared with Britain and France. Box 5.5 outlines a detailed study of the differences between the management of French and German factories.

Box 5.5 French and German Factory Management

Maurice and his colleagues carried out a comparative study of the relative status and wage payments of workers and managers in comparable factories in France and Germany. The researchers compared pairs of factories in equivalent industries (iron and steel, paper and cardboard products, machine tools, tanning) which used the same technology and were comparable in size. They were thus able to focus on national differences in hierarchy, job structures and payments.

Their results showed clear differences between the French and German firms. These included:

1 Considerably more staff were not employed directly on physically making the product in French than in German firms, and they were relatively better paid.

2 The wage differential between the lowest decile and the highest centile of employees was much greater in French than in German firms. Indeed, the difference was such that there was no overlap: the largest differential found in a German firm was still less than the smallest differential found in a French firm (2.7 times as against 3.7).

3 The number of levels in the production hierarchy was greater in French than in German firms (5 compared with 3) because there are more middle-level managers in French firms.

Maurice argues that these differences were not fortuitous but relate to differences in the educational systems of France and Germany. More top managers in France hold higher degrees, usually from the 'grandes écoles'. These are very high-status university institutes, which provide top-level technical and scientific education and which, by their extremely selective intake, provide an elite of managers for French organizations. Graduates from them are recruited directly into upper levels of companies and are paid much greater comparative salaries than in Germany. This means that there are fewer qualified supervisors and managers, who can expect to be promoted only through the middle ranks of the organization. They can never realistically aspire to join the top-management 'cadre', or set.

In Germany, equivalent top managers are often promoted in smaller steps from within the firm, which they join lower down with fewer general and more technical qualifications. Thus at the lower levels German supervisors are comparatively better qualified and better paid than their French equivalents. They can also take more technical decisions and are given more professional autonomy.

The differences show French firms to be run more bureaucratically, with orders and procedures set from above, while German work organization relies more on the professional expertise which derives from the trained knowledge and skill of more junior employees.

(adapted from Maurice, see also Maurice *et al.*)

Box 5.6 German and French Time

The German manager who arrives in Paris to negotiate a contract with a French supplier will probably have to give up any preconceived notions of setting to work immediately and concluding in time to return to Frankfurt that night. The manager will be appalled at finding that the French colleague will spend much of the morning deciding, after lengthy consultation with everyone present, where to eat lunch.

The German does not speak the French language of time, which requires evoking the whole gustatory apparatus and setting the proper inter-personal relationship before business can be taken up. If the German insists on adhering to a rigid schedule, the French will label the visitor as uncouth, someone with little appreciation of life and no feeling for people.

It is important to understand that there is nothing frivolous or trivial about such an approach. The principles of behaviour for those, like the French, who work on a multitrack system of time (as described in Chapter 2) are just as binding as for those, like the German, who work on a single track system.

They lead to different patterns. The French managers will start slowly but get faster and faster, carrying on as late as is necessary to finish the job. The Germans will start on time, work steadily and finish precisely at 5.00 p.m. (see also Box 4.1).

(adapted from Hall and Hall)

This encouragement of technical contributions from lower levels is within a framework of clear rules laying out what the responsibilities are of each level and its role in the hierarchy. The considerable emphasis on planning leads senior German managers to involve themselves in greater detail in planning concerning lower levels of the organization than is the case with British or American managers. This is the 'orders are orders' aspect of German culture, in which established goals are not questioned, but which allows for a considerable degree of self-programming by subordinates within the given parameters. It is the bureaucratic aspect of German organization structure which, for example, the Nazis were able to exploit so mercilessly in the systematic extermination of Jews.

The emphases on stability, planning and achievement are examples of the classic German attributes of orderliness and hard work. This pattern also affects their conception of time, which, as Box 5.6 illustrates, is very different from French notions, for example. The threefold combination in German management culture of planning and stability (reflecting relatively high uncertainty avoidance), hard work (relatively high task-orientation) and utilization of highly technically educated personnel (possible through relatively low power distance) appears to underlie the German achievement.

SWEDISH CULTURE AND MANAGEMENT

Sweden is the largest of the Scandinavian countries, both in numbers and in area, with its 9 million people spread sparsely over a land 1,000 miles long. Until the late nineteenth century they were an agrarian people, very independent in managing relationships with respect to the rights of individuals, underpinned by a strong Protestant faith. This stress on individuality means that Swedes are not born into a vast web of obligations to an extended family or clan, as in more collectivist cultures. The nuclear family – parents and their children – is central. As adults, individuals can personally develop their own social obligations, not have to take them on from others. Box 5.7 recounts a medieval morality tale which is the Swedish version of Romeo and Juliet. But in this case it is not a tragedy in which the lovers are trapped in their respective clans; it is a drama in which they individually forge their own future and bring about a negotiated reconciliation – a typical 'feminine', caring outcome rather than a 'masculine', fight-to-the-death one.

Box 5.7 The Tale of Ronia

Ronia loved the son of a family with which her own family had a bitter feud. The other family lived on the far side of a deep gorge separating the two houses. To miss one's footing when crossing this gorge meant certain death. Ronia's true love visited her by stealth in her house but was discovered by her father, who seized the young man and imprisoned him, regarding his prisoner as a valuable hostage in the continuing feud. To prove her love, Ronia leapt to the 'enemy's' side of the gorge, risking her life to save her relationship to her beloved and to equalize the bargaining power of the two adversaries.

Now that each father held the other's child, the breach between them could be negotiated and the lovers united in marriage.

(quoted in Hampden-Turner and Trompenaars)

A distinctive characteristic of Sweden is its late and very rapid transformation from an agrarian society into an industrial one. This transition took place from about 1890 to 1920. It came to a country where the peasants had historically been well treated (they were represented in the eighteenth-century parliament, for example) and in which there was no large middle class. Apart from the small proportion of aristocrats, everybody was much the same. So it was accepted that the high standards of living being generated would be available to all the new industrial working class.

In fact the modernization through industrialization was very successful and, in terms of per capita income, Sweden has one of the highest standards of living in the industrialized world (indeed, in the whole world, with the exception of the small-population oil States). In addition, the range of income variation is much narrower than in other developed countries, far more egalitarian. The standard of living of the lower-income groups is substantially higher than in the USA, for example, and they are better integrated into society, with less social disorganization.

Liberal and social democratic attitudes pervade the political and industrial scene. The belief that inadequate rulers could be changed has been part of the culture since Viking days, and this has developed in modern times into a constitutional monarchy. It may seem strange that such a democratic country would have retained a hereditary monarchy, but it is the very distinctive, Scandinavian 'bicycling monarchy', with much less pomp and circumstance than royal houses elsewhere. The king is regarded, and acts, as the senior civil servant he is. He is very popular, and it is commonly said that if the monarchy were abolished, he would be the leading candidate in the subsequent election for a president, or, if not him, the queen.

The absence of a many-tiered social structure leads to the feeling that those in power are quite close – this is the very low power distance value which Sweden shares with all Scandinavian countries, as shown in Box 2.5. It is characteristic, for example, that the concept of a single career structure for merchant sailors leading to 'all-officer' ships, making no distinction between officers and men, was developed and applied in Scandinavia. These values are also manifested in organizations in the style of dress and demeanour of managers (as in Box 5.8) and in the belief in the participation of subordinates. This approach is encouraged by the very high standard of education in the country, so that all managers will have good technical qualifications. There is also consultation with trade unions, and there are worker representative members on companies' boards of directors.

Box 5.8 Find the Boss

The British general manager (Europe) of an American-owned, world-wide multi-national corporation, based in Paris, described the practical difficulties of working across cultures in an international network: 'In Spain, it is comparatively easy to know who to deal with. When I visit our Spanish subsidiary company and walk through the door into a meeting of executives, I can tell instantly who is the chairman – even if I have not met him before. He has a more imposing bearing, everyone else is sitting slightly angled towards him with a respectful demeanour, and all conversation is directed to and from him.

'But in Stockholm, if I do not know the Swedish chief executive by sight, I can be in trouble. They are sitting around at ease, in casual shirts, talking generally. I can't readily tell who the CE is. It can be embarrassing.'

(from the author's experience)

Managers feel the need to obtain and analyse fully all relevant infor-mation. There is no pressure to show an assertive management style by driving decisions to an early conclusion. This does mean that decisions take longer to be made, as more people take part in the negotiations and more information is analysed; but the resulting commitment and lack of conflict are highly valued. So are concerns that things are done properly, that people matter and cannot be neglected, that the activities of working with and supporting co-operative colleagues are to be valued in them-selves. Indeed, it is held that the quality of working life should be as attractive as that of non-working life. And in Sweden, non-working life – particularly skiing and country pursuits – is very highly regarded.

These are the values in regard to **managing oneself** that have been labelled 'feminine' in Chapter 2; Sweden, again together with all the Scandinavian countries, is at the extreme 'feminine' end of the scale. This reflects its position as the leading country in the world for social welfare provisions, which are regarded, not as privileges, but as rights for all. It is typical that Swedes were the first to recognize that fathers have a role to play at the birth of their children, and therefore to introduce paternity leave from work, in addition to maternity leave. Concern for improved work conditions and more satisfying personal work experience has led Swedish factories to be in the vanguard of the movement for the design of jobs away from traditional mass production on 'Fordist' lines (Box 5.9). The wish to give autonomy to individuals and teams, and to ensure that work is as satisfying and as conflict-free as possible, is part of the 'feminine' nurturance aspect of Swedish culture.

Box 5.9 A New Way to Make Motor Cars

A Volvo advertisement read:
Henry Ford started the assembly line. Now Volvo has stopped it. For natural reasons.'

Visitors to the small town of Uddevalla on Sweden's west coast will find Volvo's latest car plant sited right by the sea.

Inside the plant, 'the greatest step forward in the history of modern car production has been taken', according to many experts.

The assembly line is gone. Instead, cars stand in workshops during assembly, a small team building a complete car.

The teams of workers see themselves as families and that is just what they

> *are. Men and women of all ages work side by side, using special, ergonomically designed machines evolved specially for them.*
>
> *The Uddevalla workers have already demonstrated that their way of making cars is more natural, and often more efficient, than the traditional assembly line. They have confirmed Volvo's belief that responsibility, involvement, comradeship and joy increase work satisfaction and raise product quality.*
>
> *Volvo's thinking is quite natural: build a car with commitment, pay attention to quality, and the owner will soon notice the difference.*
>
> (quoted in Huczynski and Buchanan)

But no country is immune to international economic conditions. The recession in the early 1990s meant that Volvo had to reduce its production operations. In doing so, it abandoned all its subsidiary plants with their innovative methods, in order to concentrate production on its major, traditionally organized factory. This may be only a temporary retrenchment, with redevelopments in a later expansionary phase, or it may be an example of the push to managerial convergence in the international motor industry discussed in Chapter 11.

The values of Swedish managerial culture (low power distance, toleration of uncertainty, individual commitment and a 'feminine' concern with the way things are done in addition to the results achieved) have produced, in the second half of the twentieth century, an economically successful country which has been the envy of social democrats everywhere in the world.

ISRAELI CULTURE AND MANAGEMENT

Israel is a small country of about 6 million people in an area about the size of Wales or the US State of Massachusetts. Something like eight out of ten of its population are Jews, the others are mainly Arab (Muslim, Christian and Druze). Israel was founded in 1948, when the British gave up their mandate to govern Palestine. The Jewish community then declared its independence and survived the immediate attacks of all the surrounding Arab states. It is unique in that it has a 'law of return' which states that it must provide a refuge and citizenship for any Jews from anywhere in the world wishing to settle, which reflects the persecution that Jews have been subjected to in many countries. Since then Israel has fought and survived several more wars, to become a stable and prosperous State with Western European characteristics.

The institutions of Israeli society have been created in the last hundred years or so by successive waves of Jewish immigrants and refugees from many countries in the world. Until the beginning of the 1930s, the original settlers from Russia and Poland did not have only – or even primarily – a nationalistic motivation; they wished to escape from anti-Semitic oppression and they came with socialist ideals, wanting to build a 'new Jerusalem' – a society based on equality and social justice. From these ideals and a strong commitment to participative democracy (forged in the experiences of living under tyrannies) have developed a number of key characteristics of Israeli economic life and work culture.

The first is that Israel is economically one of the most egalitarian countries in the world. In terms of income distribution, the share of the national income received by the richest 5 per cent of the country is smaller, and the share received by the poorest 20 per cent larger, than probably in any other country in the world. Certainly the gap is smaller than in developing countries and in Latin America, where the disparities are very wide; but it is also smaller than in North America and Europe generally, and even smaller than in such egalitarian countries as Sweden and the rest of Scandinavia.

A second characteristic is an extensive commitment to membership of trade unions as the appropriate way to protect workers' rights. Trade union membership in Israel is greater than in Germany and is right up to Swedish levels. But very distinctively, trade union ownership of enterprises is highly developed, unlike in Germany or Sweden, where it is rudimentary. The trade union confederation, the *Histadrut* (the equivalent of the TUC, the AFL/CIO or the DGB), owns some 20 per cent of the country's economy. It owns the largest building and public works undertaking, the second biggest bank, and the leading industrial enterprise in Israel: Koor Industries, a conglomerate big enough to have been on the *Fortune* 'World 500' list.

A third distinction is the existence of an extensive government sector in the economy, the biggest in any developed country other than erstwhile communist ones. The government owns, in addition to the national airline and the leading shipping company, the biggest manufacturing company (military aircraft), the largest bank, a key chemical conglomerate and so on. Thus, though the private sector is the single major part of the economy (about 60 per cent), it is considerably smaller than in other developed Western economies.

A final characteristic is the considerable tradition of co-operative enterprise. This includes, for example, the national bus company, *Egged*, which is a worker co-operative owned by its drivers. But the most famous example is of the *kibbutz* – meaning 'a gathering'. *Kibbutz* settlements are collectives, where there is not only common ownership of property but also communal living. Box 5.10 gives one version of the socialist credo which underpins life in *kibbutzim* (the plural form of the word).

Of course, how it works out in practice may differ somewhat from the ideal (see Box 5.11) but *kibbutzim* have had a great influence. Although their numbers are small (about 300 settlements, comprising about 3 per cent of the population), they provide (with other co-operative organizations) over 80 per cent of the country's agricultural output. Their factories are at the cutting edge of technology, regularly winning prizes for export achievement. They produce leaders – way out of proportion to their numbers – in politics, the government, and the defence forces, and their values are an important part of Israeli society. In terms of managing relationships therefore, Israel is, not surprisingly, the most collectivist in values of this culture slice, as Box 2.7 shows.

These characteristics have shaped Israeli work culture in a number of distinctive ways. For instance, all Israelis spend two or three years full time in the Defence Forces, followed by regular periods of part-time service. This means that a senior manager, say, may well have as a superior army officer someone who is a supervisor in the same department. These reversals of authority encourage a social levelling. The emphasis on equality combines with an anti-authoritarian attitude, nurtured when the authorities were regarded as oppressors (Tsarist and Nazi in Europe, Turkish and British in Palestine) to fashion a considerable distrust of formal organizational authority. In addition, Jews, even secular ones, inherit a culture of argument based on the traditional rabbinical training of the Talmud. The Talmud is, in effect, a series of law reports based on a religious and legal system established 3,000 years ago, but still zealously studied. However, it does not just give the final decisions of the rabbinical authorities; it presents the conflicting arguments which informed those

Box 5.10 *Kibbutz* Life in Theory

The three ideals on which the *kibbutz* is built help to guarantee that it is an egalitarian society with no social classes.

1 *Collective ownership*: *Kibbutzim* distinguish between private and public property. Private property is that which the individual needs for personal use, such as clothes, books, pictures and small items of furniture. Public property is that which the community needs for its sustenance, such as work machinery, land and motor cars. On *kibbutz*, private property is owned by each individual member, whereas public property is communally owned. In society generally, no such distinction is made. What is regarded on *kibbutz* as public property can elsewhere be owned by a private individual, who can then gain power and control over others; this results in the formation of social classes. In contrast, on *kibbutz*, since all public property is owned and controlled by the members, no social inequality exists.

2 *Collective production*: A community based on the idea of collective production is one in which everyone works for the good of the whole. Individuals do not struggle for their livelihoods, pitted against each other in dehumanizing competition; rather, they work together in harmony. On *kibbutz* no distinction is made between manual labourers and intellectuals. The *kibbutz* member with a degree in business administration is respected no more than the member who sets the dining-room table. Often the manual workers themselves are intellectuals. Even managerial roles are rotated, and industrial plants are organized on a democratic, non-hierarchical basis. One year, one person will be farming and another teaching; the next year, they will exchange positions.

3 *Collective distribution*: On *kibbutz*, wages are not paid in currency; rather, the *kibbutz* supplies food, clothing, housing and other provisions (education, vacations, medical care, entertainment, etc.) for each individual. All goods are purchased collectively by the *kibbutz* and are allocated based on the needs of the individual and the resources of the entire community. The general assembly of *kibbutz* members decides what to buy and sets policy for distribution. Thus there is no private accumulation of wealth, thereby guaranteeing equality in everyday life.

(from Ariel)

Box 5.11 *Kibbutz* Life in Practice

The *kibbutz* I know consists of about 250 people of all ages. It was founded over forty years ago, when the pioneers, including a group of new immigrants from Britain, built their living quarters and began to develop their farm. Now the members work on what is a large agricultural undertaking, with a dairy herd, battery chickens, pulse fields and orange groves, and they live in a modern village. At the centre of the village is the dining and recreation facility, which is the social hub of the *kibbutz*; to one side is the open-air swimming pool, and to the other the deep-dug communal air-raid shelter.

The *kibbutz* looks after its members from the cradle to the grave. The children are cared for in the nursery and the children's house. Later, they go to the local school on a neighbouring *kibbutz* and, as teenagers, to the regional *kibbutz* high school. The working hours for adults are usually from 6 a.m. to 3 p.m. (although this will be longer if necessary – people feel a responsibility to do what work is needed). Parents then have three or four hours with their children, before their evening pursuits (with no baby-sitting problems – it is all professionally taken care of by other members). There is no formal retiring age, older members carry on working for as long as they want. Most of the members work on the *kibbutz*, but a number work off it, for example, teaching in the *kibbutz* schools. One member is the chief speech therapist for that region of Israel; another lectures in farm management at the National Kibbutz Management School. As these have a monetary income unlike other member's, their salaries go into the *kibbutz* funds: they are then given the same personal allowances.

The *kibbutz* also has a factory – a small undertaking by international standards, employing about forty members. There was considerable discussion on whether to enter the industrial sector, since it epitomizes a good deal of what the *kibbutz* philosophy is against: alienated people having to work on components that have no intrinsic value in restricted jobs that they hate. But the factory was accepted on condition that it generated jobs that people would want to do for a socially valued product. It is a high-tech, R & D-orientated operation, contributing to the medical industry. Since in principle this *kibbutz* employs no outside workers (though accepting temporary volunteers from Israel and abroad who want to discover what *kibbutz* life is like), it has a great incentive to make capital investments in machinery as a substitute for labour, and automatic and robotic machinery is common.

One evening a week the general meeting of members takes place. In a pure form of direct democracy the meeting is supreme, all members having voting and speaking rights. The meeting takes, or approves of, all important decisions and agrees the allocation of jobs. Jobs that nobody wants (say, serving in the dining hall) are rotated, with everyone taking a turn. In principle the managerial jobs rotate too, but since there are no economic or social benefits from managing compared with doing any other job, those who are willing and good at it tend to be asked repeatedly to take the job of factory manager, *kibbutz* secretary or stores controller. If necessary, their arms can be twisted, and peer pressure is exceedingly effective in the continual close proximity of the *kibbutz*.

Nor is it quite true that there are no status distinctions. There are no formal or economic benefits from doing one job rather than another, but, human nature being what it is, informal status is important. It did not need one mother to insist firmly to me (despite the difficulties of detailed translation) that her son was not the 'cashier' but the 'treasurer' of the *kibbutz*, to bring that home.

Communal living is like living in 'one big happy family'. But that has its not so happy aspects, too: the relative lack of privacy, the gossip behind people's backs, the deep political disagreements, the marriages that break up – they are also part of *kibbutz* life. Less than a quarter of those who come to try it out actually decide to join, and the fact that all Israelis spend about two years away in army service means that many decide not to return. This does have the advantage of keeping a turnover in membership which revitalizes the group, but it is a continual battle to keep the numbers up.

This *kibbutz* is one of those that are economically viable, but many are not. The *kibbutz* federation as a whole often needs to receive large amounts of financial support from the government. The usual justification for this subsidy is that it is in recognition of the important and distinctive contribution that the *kibbutz* movement has made and is making to Israeli life. But it must be admitted that more and more ordinary Israelis resent this special treatment, and question its justification in the current capitalist world. This puts a considerable shadow over the long-term survival of the system.

(from the author's experience)

judgements. These are still debated, so the notion of argument as an inevitable part of the process of dealing with problems has a long Jewish history. All these influences combine to produce a particular Israeli view of managing authority.

Israeli managers do not issue orders to their subordinates – that would be ineffective; they inform, argue, persuade them. They expect to hear arguments in reply. They expect to be pestered with others' ideas and views in face-to-face situations. There is a great emphasis on the informal as a means of getting things done. All this is a manifestation of the extremely low power distance values in Box 2.5. Since hierarchical pronouncements are not easily acceptable, and formal decisions are often questioned, it is necessary for managers to be very much 'hands-on' operators. They are where the action is: persuading, cajoling, flitting from one topic to another incident, always being interrupted by the telephone, always in demand. They obviously enjoy coping with the moving portfolio of small tasks which characterizes the manager's job. Box 5.12 gives a typical example. And, as has been pointed out, the invention of the mobile telephone was the answer to an Israeli manager's dreams: it immediately became the characteristic status symbol, for with it they can be in contact with everyone at all times.

Box 5.12 Can You Spare a Minute?

A salesman arrived to interest a manager in his product. After waiting while the manager settled an issue with a subordinate, he then began to present his case, but was interrupted by a telephone call. After the call he restarted, but was again interrupted. After the fourth telephone call which the manager said he really must take, the salesman walked out, went to an adjoining office, telephoned and at last got an uninterrupted ten minutes of the manager's time.

(a story popular with Israeli managers)

This style of management clearly puts a lot less weight on the planning and strategic analysis aspects of the task and in this is very different from the German pattern. It is particularly the case that Israeli managers do not do much in the way of time planning. If you ask for an appointment in two weeks' time, you will be told to call the day before to see if you can be fitted in, because no Israeli manager will admit to knowing what will need to be struggled with in two weeks' time. You will be fitted in, of course, because Israeli managers pride themselves on their ability to improvise. (This is the same response as you would get from a Brazilian manager – see Chapter 2 on Managing Time – but for rather different reasons.) The improvisation aspect of Israeli culture is very important for a country which has faced regular crises through wars or waves of immigration in every decade of its existence. But it does generate a managerial culture that is better at coping with crises than avoiding them.

The socialist orientation of such a large part of the economy brings with it a high concern for workers' rights which are well provided for. It is difficult, for example, to make anyone redundant and it used to be virtually impossible. This stems from the very high uncertainty-avoidance values (see Box 2.10) which characterize Israel – among the highest in this culture slice, well above Germany. It also inevitably brings considerable bureaucratic rigidities, and any effective Israeli manager must know how to use informal methods to try to get round them.

This is known as *Protekzia* – the opportunity to use 'pull' rather than 'push' by using informal ways of getting what you want from the system more quickly than the normal bureaucratic workings will allow. For example, if you wanted a new telephone line (when these were scarce) or a permit to employ a foreign national (which is difficult because of immigrant unemployment) then if your sister was in the same class in high school as the younger brother of an appropriate manager or civil servant, you will use that avenue to bring your needs to their attention in the hope/expectation that they will do something about it especially for you. This is not financial corruption – there is no more of that in Israel than in any other Western country – for money does not change hands; but people expect to help the system along for their friends. And the smallness and openness of the country means that anyone can pick up the telephone and get through to a cabinet minister or the Mayor of Jerusalem and argue their case.

The emphasis on openness and argument in the Israeli culture (very low power distance) animates through informal improvisation what is otherwise a rigid bureaucratic system stemming from an egalitarian commitment to individual rights (high uncertainty-avoidance). This has created a very distinctive Israeli work culture which has survived effectively in an unparalleled history of turmoil.

*   *   *

The Northern European 'culture slice', with its characteristic low power distance in managing authority, individualistic approach to managing relationships with others, and relative toleration of uncertainty, has given rise to some of the most economically succesful managerial cultures in the world. The same could not be said of East-Central Europe, which is the subject of the next chapter.

Further Reading

GERMANY

Ahrens, T. 1999. *Contrasting Involvements: a Study of Management Accounting Practices in Britain and Germany*. Harwood Academic Publishers.

Campbell, A. and M. Warner 1993. 'German Management', in D. J. Hickson (ed.), *Management in Western Europe*. De Gruyter.

Ebster-Grosz, D and D. Pugh 1996. *Anglo-German Business Collaboration: Pitfalls and Potentials*. Macmillan.

Hall, E. T. and M. R. Hall. 1990. *Understanding Cultural Differences: Germans, French and Americans*. Intercultural Press.

Hampden-Turner, C. and F. Trompenaars. 1993. *The Seven Cultures of Capitalism*. New York: Doubleday; London: Piatkus.

Lawrence, P. 1980. *Managers and Management in West Germany*. Croom Helm.

Randlesome. C. 1990. 'The Business Culture in West Germany', in Collin Randlesome and William Brierley, Kevin Bruton, Colin Gordon, Peter King, *Business Cultures in Europe*. Heinemann.

SWEDEN

Czarniawska-Joerges, B. 1993. 'Sweden: A Modern Project, a Postmodern Implementation', in D. J. Hickson (ed.), *Management in Western Europe*. De Gruyter.

Hampden-Turner, C. and F. Trompenaars. 1993. *The Seven Cultures of Capitalism*. New York: Doubleday; London: Piatkus.

Lawrence, P. and T. Spybey. 1986. *Management and Society in Sweden*. Routledge.

ISRAEL

Baruch, Y. 2000. 'Management in Israel', in M. Warner (ed.), *Regional Encyclopedia of Business and Management: Management in Europe*. Thomson Learning Business Press.

Lawrence, P. 1990. *Management in the Land of Israel*. Cheltenham: Stanley Thornes (Publishers).

Other Sources

GERMANY

Laurent, A. 1983. 'The Cultural Diversity of Western Conceptions of Management'. *International Studies of Management and Organization*, 13, 75–96.

Maurice, M. 1979. 'For a Study of "The Societal Effect": Universality and Specificity in Organization Research', in C. J. Lammers and D. J. Hickson (eds.), *Organizations Alike and Unlike*. Routledge.

Maurice, M., A. Sorge and M. Warner. 1980. 'Societal Differences in Organizing Manufacturing Units: a Comparison of France, West Germany and Great Britain'. *Organization Studies*, 1, 59–86.

SWEDEN

Axelsson, R., D. Cray, G. R. Mallory and D. C. Wilson. 1991. 'Decision Style in British and Swedish Organizations: A Comparative Examination of Strategic Decision Making'. *British Journal of Management*, 2, 67–79.

Emery, F. and E. Thorsrud. 1976. *Democracy at Work*. Leiden: Martinus Nijhoff.

Huczynski, A. and D. Buchanan. 1991. *Organizational Behaviour: An Introductory Text* (2nd edn). Prentice-Hall.

ISRAEL

Ariel, J. 1985. 'Kibbutz: In search of a Jewish dream', in C. Feder (ed.), *Getting Israel Together*. Jerusalem: World Zionist Organization.

Eden, D. 1975. 'Intrinsic and extrinsic rewards and motives: Replication and extension with Kibbutz workers'. *Journal of Applied Social Psychology*, 6, 349–61.

| # The East-Central Europeans

Highlighting:
Russia
Poland
Hungary

From a global perspective, Europe is less a continent than a peninsula, with the British Isles offshore and a few jagged appendages, stretching westwards from the largest of the globe's land-masses. Across the neck of this peninsula live the heterogeneous peoples of East-Central Europe, within the precarious borders of their numerous nation-states. These include Poland (population 38 million), the Czech Republic (10 million) and Slovakia (5 million), Austria (8 million), Hungary (10 million), Romania (23 million), Bulgaria (8 million) and, pre-eminently, the great bulk of Russia (almost 150 million), at least, in this context, the European end of Russia, for as a whole Russia stretches across the top of the globe until it edges China and Japan. Then there are the Ukraine (50 million) and Belorus (10 million). Finally, there is the scattering of much smaller States from the Baltic (Estonia, Latvia, Lithuania) through the fringes of the one-time Soviet Union to the one-time Yugoslavia and to Albania on the Adriatic.

Overlaid by this complicated patchwork of States there are Western Slavs and Eastern Slavs to the north, southern Slavia (that is, Yugoslavia as it was) in the south, and in between them a wedge of non-Slavic peoples in Austria, Hungary and Romania (the word 'Slav' is used loosely here, for not all those so referred to would see themselves as properly Slavic). Three major language groups are included, Slavic, Germanic and Romance, and one of the great divides in Christendom, that between the Roman Catholic and Orthodox Churches. Catholic practice predominates in Poland, Hungary and Slovakia, Orthodox practice in Russia, the Ukraine and Belorus, Romania, Bulgaria and Serbia. The imprint of Islamic Ottoman rule remains among Muslim faithful in parts of Bosnia.

Being geographically the land route into Europe to the west, none of these territories or, in modern times, nation-states has known stable boundaries for long. The only constancy has been the constancy of change as westward migrations of peoples and the armies of many empires have trampled over these lands century after century.

In the westward movement of peoples into Europe, Germanic-speaking tribes of Ostrogoths, Visigoths, Franks and others were followed by the Huns – the name 'Attila the Hun' is still used as a symbol of terror – by Slavs, Avars, Bulgars, Magyars and many more. The Mongols, too, came in from the east in the thirteenth century.

From the south, the Roman empire had reached the River Danube, but as it fell away and its garrisons withdrew, partly under the impact of the attacks from the earliest of these tribes to reach its frontiers, so the empire of the Ottoman Turks was able to push further in. This reached its greatest extent, as far as Vienna and southern Poland, in the sixteenth and seventeenth centuries.

From the west, the spheres of the so-called Holy Roman Empire and the subsequent Germanic realm had extended into East-Central Europe in the ninth and tenth centuries.

The Ottoman grip weakened and its bounds receded during the eighteenth and nineteenth centuries under pressure from both the Austro-Hungarian empire of the Habsburg monarchy and that of the Russian tsars. Newspaper cartoons conveyed the looming presence of the latter by portraying it as an enormous growling bear. The Austro-Hungarian empire was the longest sustained influence, for in one form or another it lasted almost six centuries, at its height reaching from Italy to southern Poland, and encompassing present-day Austria, Hungary, Romania and the former Czechoslovakia and Yugoslavia. The First World War (1914–18) effectively brought to an end both these widespread yet essentially feeble autocratic regimes.

The Versailles conference held by that bloody war's victor nations in 1919 drew fresh boundary-lines across the map of Europe. Whether or not the more easterly peoples had much say in it, at least these frontiers recognized some of the nationalisms that had risen beneath the Habsburg empire and had undermined it. An era of independent nation-states was ushered in – or so it seemed. For in this troubled region, with its extraordinarily complex history, that phase of independence did not last long. From 1938 onwards, the armies of Nazi Germany swept east and with great speed enveloped the whole of central and eastern Europe in association with Hungary, Romania and Bulgaria, eventually reaching the fringe of Moscow. But, like Napoleon's soldiers a century and a half earlier, they froze there, facing the desperate, wounded bear, and retreated, exhausted.

The end of the Second World War in Europe in 1945, with a second defeat for Germany, brought yet another jostling for post-war influence among victor powers. The communist-controlled Soviet Union under Stalin sought what was in effect a ring of buffer States within its domain, to help protect it from any more ruinous invasions from the west. So Europe became divided into what for four decades was a clear west and a clear east, more or less along the line where the Red Army's advance on Germany and its satellites had stopped. West of this line the then EEC, the European Economic Community of multi-party liberal democracies, began to take shape. East of it, there were communist-ruled 'people's democracies'.

As much as anything else, it is this division which dictates that the countries of East-Central Europe shall be gathered together in a single chapter in this book. Those which fell east of the line – in fact all of them except Austria, which was accorded neutral status – have a common baseline of communist administration from which their contemporary approach to management starts out.

Communist control of the USSR (the Union of Soviet Socialist Republics) itself had been initiated earliest of all by the Russian Revolution in 1917, as the First World War moved towards its ending. Not until the aftermath of the next World War did communist rule spread any further in Europe. Then Poland, Czechoslovakia (and East Germany), Hungary, Bulgaria, Romania and Yugoslavia were brought within its grasp. Albania, too, became communist, but resisted Russian domination. Yugoslavia, like Albania, being furthest from Moscow soon broke away from Russian control. At the other extreme, much nearer to Moscow, Estonia, Latvia and Lithuania on the Baltic Sea were incorporated into the USSR itself.

The Communists imposed what was effectively single-party government in each country and proclaimed a Marxist (or Marxist-Leninist) ideology which abolished whatever independent private financial ownership (capitalism) of industrial and commercial organizations there was. It promulgated a vision of a more egalitarian society without exploitation by financial market forces. The next section of this chapter examines the form of management that resulted.

The peoples of East-Central Europe were repeatedly restive under Moscow's domination. Fundamentally, it was the Red Army which held the political and economic system together. Hence anti-communist revolutions spread fast, once the Soviet Union had signalled that Moscow would no longer use the Red Army to impose uniformity among communist administrations. Not just uniformity but communist rule itself was thrown off with astonishing speed, mostly inside a single year, 1989.

MANAGING THE COMMUNIST WAY

The Communists had taken over what were largely peasant societies. To the English eyes of one of the authors, the sight of medieval strip-farming in Poland in the second half of the twentieth century was like rounding a corner and meeting a Roman soldier, an unreal encounter with something that belonged only in a history book. In the poorer parts, the peasant villagers just kept themselves alive, with a little to spare now and then, enough at least to be taxed to pay for aristocracies and empires; but, outside the more sophisticated of the capital cities, most people were far below the way of life of the urbanized nations in Western Europe. The most substantial industry was in a central belt from eastern Germany through southern Poland into western Czechoslovakia. Much of it had been State capitalist, often begun by a regime wanting to make arms for the inevitable next war, the State having then continued its protection.

So although the vestiges of private capitalism were abolished by communist administrations, except for personal craftsmanship or services and personal cultivation of small plots of land, this was not so great a change as it would have been if made in the West. Even though the communist system did not call for entrepreneurial management of the kind demanded by competitive capitalism, that was no big loss either. Those in charge were more accustomed to administration in State-led bureaucratic forms of organization (using the negative meaning of that word).

Under communist State ownership, the pace of industrialization was forced. Especially this was the case in heavy industry, such as steel and engineering, together with extracting coal and oil, partly because that was seen as the fastest way to boost economies through the early stages of development, partly because (once again) it was desired for armaments. In Czechoslovakia, where there were already more advanced and diverse industries, they were nevertheless subjugated to this policy. Furthermore, Soviet central planning focused the flows of trade between the eastern States in a form of exchange that was widely felt to favour the industrialization of the Soviet Union itself.

The communist managerial ideal was of a 'democratic centralism', under which decisions made at the top of a unified national administration, in the interests of the working class, would be carried out – after due consideration of comments from below – by workers committed by common ownership to common aims. They would not be alienated from their work by someone else owning what they were doing.

Since communist management began in the Russian-led Soviet Union, the system which attempted to put the ideal into practice was primarily on the Russian model. This was a model which took shape in a culture that, both under the tsars and before the tsars, had had no real experience of anything other than autocracy. Its way of **managing authority** and **managing uncertainty** was by two main interlocking features, dual hierarchy and planning.

The **dual hierarchy** paralleled every layer of line management with Communist Party organs, step by step from top to bottom. Box 6.1 gives a hugely simplified picture of this dual command of a 'command economy'. Under the Council of Ministers and the Supreme Planning Council, there were numerous ministries, several times the number usual in market capitalist systems, since every single economic activity had to be administered instead of being left to supply and demand. There were ministries for every product and every service: for steel, metal fabrication, textiles, foods, transport, and so on, as well as for health, education, defence, etc., as is normal elsewhere. These ministries subdivided into under-ministries, which regulated the numerous industry boards, one for each industry, to which the actual operating organizations reported.

At every level, there were parallel Communist Party Committees, the leading leg of the dual hierarchy. They were chosen from among Party members at each level (in the Soviet Union, for example, about one in

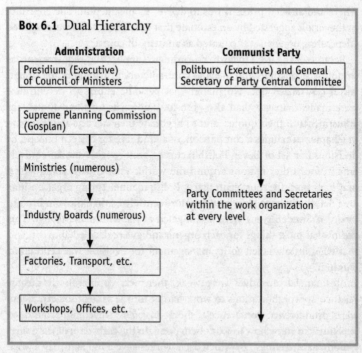

Box 6.1 Dual Hierarchy

Administration	Communist Party
Presidium (Executive) of Council of Ministers	Politburo (Executive) and General Secretary of Party Central Committee
Supreme Planning Commission (Gosplan)	
Ministries (numerous)	Party Committees and Secretaries within the work organization at every level
Industry Boards (numerous)	
Factories, Transport, etc.	
Workshops, Offices, etc.	

ten of the population had the status of membership). In each factory there was a factory Party Committee, with a Party Secretary, representing the Party Committees at each workplace below. These were made up from employees in each section: a drawing office committee, a canteen committee, a committee in each production workshop, and so forth. This division of power at every level of work was designed to ensure ultimate Communist Party control so that political aims should be uppermost.

Those aims were implemented by legally enforceable *planning*. Management everywhere revolved around 'The Plan'. This was what the dual hierarchy had to formulate and carry out. Five-year national plans setting broad targets of growth were broken down into yearly and quarterly plans, and into more detailed targets at each level down the hierarchy, until eventually each workshop or equivalent had its monthly or weekly quotas. Every factory had its instructions on what to produce, what materials, finance and labour it was to receive, and at what prices, and where and at what prices it was to deliver its production. The enormity of the task is suggested by an estimate that 24 million items were covered (depending on what was counted as an item, of course!).

Because of the need to try to co-ordinate supplies and requirements as smoothly as possible, and to avoid contradictory instructions, the system was a centralized one. No matter that periodic efforts to decentralize were made, managers had always to look upwards for their quotas, for adjustments to their quotas, and to negotiate their next quotas. Box 9.15 in Chapter 9 includes a comparison, of a kind rare for eastern Europe, of decisions in a set of eleven Polish factories, with roughly similar equivalents in four other nations around the world. Though it is India which may have been the most centralized, Polish manufacturing organizations are reliably shown to have been far more centralized than those in Britain, Japan or Sweden (they were investigated at the end of the 1970s). This meant that most things for each organization were decided above it, and that what little was left to its management for decision was centralized within it.

As financial incentives were weak, there was comparatively greater reliance upon exhortations to work harder for the sake of society. There were productivity conferences, shock brigades travelling around to explain or to show how to work better and, in the early days of the Soviet Union, 'Saturdayings', by which each worker gave a full Saturday's work to the cause (this became just a routine six-day week). Most famous were the 'Stakhanovites'. These workers emulated a miner named Alexei Stakhanov who was deemed to have produced a phenomenal tonnage of coal. Individuals or organizations who did well were given the Order of Hero of Socialist Labour or the Order of the Red Banner of Labour.

As the ultimate negative sanction, the threat under capitalism of unemployment was replaced by the threat of the '*gulag*' (labour camp), to which those who fell foul of the system were removed.

SUCCESSES AND DIFFICULTIES

The communist system of management succeeded in transforming peasant economies into industrial economies in a historically short time, most of all that of the Soviet Union. The USSR led the other eastern nations in a dramatic increase in sheer volume of production until, in the mid-1980s, their combined manufacturing total was claimed to be 40 per cent of world industrial output. Relative to where they had been at the start of the century, most of their populations had a higher standard of living and greater security, with assured jobs and free health and education services.

These were the intended consequences of the system. Its unintended consequences were often oppressive. They were discovered quite quickly, early in the experience of each country. Box 6.2 shows that the Poles were already deeply troubled after less than a decade, and Box 6.3 reveals Lenin's personal misgivings only five years into Russia's experience.

Box 6.2 Early Problems: What the Poles Found

In 1956 the Polish United Workers Party (i.e. Communist Party) at its Seventh Plenary Session declared:

An excessive centralization of the planning and administration of the economy has taken place, as well as . . . the bureaucratization of the methods of leadership. These phenomena have hampered the initiative of the masses . . . have caused waste and have retarded technical progress and economic expansion in general.

(from Singleton, p. 118)

Box 6.3 Earlier Problems: What Lenin Saw

In letters as early as 1922 Lenin wrote:

We are sinking in the dirty marsh of bureaucracy, in the writing of memos, in deliberations on decrees, in the writing of decrees, and in this 'sea of memos' the real job is sinking.

Even more vituperatively:

Everything in our country has sunk in the stinking mud of the ministries. To fight it effectively, great authority, wisdom and iron-hand ruling are required. The departments are bullshit, the decrees are also bullshit.

(from Kiezun, pp. 45 and 46)

As Lenin found, a system not governed by prices had to be governed by paper. All the information that went into The Plan for each enterprise, all the details of The Plan, and all the arrangements for fulfilling The Plan, were on paper. Management was disproportionately *paperwork*.

Each management had to negotiate its Plan up the hierarchy. As anyone with experience of a large administrative system will know – and the systems in eastern Europe were largest of all – the tactics are for those below to overstate what they need in anticipation that they will get less than they ask for, and for those above to allocate less than is needed so as to give themselves a margin to concede later or so that they can claim to have been stringently economical.

Since the entire system worked by this **bureaucratic bargaining**, the faults of such bargaining were magnified. Managements overstocked both materials and finished production, and declared less than they had, in order to cope with the uncertainties of the system. If it broke down somewhere, they had a better chance of being able to meet their planned quotas and of avoiding penalties for failure, if they had something in hand. Even better, they arranged for, say, components to be made in their own workshops, even if strictly outside The Plan, rather than depend on someone else to carry out instructions under The Plan to deliver them. So duplication arose. Box 6.4 shows yet another way of getting around the system when it failed.

Box 6.4 Oiling the Wheels by Greasing the Palms

A factory of 3,000 employees making welding machines, on the western boundaries of the Soviet Union, got its principal raw material, steel, from a steelworks in the Ural mountains, far to the east. A new steelworks was being built in Uzbekistan which, under The Plan, would take over. On the planned date, supplies from the Urals ceased, yet supplies from Uzbekistan did not arrive. The steelworks there had failed to meet its planned date for starting production.

The managers of the welding machines factory were desperate: their workers were idle. There were no ways out, such as laying off employees without pay, or buying steel elsewhere. If they failed to produce their quota, then their personal incomes would suffer and the factory's allocations of supplies next year might be cut. Pleadings with their Industry Board and Ministry got nowhere. They resorted to visits by rail to the Urals to see personally the suppliers with whom they had longstanding relationships, with a little *blat*.* This worked. They got further supplies to help them through the hiatus.

* *Blat* means reciprocal favours, such as cases of vodka, help with arranging a stay in a State holiday resort, or an understanding about further favours when the next problems in The Plan have to be got around.

(from the personal story of the deputy production controller in the welding machine factory, as told to one of the authors)

Many of the difficulties are exemplified in the factory in Moscow which is pictured in Box 6.5. Though none of them are exclusive to the communist way of managing and may be found in organizations of all kinds everywhere, they were multiplied and magnified in the nations of East-Central Europe by the enormity of the omnipresent system.

Box 6.5 Manufacturing Communism

To walk around these production departments is to be transported back to the last century. They are dark and dingy and the noise from the antiquated machinery can be deafening ... many of its own employees liken it to an industrial museum. Indeed, some 40-year veterans have spent their entire working life on the same machine.

This was 'Rezina' in 1991, a Moscow factory of 3,500 employees that had been run under the communist system for over seventy years. It made numerous rubber goods, such as pipes, hoses, washers, gaskets and conveyor belts, in a six-storey building and some linked subsidiary sites. It was well known both for being in 'the vanguard of the working class', and for bad working conditions.

It was under the jurisdiction of the Ministry of Chemical Industries, which connected it with a single dominant supplier plant for its main raw material, synthetic rubber, and a set of main recipients for its products, including the three principal car producers and the former USSR's large agricultural conglomerate. It was also under the control of the Party, whose representatives had a suite of offices and conference rooms, with a receptionist, in an administrative floor of the building.

Rezina's operating problems were not sales, since its products were routinely distributed; rather, its problems were getting adequate materials, equipment and personnel. The synthetic rubber, for example, arrived in railway wagons in 30-kilogram bales (there was no freight container system). These had to be manually unloaded on to a fork-lift truck. It was such heavy work that labour turnover was high and, at times, soldiers had to be used to do it. Further, Rezina did not have enough trucks to smoothly offload everything that arrived by rail, so there were transport bottlenecks that caused production to be stopped in the manufacturing workshops. This undermined effective planning and production control. In any case, the most sophisticated machine in the planning department was an electric calculator long obsolete in the West, while abacuses were used to make calculations.

The outcome was that output, number of employees and financial performance had all been declining for some years.

(synthesized from Burawoy and Hendley)

In the end, the rising aspirations of the 'masses' for greater quality and variety of goods and services, and for greater freedom of choice in life, which were heightened as they became more aware of standards in the West and in Japan, were more than the system could fulfil.

DIFFERENT WAYS OF MANAGING THE COMMUNIST WAY

To many outsiders, the system appeared uniform and monolithic right across East-Central Europe. It began in each of the other nations modelled on the Soviet system at its Stalinist zenith. As the poster slogans put it, 'with the Soviet Union as our guide and leader'.

However, it was not long before national differences, historically derived from culture and politics, began to show through. First and foremost – and most different – was Yugoslavia, the southern Slav federation of Serbia, Bosnia-Herzogovina, Croatia, Macedonia, Montenegro and Slovenia. Yugoslav guerrilla partisan forces had themselves speeded the departure of the occupying German army in the Second World War, and they took over government. Peasant in origin, independent in outlook and, as mentioned earlier, far from the Soviet Union, in less than three years they had broken away from Moscow's dominance.

They instituted a more devolved system, more open to commerce with the West. Most memorably, they launched worker self-management. For four decades the world followed the wavering fortunes of this experiment with interest, with hope, with disappointment.

In outline, a general assembly of all the employees in each establishment (who nominally owned its means of production) had to be consulted about major contracts and investments. The assembly elected a workers' council which formally decided policy on output, finance and pay and, most remarkably, elected the board of management, including its chairperson, the managing director or chief executive, whose position had to be advertised. This did engender at its best more participation and influence by lower-level employees than anywhere else in Europe, east or west. Even so, the fundamental differences in the nature of jobs in organizations step by step down the hierarchy eroded it. Workers doing limited routine jobs did not sufficiently understand more complex issues and became apathetic. Their representatives, handed sheafs of words and figures, could not understand enough to make an intelligent contribution. Those who by experience or training came to understand, and spent a lot of time sitting in offices and committee rooms instead of at the workbench, ceased to be workers quite like the workers they were intended to represent. In any case, managers could present information in ways favourable to their own viewpoint, and overwhelm discussion by their superior verbal skills.

The other nations did not go so far. Poland and Hungary probably had the least rigid and autocratic approach to management, as the very broad characterization in Box 6.6 suggests. This groups six of the nations in pairs according to degree of autocracy in management, as indicated by bureaucratization (numbers of regulations, instructions and forms), centralization (proportion of decisions permitted at higher or lower levels), criticism (the numbers of claims and proposals for improvement submitted at staff meetings), self-discipline (absenteeism and forms of strikes and conflict), propaganda (assertive exhortation from the top), productivity (output per worker), and employee purchasing power. The last mentioned was a comparison of proportion of average pay required to buy a 'standard shopping basket' of goods and services, avoiding the often insuperable obstacles to using national statistics. The grouping must be treated with caution as the evidence for it is so slender and it rests on the judgement of its Polish author, but it offers a rare overview.

Poland and Hungary are shown as having the least bureaucratized and centralized management with the least docile (or most troublesome)

Box 6.6 A View from Inside

	Autocratic	Autocratic and Self-Disciplined	Less Autocratic
		MANAGEMENT STYLE	
	Bulgaria & Romania	East Germany & Czechoslovakia	Poland & Hungary
Bureaucracy	Very high	High	Lower
Centralization	Very high	High, with exceptions	High, with elements of decentralization
Criticism (Speaking out)	Low	Low	Higher, especially at times in Poland
Self-Discipline (Motivation)	Less strong	Strongest	Less strong
Propaganda (Exhortation)	Banners, pictures of leaders, slogans	Banners, slogans, pictures of leaders; less in Czechoslovakia	Poor visual propaganda (except in Silesia)
Productivity	Lowest	Highest	Medium
Employee Purchasing Power	Lowest	By far the highest	Not so low

for footnote see foot of opposite page

workforces. They have relatively individualistic cultures in which people did not passively operate a uniform system that was perceived as imposed from without.

Hungary was notable for the extent to which it succeeded in decentralizing decisions to the management of each establishment; and Poland, too, moved in this direction. Managers had considerable discretion in preparing their own plan, choosing sources of supplies and deciding prices (within limits). Managerial performance was assessed in financial terms, and employee pay depended on the results. This degree of 'market socialism' had some periods which economically were comparatively successful, but it remained within an overall central control and the improvements were not sustained.

Most successful economically, though, were the East Germans and the German-influenced Czechs, as mentioned before, the purposeful and rule-abiding Germanic culture being as effective a soil for economic growth, relative to nations with the same or similar system, as in the West. Both had a relatively urban industrial basis and, it may be said, the most significant Protestant Christian traditions in eastern Europe.

Bulgaria and Romania, however, shared much of the autocracy traditional in their Orthodox Churches and left to them by centuries of Turkish rule. Despite a policy in later years in Romania of 'openness to the West', and a toying with worker self-management in Bulgaria, both were subject to relatively tight, even ruthless, administration.

The Soviet Union itself was not unchanged, of course. It edged slowly away from the highly top-down approach under Stalin to a marginally greater discretion for local collectives, and eventually to the upheavals of *glasnost* (greater openness of information and discussion) and *perestroika* (restructuring and reorganizing) at the end of the 1980s and beginning of the 1990s.

Footnote to table opposite:
This table is a modified version of that given by Kiezun (pp. 308/309). Since to carry out direct comparative research required official permission, and to obtain that required tediously protracted applications and the allaying of official suspicion, with the foreknowledge that anyway permission would almost certainly be refused, Witold Kiezun in 1976 undertook an unofficial personal enquiry. Through personal contacts he arranged for a machine-tool factory to be studied in each of Poland, Hungary and East Germany, and the results passed to him; and where even that was impossible, as in Czechoslovakia, Bulgaria and Romania, he persuaded a management professor in each country to answer questions in the light of his own experience and enquiries. He himself was a very prominent national figure in Polish management training at the time. The table summarizes the results he obtained.

TRANSITION

It was plain that the disintegration of the Russian-dominated system left much industry technically backward by comparison with that in Western Europe. Pollution of air and water was far worse, and there was a comparatively poor infrastructure of roads, energy supplies and services. The material standard of living was much lower. The East Germans and neighbouring German-influenced Czechs were best off, just as the West Germans had taken the economic leadership of the EC. The other eastern countries were probably less well off than Greece, Ireland and Portugal, the poorest of the EC nations.

In order to make these economies more efficient, a fundamental change from public to private ownership was considered essential. **Privatization** on such a scale, of every potential organization in entire economies, is unprecedented. Former British Prime Minister Margaret Thatcher set out to show how to do it, but even her government had only a comparative handful of nationalized undertakings to sell, and it sold them one at a time. Conversely in the previously planned economies, units can be so large and can incorporate so much of their own 'suppliers' and 'users' (vertical integration) that it is difficult to separate them into disposable pieces. Where do they begin and end? For instance, in the former Soviet Union, the Kama River truck factory covered nine square miles, and is said to have been larger than the combined capacity of all the equivalent American manufacturers.

Abolishing planned prices so that each management can decide its own, and withdrawing subsidies, is a further step towards a market economy, but it frequently results in inflation. With the opening of markets, managements have turned to the West for supplies and to sell whatever is saleable there, so that trade with the West has increased and that among the eastern nations has decreased. Though joint ventures with western companies are multiplying, capital to renew outdated plant is scarce, and severe unemployment is entailed as managements jettison the underemployed people they were previously required to pay.

Given the diversity of the lands and peoples of East-Central Europe, it is hard to pick any true exemplars. Three have been chosen for portrayal: the largest and two which show the greatest contrast with it. Compared with the others, these are also the three countries about which more material is available in English. They are:

Russia
Poland
and Hungary.

RUSSIAN CULTURE AND MANAGEMENT

How often has it been said that Russia sprawls halfway around the top of the globe from the Baltic to the Pacific? It has already been said in this chapter. It just cannot avoid being said again. Non-Russians find it difficult to separate Russia from the USSR, because it was three-quarters of the area of the communist USSR for the nearly seventy years of the Union's existence, until 1991. It also produced three-quarters of the Union's industrial and agricultural output and contained a good half of its nearly 300 million people. Nevertheless, there were many other peoples in the USSR and, even within its own borders, Russia – or, strictly, the Russian Federation – includes numerous minorities, some constituted as subsidiary republics and regions.

Russia was not always so. It had small and perilous beginnings as conquerors trod to and fro across the lands which it itself eventually conquered.

The Slav peoples who had populated what is now the west of Russia in the fifth, sixth and seventh centuries were overwhelmed by Mongols and Tartars in the thirteenth century. The two-and-a-half centuries of Mongol rule and domination which followed are widely held to have instilled an acceptance of absolutist authority into the nascent Russian culture. By the time the Grand Duchy of Muscovy threw off the Mongol grip, both the subject Russian princes and their peasants were well used to authoritarianism and to the assumption, which the Mongols had brought with them, of a divine dispensation to rule in such a fashion. In the sixteenth century, its imperial pretensions were symbolized when the title of tsar began to be used, a word derived from the Latin 'Caesar', with all the grandeur which that implied. Russia came to be treated as a gigantic royal estate owned by the tsars. There was never a feudal system which, elsewhere in Europe, did carry some notion of mutual obligation, not only of peasant to lord but of protection and patronage by lord to peasant. So authority was even more top-down. By the seventeenth century, most peasants had been reduced to serfdom, a condition of virtual slavery. It was a social structure paralleled by that of the Patriarchal Orthodox Church, which had evolved a similar form and view of religious authority.

In this patrimonial empire, a great deal depended on what each particular tsar was personally able and willing to do. The problem with such a personal conception of authority was, of course, that decrees signed in Moscow were either not known of hundreds or thousands of miles away, or they were impracticable or were ignored, or all of these. Nor did serfs work with enthusiasm. They were not paid to do so (see Box 6.7).

Box 6.7 Whipping up Enthusiasm

John Perry, an English engineer brought in by Tsar Peter to supervise canal construction and other projects, commented on 'the custom of Russia' of demanding work without pay. When he asked that the better labourers be paid in recognition of that: 'I have received for answer, particularly by my lord Apraxin . . . that there was no such precedent for the giving of money out of the Tsar's treasure for men to do their duty for which they were sent; . . . and if they did not do their work when required, they must be beaten to it.'

(from Bendix, p. 164)

The system was ultimately less efficient than its rivals, industrially and militarily. Revolution in 1917 led to Bolshevik (communist) rule.

This substituted the authority of the Party for that of the tsar, over a more thoroughgoing and, by comparison, modern bureaucratic system of administration. Yet the parallels of the communist, centrally planned control which has been described, with what had preceded it, are unmistakable. Especially was this so when Stalin forced the pace of industrialization and urbanization from the mid-1920s to the mid-1930s at great human cost in long hours, poor pay, bad working conditions and, in the countryside, the eviction and even starvation of peasants during the compulsory collectivization of farming. To a point, this industrialization worked, for it was the foundation of the USSR's victory over the Germans in the Second World War, and of its superpower status with nuclear bombs and spacecraft soon afterwards.

Box 6.8 Studies of Russian Values

Studies using the concepts of Hofstede as described in Chapter 2 have found that the Russian culture is distinctive. Two studies, one by Bollinger and one by Elenkov, found that the Russian way of **managing authority** is very high at the authoritarian end on power distance, being comparable to that of many developing countries. In terms of **managing relationships**, it is found to be on the collectivist side – comparable to Japan. But, unlike Japan, in **managing oneself** it is at the 'feminine' end, emphasizing good relationships with colleagues rather than high achievements. In **managing uncertainty**, it is at the high uncertainty avoidance end, comparable with France. These basic values can be seen working out in both the Tsarist and the Communist regimes, and may be expected to influence subsequent transformations.

(from Bollinger; and Elenkov)

The ingrained top-down managing of authority (as indicated in Box 6.8) had and has as its cultural antidote an approach to managing relationships which shows a high degree of collectivism (see Box 6.8 again) which helps to make insensitive authoritarianism endurable. Russians **manage relationships** in and out of work in a comparatively warm, open manner, emotionally expressive, share and share alike. Arguably, this, together with an ability to submerge self in a common cause, originated in the necessity to work together for survival in the first bleak, and scattered Slav settlements, and was sustained by mutual loyalty under Mongol sovereignty. Here again, the national Russian Orthodox Church is woven into the cultural pattern. Confession of sins is often communal, in public, as against the curtained privacy of the Roman rite, and the creed or statement of belief does not begin 'I believe', as does the Apostles' creed, but 'Let us love one another'. It was an emphasis just as well suited to atheistic communism, which maintained the traditional precedence of collective duties over individual rights in the service of Mother Russia.

Collective folk humour brought impersonal communist management down to human level. Employees saw through low productivity and weak material incentives: as they said, 'We pretend to work and they pretend to pay us.' The queues in the shops were not pretence, of course, but they too could be made light of (see Box 6.9).

There is a seeming contradictoriness in the Russian way of **managing**

uncertainty. Like the tsars, the Communists governed by issuing copious written decrees from the Kremlin which were supposed to be universally applicable and acted upon. An uncertainty-avoiding culture (which the researchers of Box 6.8 found) and a large-scale bureaucratic administration acted together in the same direction. Every workplace bulged with manuals of rules and detailed instructions. Lists of regulations covered the walls, along with pictures of leaders whose portraits were meant to inspire greater efforts. However, little attention was given to these regulations, whether they prescribed standards of quality, standards of safety or whatever, by an essentially non-orderly workforce. Especially was this so when livelihood depended on cutting corners and cheating a little to meet The Plan. Not here the comparative conformity and tidiness of workplaces in, say, Germany or Japan. The scene is implicit in the description of the Rezina factory in Box 6.5.

Box 6.9 Laughing on Queue

Two Russians had been queueing for two hours for some soap. One became exasperated, and stamped off. 'Where are you going?' called the other. 'To shoot Gorbachev,'* was the reply. Half an hour later the same Russian returned, looking even more frustrated. 'Didn't you do it?' the other asked. 'No,' came the furious answer, 'the queue there was even longer.'

* Communist Party General Secretary

(typical witticism of its time)

Russian dominance of management ran throughout the Soviet Union. There was a 'Russification' of management, with Russians appointed disproportionately to managerial posts, especially in vital manufacturing, in the other republics as well as in Russia itself.

Like managers worldwide, the Russian manager worked hard and long hours. As a large proportion of each manager's income, up to one-half of it, depended on meeting set quotas, managers could not afford to fail. They were highly stressed by The Plan – which no doubt accounted for some of the famed Russian consumption of vodka. In addition to the risks of transfer or demotion taken by managers in other countries, they faced the penalties of loss of Party membership, or even of imprisonment, if they failed in such a way as to be deemed to have contravened national policy. Whilst they could not be thrown 'on to the street' in quite the same manner as in the West, they could be moved abruptly sideways or downwards, and since holding the Party card was virtually a condition of being considered reliable enough to hold a managerial post, its removal could be a severe penalty. After rapid mobility around and up the new system in the years before the Second World War, when it grew fast and constantly needed more managers and administrators, promotion slowed to a crawl as the system consolidated, with seniority ever counting for more.

Once the devastation and casualties of that war had been made up for, labour was again comparatively cheap. Performance was often achieved by the wasteful use of personnel. Manual labour was easier to obtain than expensive equipment (the Rezina factory again illustrates this). Further, in pursuit of short-term attainment of plan, maintenance or improvements could be set aside, and frequently were, with deleterious longer-term consequences.

From the early 1990s onwards the awkward transition towards a market-orientated economy began to take place. Various forms of private ownership, illegal during Communist times, were allowed. Individuals gained the right to start their own businesses, to buy shares in enterprises which had been state owned, to own houses. But it was the enterprise directors, the government officials (the former Communist party leaders) who gained most of the land and property. Prices, which had been controlled, were freed and the resulting inflation was phenomenal. In 1992 the inflation rate was 2,600 per cent, annual interest rates exceeded 100 per cent, and taxes increased dramatically. Inevitably, consumer demand dropped, production fell, and enterprise debt increased causing much hardship. But the official unemployment rate stayed below two per cent, showing that the traditional Communist (and Russian) reluctance to lay off workers continued. There followed a period of relative stability. But the unresolved problems of oppressive tax policies, government instability, and coping with the market economy led to another financial crisis in 1998. The government defaulted on loans, the stock market collapsed, the rouble was drastically devalued (again) and many people's savings became worthless.

The difficulties of Russian managers having to operate in this transitional phase are considerable. Planning is a basic management function necessary for making decisions to secure the future. Now that central government plans no longer exist, the managements of enterprises must plan for themselves. But it is very difficult to do so because of the high level of uncertainty in the environment. Companies are closing every day and are unable to deliver their commitments. A supplier may not be able to deliver because its own supplier has gone bankrupt. A dishonest supplier may take advance payment for goods and then disappear. Since production planning is difficult, a common uncertainty avoiding practice is to have the finished goods in stock and then look for a buyer. The lack of trust means that once a buyer is found, the producer will want payment in advance and will only then ship the goods. Credit is haphazard. Banks have experienced a large number of bad loans, and are loath to issue credit except on the basis of personal contacts and in return for a share of the ownership. Hence lateral networking becomes increasingly important for the managers – not just upwards in the Ministry and the Party, which was the priority before. All of these factors slow up economic development.

The Russian style of management is authoritarian (high power distance, as in Box 6.8) and attempts to be participative have not worked very well. It is also paternalistic and Russian managers often treat their subordinates as if they were children. They look after them, but they are also continually checking and correcting them. Verbal abuse is common, although Russian emotional openness means that employees are not precluded from answering back. Russian managers are unlikely to decentralize as they wish to preserve their power. There are few management meetings, the pattern is for the General Manager to meet the individual managers separately, a not very efficient method of co-ordination. For their part, subordinates are unlikely to welcome responsibility as they do not have the necessary skills and see no obvious rewards. So typically when the General Manager is off the premises work will continue as long as there is no need for a non-routine decision. Should such a decision be needed, work will grind to a minimum and may even halt altogether.

Because the market is so inefficient, networking (as we have seen) is key and managers are loath to allow others access to their own networks of suppliers, banks, and customers – in case they steal the business. The Russian management jungle is illustrated in Box 6.10. It also still has within it the illegal 'grey market' which sprung up because of the rigidities of the former system, and the Russian 'mafia' remains very strong.

As things stand at the beginning of the twenty-first century, it is clear

Box 6.10 The Russian Management Jungle

Moshe Banai of the City University of New York has been conducting a long-term study of the changes taking place in management practices in the Russian Republic of Tatarstan. He finds that while some formal changes have taken place to make enterprises more like Western ones, the Russian management culture means that these changes have only limited effect in the very harsh reality of current economic activity.

For example:

● government officials who still control some major resources (e.g. credit, heating) prove deliberately obstructive unless offered 'inducements', forcing the manager to deal with illegal enterprises in the 'grey' market;

● employees do not have the skills and work performance to justify large wage increases, so they hop jobs to improve income even slightly. Managers have to have a steady stream of workers to keep lines going, so they hire labour indiscriminately. In any case, a great proportion of salary is paid 'under the table' to avoid taxes;

● all firms need security measures – against internal theft and damage, and against external 'hooligans'. Most security is provided by:

  i   government agencies, such as the police;

  ii ex-government agents who have become private operators; and

  iii illegal 'mafia' groups who extort money for 'protection'.

  The distinctions between these three types of providers are not always clear;

● to cope with high tax rates and extortion payments, businesses have to keep three sets of books: one for the owners, one for the government and one for the illegal groups;

● senior managers or owners do not allow others to get involved with more than a fraction of the critical tasks. They wish to control all business relationships themselves in case their subordinates make contacts which allow them to establish their own networks and eventually steal the business. For example, an American businessman who developed an oil bartering business in the Ukraine, identified a young person with managerial potential and trained him for over a year to take charge of the subsidiary. Once the employee was ready for the job, he opened his own barter firm and took with him all the major customers.

(from Banai)

that the transition is working so poorly that progress toward the free market system may well have stalled. A current estimate is that the GDP per head is 30 per cent less than it was before the reforms began, and there is even talk of re-nationalizing some of the large enterprises. But it is unlikely that Russia would return to a Communist system; for one thing the leading politicians, and the top managers of banks and large enterprises, are former party officials who have personally done very well out of the change so far and would have much to lose. The general consensus of outside observers is that it will take a generation (i.e. 10–15 more years) before the young managers who have not experienced the Communist system get to positions of power and the Russian economy and management begin to work in anything like an efficient way.

POLISH CULTURE AND MANAGEMENT

Third most populous nation in this area of the globe, after Russia and the Ukraine, Poland lies in north-east Europe, surrounded by Germany, the Czech Republic, Slovakia, the Ukraine, Belorus and Lithuania (and even a tiny detached piece of Russian territory that is perched on the edge of the Baltic). From it have arisen Copernicus and Chopin and the Curies and, from an overwhelmingly Roman Catholic land as contrasted with the Orthodox churches of Russia and the Ukraine, the first non-Italian Pope since 1522.

The appearance, disappearance and reappearance of Poland over the centuries typifies the instability of this part of Europe. During its 'golden age' in the fifteenth and sixteenth centuries, it dominated the region, at its height reaching from the Baltic Sea to the Black Sea. At the start of the seventeenth century, a Polish army actually occupied Moscow briefly. Thereafter Poland fell more and more under foreign control itself. During a curious elective monarchy, when the royal incumbent was chosen by the nobles, choices from among other European dynasties tended to pursue their own interests rather than those of the Poles. In 1797 the country was partitioned between Austria, Prussia and Russia, and it did not regain independence until after the end of the First World War.

This short-lived independence was instantly lost as the Second World War began in 1939 with invasion by Nazi Germany, and division of the country between Germany and the USSR. The desire, shared by Hitler and Stalin, to control and even suppress the Poles overcame the animosity of their fascist and communist ideologies.

After huge loss of life, including the extermination of Jewish people, during the total German occupation which followed Nazi Germany's attack on the Soviet Union, the Poles again achieved independence of a sort at the war's ending. But it was restricted by the surveillance of the USSR, and by the imposition of a Russian-style communist political and economic system.

However, this was no passive imitation. Box 6.2 has shown that as early as 1956 Polish discontent had surfaced in official declarations of protest. There were, of course, the strains in the centralized management system itself. The dual hierarchy (Box 6.1) could pull managers both ways so that they resorted to all sorts of manoeuvres between their line superiors and their Party bosses. Box 6.11 describes the predicament in which one bank manager found himself.

Box 6.11 Banking on it

When the local branch manager of the National Bank of Poland refused to lend any more to an enterprise which was not doing well, the local Party Secretary intervened to reverse the decision (this was during the 1960s); he was not willing to risk the political consequences if wages were not paid. For his part, the bank manager pointed out that he had acted in accordance with directives from bank head office.

Eventually, the manager contacted the president of the bank (an instance of the centralizing pressures in the system). The president advised more or less as follows: 'If you decide against the opinion of the Party's Secretary, sooner or later he will come to me to make a demand for your dismissal from the post because of your lack of co-operation with the Party, and I, of course, will dismiss you. On the other hand, if you decide in accordance with the Secretary's suggestion, I will send an enquiry commission to you and they will find out that you are not carrying out my instructions and, consequently, will also demand your dismissal.' 'Then what shall I do?' asked the manager, to which the president replied: 'Obey the Party and count on my generosity. I have to obey the Secretary's proposal for your dismissal, whereas the enquiry commission is under my supervision and I have the power to reject their recommendation.'

(from Kiezun, p. 197)

Poles were always striving for greater latitude within the system. Compared to most others in East-Central Europe, they seemed more ready to speak out against its defects, they were less committed to it, and theirs was, if anything, less ponderously bureaucratic. From 1956 onwards there were periodic convulsions which yielded step-by-step relaxations. Strikes and riots in that year brought the legalization of workers' councils in workplaces, along similar lines to, but less effective than, the Yugoslav councils which were outlined previously in this chapter. Although their powers were gradually attenuated by a mixture of Party moves to recover greater control and of employee indifference, they outlasted the communist regime. Then after another wave of strikes in 1970, a degree of financial autonomy was permitted to working establishments. Finally in 1980 came the extraordinary phenomenon of 'Solidarity'.

The Gdansk shipyard which had sparked the 1970 riots was once more the source of the action. From being ostensibly a trade union, the symbolically named Solidarity became a mass opposition movement which at its peak claimed almost ten million members. It demonstrated again, as had resistance inside and outside Poland during the Second World War, an ability to organize against the system, against the odds. Although in 1981 martial law was imposed to try to shore up the regime, and the leaders of Solidarity were imprisoned, when 1989 arrived Poland had a non-communist prime minister and a government not controlled by Communists.

The managers who emerged from beneath the regime presided over a manufacturing industry which, as in Russia, had a high proportion of very large plants, vertically integrated, ill-equipped, and heavily polluting. Managers were for the most part well educated, though not in what the Anglo West regards as business studies; but a recognizably Polish style of management has hardly had a chance to develop. Industry had begun and administration had taken shape in the nineteenth century under foreign rule when the country was partitioned three ways. After 1939, it had been built up for military purposes during German occupation, and had then operated under a command economy of essentially foreign (Russian) design.

So managers are used to **managing authority** more autocratically than in most of Western Europe, within a centralizing hierarchy (the evidence for this in Box 9.15 has already been mentioned). Yet they manage in a culture more *individualistic* than that of the Russians, in which people are prone to resist authority (see Box 6.12). Even Stalin is said to have remarked to Churchill that 'Communism for Poles is like a saddle for a cow.' There is something reminiscently French about looking for an authoritative lead whilst being individualistically suspicious of it. Authority is needed to hold things together, but it is distrusted after so many centuries when it was imposed from without.

Box 6.12 Studies of Polish Values

A study using the concepts of Hofstede (as described in Chapter 2) found that in the Polish culture **managing authority** is very high, at the authoritarian end on power distance. In terms of **managing relationships**, it is found to be on the individualist side. In **managing oneself** it is on the 'masculine' side placing some emphasis on the achievement itself rather than the process which brought it about. In **managing uncertainty**, it is at the high uncertainty avoidance end. This general cultural pattern places Poland in the group which Hofstede labels 'More developed Latin' – comparable with France and Brazil. The link appears to be the influence of Roman Catholicism, which would have helped to keep Poland different in culture from Germany, to its west, and Russia, to its east. According to this study, therefore, Polish managers try to control an individualistic and assertive workforce in an authoritarian and bureaucratic way – a potentially fraught combination as Polish history shows.

(from Nasierowski and Mikula)

Such a people are ready material for the opportunities for enterprise in an open economy. Even under communist central planning, private business had increased as the system gradually relaxed, far more so than in Russia. Moreover, there were a large number of co-operatives. So in 1989 the Poles leapt into their economic 'cold bath' with alacrity, even though some were hesitant. Despite inflation and unemployment, queues in the shops disappeared and exports expanded. At first there was some 'spontaneous' privatization of ownership, which took advantage of a change of State ownership to company format to arrange 'insider deals'. Members of the communist '*nomenklatura*' elite are said to have acquired shares at knockdown prices. A stop was put to this, but it accelerated official privatization, albeit under more careful control. Most often companies have been formed by employees to lease or buy the assets of State establishments that have been wound up for the purpose. There are provisions for employees to buy shares at discount prices, and to require workers' council agreement in certain situations. Poland has been swarming with Western consultants trying to arrange sales to Western capital, and the Ministry of Privatization advertised its wares in the Western financial press. Though some expected the process to go even faster, and private ownership of small businesses and in the retail trade is easier to accomplish than for larger undertakings, private business is overhauling the State sector.

Not all Polish managers could cope with the new free-market situation, but many could and did well. There were reforms in both the state and private sectors with, as Box 6.13 shows, success stories. But the mere fact that these cases are highlighted underlines that the professional standards of management (particularly in strategy and marketing) in general lag considerably behind the West.

Box 6.13 Success Stories

Krzysztof Obloj, a Polish academic commentator, describes two successful firms (one state-owned, one private) which survived and prospered after the 'shock therapy' of deregulation.

The state-owned Szczecin shipyard was almost bankrupt when the changes took place. But the management designed and carried out an effective turnaround strategy using the management technique of SWOT analysis (i.e. identifying the Strengths and Weaknesses of the enterprise, and matching them with Opportunities and Threats in the environment). From this analysis medium priced, medium sized container ships were identified as an appropriate niche in the market. To operate successfully the size of the enterprise had to be reduced and unwanted production facilities leased out. Costs had to be cut (e.g. non-productive assets, such as apartments and technical schools, were sold or given away), and credit re-negotiated with suppliers and banks. Workers were concentrated on the core activities of building ships and the traditional payment scheme was changed to a skill-based system that increased the quality of work, reduced overtime costs and created the incentive for continuous improvement and training. A re-design of the production process, allowing many tasks that were previously done sequentially to be done in parallel, together with a reduction in the number of ships built at any one time, enabled the time needed to build a ship to be cut by more than half (from 26 months to 11 months), and the firm to prosper in its new market.

The strategy of Ambra S.A. a private company, was to produce quickly a large volume of low-to-medium quality sparkling wines at lower cost than their competitors and then market them strongly. The marketing department developed a range of fancy glittering labels that attracted attention in stores. When their competitors caught up, Ambra strengthened their sales force which promoted the products to retailers, obtained the best shelf space in stores, offered merchandizing support, and negotiated long-term contracts with the newly developing chain stores. By the end of the decade, the company dominated the market.

(from Obloj)

By the beginning of the twenty-first century, Poland's GDP per head was 20 per cent up on what it was at the fall of the previous regime. At completely the other extreme from Russia, the country's managerial culture has thus been the most successful of the former Communist countries in adapting to the new economic climate.

HUNGARIAN CULTURE AND MANAGEMENT

In Europe, the mountains to the east of the Alps form a crescent which encloses a fertile plain – the Carpathian basin. Somewhat over a thousand years ago, a number of nomadic tribes crossed into this sparsely populated area from the east and settled for good into a pastoral–agricultural lifestyle. The Europeans to their west mistakenly thought they were the descendants of the Huns who had occupied the area many centuries before. They called them Hungari, and so the area came to be known as Hungaria (in English, Hungary). The people called themselves Magyar after the name of the dominant tribe.

After the settlement western influences began to penetrate. Christianity was adopted as the official religion, and the Kingdom of Hungary was recognized by the Pope and the Holy Roman Empire. The power of this kingdom, being in the strategically important, but geographically vulnerable, south-eastern corner of Europe, waxed and waned over the following centuries. A low point was the three-way partition of the country in the sixteenth century – between the occupying Turks, the

Habsburg Holy Roman Emperors, and local Magyar barons. By the nineteenth century, when the Holy Roman Empire had evolved into the Austrian Empire, an agreement was reached to establish the Austro-Hungarian dual monarchy. The Emperor of Austria became, separately, the King of Hungary, and considerable devolved sovereignty was given to the country. But the Habsburg connection meant that Hungary was on the losing side during the First World War.

Following the First World War, the Peace Treaty of 1919 recognized the constituent nationalities of the Habsburg Empire and established independent states, including Romania, Serbia and Czechoslovakia, which between them took more than 70 per cent of Hungary's former territory – leaving it with an area about one-third the size of Britain. These frontiers hold today, and it makes Hungary unique in being bordered on all sides by its own former territories, each with Hungarian speaking minorities. About 10 million Hungarians live in Hungary, but about four million live in the surrounding countries. The resentment towards the Allies, generated by the peace settlement, determined that Germany was the prime influence on economic development between the wars and contributed to the country being ruled at that time by a Fascist, Nazi-sympathizing regime. This meant that Hungary was, again, on the losing side during the Second World War.

Before the Second World War Hungary had been primarily an agricultural country, and it continues to be a net exporter of food. Much of the industry that did exist was destroyed during the war. At the end of the war the country was occupied by the Red Army of the Soviet Union, and Communist rule was established in 1948. With the advent of the Communist regime, the remaining industry was nationalized and the farms collectivized with much repression. In typical Soviet fashion, the country was then industrialized with the emphasis on heavy industry fitting into the Soviet bloc's Comecon system of planned reciprocal trade between the Communist states. Hungary specialized in buses, electrical equipment, pharmaceuticals and foodstuffs. The Hungarian economy and its industry were run in the way described for the Soviet Union earlier in this chapter. The managerial objective was to fulfil the demands of the centrally established plan, the emphasis being on quantity not quality. Thus, as described in Box 6.14, the Hungarians provided the Russians with buses which were, by Western standards, of poor design and low quality, and received other low quality capital goods in return.

At first, consumer goods were relatively neglected in this system, but in the 1960s they received more emphasis. After 1968, with the introduction of the so-called 'New Economic Management System', economic decision-making began to be more decentralized. Profitability, rather than the attainment of established quotas, was introduced as a leading criterion for judging the performance of a factory. Although this was not applied consistently, Box 6.6 shows Hungary was one of the less bureaucratic of the Communist regimes with regard to industry. There were elements of decentralization, and some degree of outspoken criticism was tolerated.

BOX 6.14 The Comecon System

The production manager of the Budapest factory of Ikarus – the largest Hungarian bus manufacturer (i.e. bodybuilder and assembler) described working in the Comecon system:

... about 90–95 per cent of our production was produced for the socialist countries. In these places in all the countries, the quality was not in first place. That is why we did not think about it, it was not necessary. It was an exchange in the socialist market, as we handed over to the Russians a bus, which was not very high quality, and we received a Lada passenger car and a tractor, which were also of not very good quality. The quantity was first, quality did not matter.

He also described resulting present-day effects:

Now the bigger part of our production goes into a market where quality is a requirement ... That is why we suffer so much today, because all of the people have in their mind just the work, not the good quality. Today, to make some people work hard and exactly is very difficult. After 40 years, everything is very hard in the brains. It is difficult to change now.

(adapted from Wallace)

Hungarian Language and Culture

These liberalizing tendencies were possible, even in Communist times, partly because, historically, there was always a considerable degree of wiliness in Hungarian culture. The people have experienced hundreds of years of occupation and oppression by other nations. They had, therefore, to learn to use their wits. Part of their resistance is due to the use of a very distinctive language, nothing like those used by the surrounding Germanic or Slavic countries but one with links to Finnish. Although Latin script is used, it is very difficult for foreigners to recognize words. There are imported words like *posta* and *menedzsment* (management) but the Hungarian words for hotel, police, economics, production, and so on are not immediately recognizable. A few words have been exported: goulash and paprika have become international; and so has the word 'coach', originally applied to a four wheeled carriage as developed in the Hungarian village of Kocs (pronounced coach).

With this culture, the way of **managing authority** was subject to considerable strain in the Hungarian Communist system. The traditional anti-authoritarian culture of Hungary (shown as the low power distance in Box 6.15) was in conflict with the imposed centralized 'vertical' system. The outcome over the years was an imposition of authority less heavy-handed than in other Communist nations.

Box 6.15 Studies of Hungarian Values

Studies using the concepts of Hofstede (as described in Chapter 2) have found that the Hungarian culture may be classed with the Northern European group of Chapter 5. (In this it is different from Polish culture which has more affinities with the Latins of Chapter 4.) Research by Varga found that Hungary was low on power distance in regard to managing authority, high on individualism in managing relationships, high on masculinity in managing oneself and medium on uncertainty avoidance. This pattern is very similar to the German culture described in Chapter 5. A later study (by Bakacsi and colleagues) found a very large gap between what Hungarian managers said was the present power distance in organizations (very large, i.e. authoritarian) and what they would like it to be (small, i.e. participative). This seems to be the legacy of the Communist system.

(from Bakacsi)

Hungarians have been creative as inventions such as the Biro ball point pen, the Gabor hologram and the Rubic cube illustrate. They value individual innovativeness and flexibility. **Managing relationships** in this culture puts the emphasis on individualism (as in Box 6.15). But to those who have had to try and deal with Hungarians, either as rulers (like the Austrians), or as ruled (like the Romanians), this individual shrewdness and wiliness is easily interpreted negatively as untrustworthy 'slipperiness'. Their reputation is characterized by the classic caricature that they are so slippery that 'if a Hungarian goes into a revolving door behind you, he will still come out in front!'

Goulash Communism

These characteristics led Hungary in the 1980s, even under nominal Communism, to accelerate its move away from a centrally planned economy to one taking more and more account of the free market, particularly encouraging the small private firm sector. It led the Communist bloc in doing this, and the phrase 'Goulash Communism' was coined to describe what was the most liberal Communist regime of that time. In 1989 Hungary undertook a peaceful transition to a democratic multi-party system.

After Communism

The hangover from the Communist system is pervasive in enterprises, and the management problems of transition are considerable. Managers often have to use outdated and poorly functioning machines. They operate in a semi-controlled labour market, restricted by government regulations on wages and benefits, with poor worker motivation. Yet they have now to cope with demands for a greater variety of goods, made to higher quality standards and delivered more quickly, while faced with greatly increased competition.

The experience of Goulash Communism in the 1980s helped managers to begin to understand market mechanisms and to try to operate in them. After 1989 when, in practice, the state abrogated its role as the owner of all enterprises, many managements took the opportunity of the absence of effective controls to use their firms for personal short-term gains. They paid themselves high salaries, employed excessive numbers of workers and, in many cases, just appropriated the enterprise's assets.

An extreme example of this phenomenon was the spate of what were called 'spontaneous privatizations' which took place after the Communist regimes fell. Managers sold or leased the firm's assets to nominal companies in which they personally owned large blocks of shares. It happened in all post-Communist countries, but happened more quickly and more widely in Hungary than elsewhere. It led to the ironic situation that top managers, inevitably mostly former leading members of the Communist Party, were becoming rich capitalists practically overnight. There were public objections and, in 1990, government controls to limit this practice were established, but since these new enterprises were often set up as joint ventures with foreign firms, there are those who argue that it is necessary for this process to continue if the transition to a free market economy based on Western standards of efficiency is to be maintained. It is an argument comparable to that used by the British Conservative government in the privatizations of the 1980s and 1990s. This gave considerable financial incentives for firms to buy British public utilities such as the electricity, gas and transport industries, on the grounds that this was the only way to make them efficient. And in Hungary too, public utilities were privatized in the 1990s.

In these circumstances of great economic change in Hungary, managers of enterprises which remain in state hands have to try to borrow as much credit as they can for as long as they can to keep their organizations going and their workers in jobs. For a time the government rationed credit from the state banking system, so inter-firm credit (a form of bartering) supplemented it. One effect was that such firms had to continue to deal with the other firms in the supply chain that they already knew. This meant fewer changes in suppliers and customers post-Communism than might be expected. Firms obtained raw materials and parts from their established suppliers who extended them credit and, in turn, they supplied their established customers on credit. This allowed enterprises to keep going longer – even if they were grossly non-competitive in international terms. Indeed, if Western accounting procedures are used (including proper replacement value of stocks and provision for re-equipment in the longer term) it is likely that some firms are still not adding value through their activities. They are 'value subtractors': that is at world prices the value of the resources they consume is more than the value of the products they produce.

The way out of this situation is to export goods to the West to obtain hard currency. Many firms in Hungary have succeeded in doing this. It may happen as part of a joint venture in which Western know-how is used to make products to the appropriate standards. It will draw on the relatively high levels of education in which the Communist state invested, together with the Hungarians' own achievement orientation (high masculinity in Box 6.15) put to business uses. The example of General Motors in Hungary (Box 6.16) shows what can be achieved by a forceful multinational corporation setting its worldwide standards, and recruiting high quality workers and managers.

Box 6.16 General Motors in Hungary

In the early 1990s as part of its globalization strategy, General Motors (GM), the US multinational corporation, decided to begin production in Hungary of its Opel Astra car to serve East European markets. It did this by buying an almost completed Hungarian factory site, expanding its capacity and running it according to GM world-wide standards. GM Hungary set up a system of operating principles which were quite new to the Hungarian industrial culture, as inherited from Communist times. They included:

- produce high quality products;
- exceed customer expectations;
- concentrate on the core business with outsourcing of other activities (e.g. central plant maintenance, plant security, car forwarding, payroll, rental and cleaning of safety clothing);
- operate a 'lean' organization (i.e. only 3 levels between the managing director and shop floor employees, *viz*: managers, co-ordinators, team leaders);
- no segregation between hourly paid and salaried employees; all employees have a performance related element of their pay through benchmarking with other GM Europe plants;
- operate a continuous improvement process, in which all employees are expected not only to perform their tasks but also to suggest improvements.

In order to achieve these aims, GM decided to recruit the best people in Hungary and advertised widely. The qualities they were looking for in middle managers included initiative, flexibility, teamwork spirit, and the ability to communicate and to work under pressure. The 300 or so applicants for the posts of co-ordinators were subject to a rigorous selection process to obtain the 14 required. Those selected were placed on a training programme, lasting between 15 to 27 weeks, which included general orientation and on-the-job training both in Hungary and in other GM Europe plants.

After a year GM Hungary was ranked among the best Opel Astra producers as far as quality was concerned, and GM headquarters was satisfied with its level of productivity.

(adapted from Balaton)

But it is not always possible simply to start from scratch with a green-field site. Many foreign companies go into collaboration with an established Hungarian firm in a joint venture to serve new markets. They then find considerable difficulties in attempting to switch the established management culture into a new mode as Box 6.17 shows. This reports a study of joint ventures and finds that many of the old habits die hard.

Box 6.17 Managing in China and Hungary

John Child (an expert on Chinese management) and Livia Markoczy (an expert on Hungarian management) compared the behaviour of local managers in China and Hungary who were participating in international joint ventures in collaboration with foreign firms. In spite of the fact that the cultures of China and Hungary are so different, they found remarkable similarities between them flowing from their similar economic histories in the second half of the twentieth century:

1. *Reluctance of local managers to make decisions and accept responsibility* – Managers in both countries are very defensive and have a mine of excuses which they regularly use. They attempt to ensure that the foreign partner takes the risk of blame for any possible failure, by requiring formal written authorization for every decision.
2. *Reluctance of local managers to communicate, particularly information on problems* – There is an emphasis on written communication, rather than informal rapid communication focused on problem solving. But much of the written communication is bureaucratic form-filling suiting the needs of higher authorities, rather than the operational requirements of the enterprise.
3. *There is no effective labour market, and personnel practices are not geared*

to business objectives – Restrictions were placed on recruitment and dismissal. The socialist philosophy that everybody has a right to work leads to much indiscriminate hiring of staff. There is also considerable resistance to personal incentives related to performance, and it is extremely difficult to dismiss inadequate staff.

Child and Markoczy regard the similarity of these problems as being due to the state socialist (Communist) political and economic environment which both countries have experienced for over 40 years. The environments have been highly centralized by government economic regulation. This means that individual enterprises have had much more incentive to look upward to the government ministries to obtain their resources, than sideways to their suppliers or customers. The key objective has been to keep in well with the ministry, and political approval was more important for survival than economic viability. In these circumstances, the system of industrial governance can outweigh national cultural differences in affecting managerial behaviour.

(from Child and Markoczy)

Hungarian managements have succeeded in coping in various ways with the new economic environment. This leads to a range of types of companies and managers as shown in Box 6.18. Management in Hungary is not easy, but economically the country is developing sufficiently to be able to enter the European Union.

This is a measure of the resilience of its national and managerial culture.

Box 6.18 Who Are the Managers?

A survey of top post-communist Hungarian business managers by researchers Csite and Kovach found that they fell into four groups:

1. *Clientele* is the name given to the group of managers still in state or publicly owned organizations, where they have no personal stake. They are older, have good academic qualifications often in economics. They are most likely to have been communists and maintain strong ties with politicians whose clientele they remain.
2. *Entrepreneurs* are owner-managers of privatized domestic firms. They are relatively young. Fewer have formal qualifications and many were former blue collar workers. They have the lowest proportion of ex-Communist

party membership, since the majority of them were already obtaining income from the emerging private sector under 'Goulash communism'.

3. *Technocrats* gained significant ownership stakes in the privatization process through management buy-outs and employee share ownership schemes. They are often ex-communists though their educational attainments are not as high as the other groups.

4. *Subordinates to foreigners* hold managerial positions in foreign owned firms with no stake themselves. They are quite young, are highly educated with well-developed language skills but little personal wealth.

The economic evolution which the post-Communist system is undergoing produces a much wider range of types of business managers than before.

(quoted in Mako and Antal-Mokos)

*   *   *

Nowhere else presents so complicated a past preceding so complicated a present as does Eastern and Central Europe. Direct research comparing the approach to management in one society with that in another is rare and, during the communist era, virtually nonexistent, though there is everywhere a shared past of authoritarian management exercising central control. Breaking away from this, the characteristic ways of managing and organizing to be expected from peoples of differing cultures have yet to emerge sufficiently distinctly and consistently to be readily recognizable and contrastable.

Yet the countries within the East-Central Europe slice of the diagram at the end of Chapter 2 (Box 2.13) do not have as great a cultural similarity among them as is found in most of the other slices, and they are poised uneasily between its individualistic side and its more collectivistic side. However, there is no doubt about where the Asians, whose approaches are discussed in the following chapter, should be positioned. They are collectivistic.

Further Reading

GENERAL

Batt, Judy. 1991. *East Central Europe from Reform to Transformation*. Pinter.

Hill, Ronald J. 1985. *Soviet Union: Politics, Economics and Society*. Pinter.

Kiezun, Witold. 1991. *Management in Socialist Countries: USSR and Central Europe*. De Gruyter.

Richman, Barry M. 1965. *Soviet Management*. Prentice-Hall.

Singleton, F. B. 1969. *Background to Eastern Europe* (revised edn). Pergamon Press.

Sword, Keith (ed.). 1991 *The Times Guide to Eastern Europe* (revised edn). Times Books.

RUSSIA

Banai, M. 1997. 'Children of the system: management in Russia', in T. Clark (ed.), *Advancement in Organizational Behaviour: Essays in Honour of Derek S. Pugh*. Ashgate.

Bendix, R. 1956. *Work and Authority in Industry*. Wiley (revised 1963, Harper).

Berliner, J. S. 1998. *Soviet Industry from Stalin to Gorbachev*. Edward Elgar.

Bollinger, D. 1994. 'The four cornerstones and three pillars in the "House of Russia" management system'. *Journal of Management Development*, 13,2, 49–54.

Elenkov, D. S. 1998. 'Can American management concepts work in Russia: a cross-cultural comparative study'. *California Management Review*. 40, 4, 133–55.

Granick, D. 1960. *The Red Executive: A Study of the Organization Man in Russian Industry*. Macmillan.

Puffer, S. M. (ed.). 1996. *Business and Management in Russia*. Aldershot: Edward Elgar.

POLAND

Gupta, K. L. and R. Lensink. 1998. *Financial Reform in Eastern Europe: A Policy Model for Poland*. Routledge.

Nasierowski, W. and B. Mikula. 1998. 'Culture dimensions of Polish managers: Hofstede's indices'. *Organization Studies*, 19, 3, 495–509.

Obloj, K. 2000. 'Management in Poland', in M. Warner (ed.), *Regional Encyclopedia of Business and Management: Management in Europe*. Thomson Learning Business Press.

HUNGARY

Antal-Mokos, Zoltan. 1998. *Privatisation, Politics, and Economic Performance in Hungary*. Cambridge University Press.

Child, J. and L. Markoczy. 1993. 'Host-country Managerial Behaviour and Learning in Chinese and Hungarian Joint Ventures'. *Journal of Management Studies*, 30, 4, 611–31.

Mako, C. and Z. Antal-Mokos. 2000. 'Management in Hungary', in M. Warner (ed.), *Regional Encyclopedia of Business and Management: Management in Europe*. Thomson Learning Business Press.

Markoczy, L. 1994. Modes of Organizational Learning: Institutional Change and Hungarian Joint Ventures. *International Studies of Management and Organization*, 24, 4, 5–30.

Other sources

GENERAL

Daniels, John B. and Lee H. Radebaugh. 1992. *International Business: Environments and Operations*. Addison-Wesley.

Harris, Philip R. and Robert T. Moran. 1991. *Managing Cultural Differences* (3rd edn, Ch. 16). Gulf Publishing.

IDE International Research Group. 1981. 'Industrial Democracy in Europe: Differences and Similarities Across Countries and Hierarchies'. *Organization Studies*, 2, 2, 113–29.

Kuc, B., D. J. Hickson and C. J. McMillan. 1980. 'Centrally Planned Development'. *Organization Studies*, 1, 3, 253–70; and Ch. 5 in D. J. Hickson and C. J. McMillan (eds.), *Organization and Nation: The Aston Programme IV*. Gower, 1981.

Maruyama, Mayoroh (ed.). 1993. *Management Reform in Eastern and Central Europe*. Dartmouth.

Petkov, K. and J. E. M. Thirkell. 1991. *Labour Relations in Eastern Europe*. Routledge.

Singleton, Fred (ed.). 1987. *Environmental Problems in the Soviet Union and Eastern Europe*. Lynne Riener Publishers.

Tayeb, Monir H. 1992. *The Global Business Environment: An Introduction*. Sage.

RUSSIA

Burawoy, Michael and Kathryn Hendley. 1992. 'Between Perestroika and Privatization: Divided Strategies and Political Crisis in a Soviet Enterprise'. *Soviet Studies*, 44, 3, 371–402.

Kemp, Tom. 1983. *Industrialization in the Non-Western World*. Longman.

Miller, Wright. 1973. *Who are the Russians?: A History of the Russian People*. Faber & Faber.

POLAND

Fryman, Roman, Andrzej Rapaczynski and John S. Earle *et al.* 1993. *The Privatization Process in Central Europe*. Central European University Press.

Mroczkowski, Tomasz (guest ed.). 1991. 'Polish Economic Management in the 1980s: the Quest for Reform'. *Special Issue of International Studies of Management and Organization*, 21, 2.

Poznanski, Kazimierz Z. 1992. 'Privatization of the Polish Economy: Problems of Transition'. *Soviet Studies*, 44, 4, 641–64.

HUNGARY

Bakacsi, G. 1999. 'The Pendulum Effect: Culture, Transition', Learning, in C. Mako and C. Warhurst (eds.), *The Management and Organization of Firms in the Global Context*. Budapest: University of Gödöllö and Budapest University of Economic Sciences.

Balaton, K. 1994. 'Implementing Corporate Management Systems Abroad: General Motors in Hungary', in C. Mako and P. Novoszath (eds.), *Convergence and Divergence: the Case of Corporate Culture*. Budapest: Institute for Social Conflict Research, Hungarian Academy of Sciences.

Wallace, T. 1994. 'From Russia With Love: the Case of Ikarus and the Hungarian Bus Industry', in C. Mako and P. Novoszath (eds.), *Convergence and Divergence: the Case of Corporate Culture*. Budapest: Institute for Social Conflict Research, Hungarian Academy of Sciences.

7

The Asians

Highlighting:
China, with the Nanyang (Overseas) Chinese including Hong Kong
Japan
South Korea
Indonesia

Most people living are Asians. Certainly that is so if this region were taken to include India (in this book India is placed in Chapter 9). Around the western rim of the Pacific Ocean stand China, the most populous nation in the world (around 1,250 million), Indonesia, by far the most populous Islamic nation (well over 200 million, lying fourth behind China, India and the USA in size order), Japan (127 million), and many densely populated, smaller States . . . in all, at least half the population of the planet.

Asians inherit the world's oldest continuously extant civilizations, most obviously in China, but also in Japan and India too. Although the peoples of the 'New World' Americas have customarily regarded their European forebears as being from the 'Old World', Asia is a far older world. It was far advanced in philosophy and technology until it was overtaken in the last three centuries or so by the scientistical Euro-American culture. This first made itself felt in imperialist forays by the Europeans – and indeed by the Americans – which resulted in colonization spreading northwards until it covered what are now Papua, Indonesia, Singapore, Malaysia, Burma, Laos, Cambodia, Vietnam, and the Philippines. Yet China as a whole was never colonized, although it had to concede trading rights and lease coastal territories (Hong Kong and Macao coming to be treated as British and Portuguese colonies) and to submit to foreign influence generally. Korea, too, was intruded upon, but Japan remained entirely untouched, symbolizing its unique freedom from foreign interference and from the turbulence that overthrew continental regimes by its own religious forms (Shinto) and its stable monarchy. In this it was curiously similar to that other island nation at the other end of the land-mass, Britain.

ORIENTAL IDEOLOGIES

In 1948 the Communist People's Liberation Army completed its conquest of China. Although ostensible communism did penetrate down into some of the smaller nations of east Asia, south of China, it never crossed the seas to the island states. So, with the collapse of communism in the Soviet Union, China was left not only as the world's most populous nation but as its foremost exponent of a communist system.

However, atheistic communism is a phenomenon of the second half of the twentieth century and, some would say, so far a superficial one. Centuries before its appearance, Spanish colonization had originated Asia's sole predominantly Christian nation, the Philippines, where the majority of the population profess the Roman Catholic version of the faith, and Islam had spread via what are now Pakistan and Malaysia to Indonesia. Most hallowed by time is Buddhism, a development from Hinduism. It was taken across the mainland into China, blending there with Taoism, and thence to Japan to interweave with Shinto.

Intertwined with Chinese Buddhism, Confucian ideals prevailed, arguably of much greater significance for the approach to management than the specifically religious elements of Asian culture.

Confucius, who died in 479 BC, was a moral philosopher rather than a religious prophet. He was concerned with precepts for the right way to live rather than with beliefs, a separation strange to those in the Judaeo-Christian-Islamic tradition, for most of whom the moral and the supernatural are inextricably interwoven. In his ideally cultured and courteous world, everyone knew their place. Loyalty to others and reciprocity, doing for others what is proper in return for what they do for you, were emphasized. Loyalty and reciprocity upheld five basic relationships in society: those between ruler and subject, father and son, husband and wife, elder brother and younger brother, and between older friend and younger friend. There should be due respect for the authority of the senior in each relationship – usually the elder, since age is respected.

The influence of these precepts on Chinese culture can be gauged by the fact that in modern, Westernized Hong Kong, two and a half millennia later, it is customary to identify which of male twins is born first so that, when the second-born learns to speak, he can use the conventional form of address to his 'elder' brother.

Box 7.1 Managing Harmony

	Percentage agree or strongly agree among		
	Indonesians	**Japanese**	**Americans**
1. Avoiding open conflict is a major task of management	64	50	24
2. Most conflicts in a company can be productive	21	29	64

Responses to a questionnaire given respectively to 96, 50, and 50 managers from three countries on courses at the INSEAD business school, Fontainebleau, near Paris, by A. Laurent, and quoted by Hofstede.

THE ORIENTAL WAY

This stress on **managing relationships** in a harmonious manner runs throughout Asia. An example in China itself appears in Chapter 2 in Box 2.6. It is a considerateness that extends from north to south, from Japan to Indonesia (see Box 7.1); and, in between, the Filipinos are noted for the importance they give to smooth relationships and personal dignity. It is vital in work as much as outside it to maintain a good network in which you yourself are accepted and respected. Of course, that is so for anyone in any society: Chapters 8 and 9 show it as a general feature of Arab society and of developing countries, but nowhere is it more crucial to life than in Asia.

The Anglo (especially American) notion that a certain amount of difference of view, openly expressed in argument, can be productive, by leading to fresh ideas and keeping managers 'on their toes', is alien to the Asian outlook; much better to preserve harmony among colleagues so that they can collaborate constructively. Much better to avoid directly contradicting others, especially superiors, in any way that makes them 'lose face' socially, and then they will do the same for you. After all, there is no need bluntly to say 'No'. It is possible to say 'Yes' in a manner that indicates understanding but not agreement. A subtle concurrence of view, if not positive consensus, is sought – notably in Japan, which is discussed later. Thus, too, the greater difficulty compared to Anglo and European managements in singling out some individuals above others, for this is always liable to cause friction. Direct and open appraisal of the work performance of individuals, and differential payments, sensitive matters anywhere but more so here, are preferably avoided, as is dismissal as far as possible. Family ties and friendships among employees have always to be taken into account, too.

Mutual trust and confidence must be patiently built up in relationships. First and foremost it is the person with whom business is being done who matters; hence, as discussed in Chapter 2, the time and trouble taken in entertaining and getting-to-know-you conversations preliminary to business talks.

It is this ingredient in culture, more than anything else, which brings the Asian societies together at the collectivistic end in Box 2.7 and gathers them in the same slice of the 'culture cake' diagram (Box 2.13).

However, harmony does not assume what the prevailing Western management literature calls participation. After all, in the West there can be conflictful participation, in which differing views are strongly expressed and may not be reconciled. In Asia, respect for seniority of person and of position means **managing authority** firmly from the top. That is how Confucius would have wished it in China.

That is why none of the Asian countries is at the low end of the power distance spectrum in Box 2.5, and why at the high end Malaysia and the Philippines are among those countries with the greatest power distance of all. For, in addition, both were subjected to colonial authority (from the British and from the Spanish) and they respect, too, the authority inherent in Islam and in Catholic Christianity.

Although these similarities can be discerned in Asia as a whole, particularly when contrasting it with Western societies, Asians are no more uniform in culture than are Westerners. The sharpest contrasts occur in **managing oneself** and **managing uncertainty**.

It was shown in the section in Chapter 2 on managing oneself that the Asian societies (including the three mainly Chinese-populated islands of Hong Kong, Singapore and Taiwan) are middling on the characteristic which has been called masculinity–femininity. Japan, however, stands out as different in this respect. It appears as one of the most masculine of nations, perhaps the most masculine of all. So, among Asians, the Japanese seem to have the most self-assertive drive for success and recognition.

Further, Japan appears as highly uncertainty avoiding (in Box 2.10), contrasting especially with the Chinese in Hong Kong and Singapore who – not surprisingly for commercially entrepreneurial, émigré people – are more 'uncertainty tolerating'. This unique Japanese combination of anxiety-propelled (uncertainty avoiding) assertive drive for personal well-being, attained loyally through group well-being, separates it from the other Asian cultures in the 'culture cake'. As has already been commented, it seems likely to lie behind Japanese economic prowess.

So may their **managing of time**, in which they have evinced a patience to work for the future, though in this the Chinese are similar. Asians do not have the 'immediatist' need for returns here and now, as found in Brazil, for example.

RACING DRAGONS

Even so, some got quick returns when the second half of the twentieth century witnessed the fastest economic sprint ever seen, by what became known as the Five Dragons of Asia (sometimes dubbed the Tiger economies). One big one and four small ones, they are Japan, and South Korea, Taiwan, Hong Kong and Singapore. Their astonishing economic success was the more spectacular for not being based on domestic raw materials or on large domestic markets. It was an export-orientated achievement in manufacturing which took on the established manufacturers of the USA and Western Europe at their own game in their own home markets, and usually beat them on both price and quality. As a result, it was not long before Japanese and Hong Kongese banking rose to parallel prominence in world finance.

Not far behind looms the Giant Dragon, China itself, where the more market-led areas of the economy of the People's Republic, which have been opened up in the east and south since the death of Chairman Mao Tse-tung, have boomed at comparable or even greater rates.

Despite the economic setback of the 1990s, when the dragons faltered and slowed, even slipped back, they held a place in the world at the beginning of the 21st century that was unimaginable fifty years before.

All the Asian societies were 'late developers', industrializing centuries later than their Western competitors but thereby able to take whatever suited them from the latest of Western management methods without the same degree of hindrance from earlier and now outdated practices. Whilst this probably was an advantage, it could be so only if traditional social patterns also adapted quickly. In the ancient Chinese and Japanese cultures in particular, there was historically a low regard for trade. Aristocratic position, wealth in land, position in the administration of court or state counted for more. Indeed, whilst some merchants became wealthy and thereby prominent citizens, they remained low in social status, especially in Japan. This had to change. A new regard for business and its managers had to arise.

How can this extraordinary economic and social transformation have been accomplished? What made it possible? This is a question that has been and is much debated. It is one so large in its ramifications that it is unlikely ever to get an agreed definitive answer. Obviously, economic conditions played their part. Though the Five Dragons lacked raw materials, the boost to air and sea transport given by the Second World War enabled them to produce for overseas markets and made Western investment in the labour forces of the smaller dragons an attractive proposition. The overall effect was to shift the focus of world manufacturing from west to east.

Equally obviously, cultural predispositions are highly likely to have been a vital factor. It was suggested earlier (in Chapter 2) that if culture is a key to economic performance, then it is not any culture that will do, but the one which happens to be appropriate to the political-economic conditions of the period. Can it have been the Confucian element in the Chinese and Chinese-related cultures which was and is appropriate? Though collectivistic rather than individualistic, its extolling of harmonious, abstemious, reciprocal loyalty was not far in its suitability to industrialization from the 'protestant ethic' of Anglo-Germanic Protestant Christian Europe, which has been held to have spurred the entrepreneurial spirit of the latter's industrial revolution by extolling thrifty hard work. It is noticeable that neither the Catholic-dominated Philippines, where people blend work and leisure in a more easy-going manner, nor Islamic Indonesia, have yet shared in the economic boom to the same degree.

It has been claimed that the specific Confucian feature which directly contributed most may have been identified. This has been called 'Confucian Dynamism' (Box 7.2). Did it and does it so dispose the outlook of sufficient people in the dragon societies that, given the right conditions, a lightning industrial revolution was possible, so successfully that their products, from clothes to cameras and computers to cars, flood shops and markets worldwide?

Illustrative nations select themselves. The two largest dragons stand out, and one of the smaller that lies between them can be included, and for contrast another large nation that is racially different. They are:

China, with the Nanyang (Overseas) Chinese including Hong Kong,
Japan,
South Korea,
and Indonesia.

CHINESE CULTURE AND MANAGEMENT

Over one-fifth of the human race live in the world's largest communist State, the People's Republic of China. They are especially crowded in coastal regions and, further inland, in the more fertile plains along the River Yangtse and its tributaries. Though there are no fewer than fifty-five recognized ethnic minorities, most people, well over 90 per cent, are Han Chinese. Despite increasing urbanization, the bulk are peasants making a living from the soil, industry being mainly in northern, coastal and southern areas.

The continuity of a civilization traceable back over more than three thousand years is partly due to the development of its unique script of thousands of characters. This is used and understood throughout China, literacy being over 75 per cent, even though speech differs from place to place.

Societal continuity is also due to the influence of Confucian ideas down the centuries, as pervasive as Graeco-Roman-Judaic thought has been in the West.

Box 7.2 Dynamic Confucius?

How far is research itself culture-biased? This was a question asked by Bond, a Canadian academic who has long worked in the Far East. Most questionnaires use questions worked out by Westerners, and this was so even for those that were the basis of the research by Hofstede described in Chapter 2. Do they miss essential aspects of Eastern cultures by not asking the right questions?

Bond wanted to start the other way around, with a questionnaire that, if it was biased, would have an Eastern bias. So he asked Chinese social scientists in Hong Kong and Taiwan to specify Chinese values, from which a questionnaire was constructed in Chinese (and then translated into English and other languages, the other way round to the usual sequence). The questionnaire was given to 100 students (50 male, 50 female, studying a variety of subjects) in each of 22 countries, plus China added later to make 23.

Four cultural characteristics emerged. One was similar to Hofstede's power distance (Box 2.5), but with an Asian emphasis on moderation in the use of the authority conferred by status. Another was related to his individualism/collectivism (Box 2.7) and a third to his masculinity/femininity (Box 2.9), but with an Asian emphasis on courteously restraining over-assertiveness. But the fourth seemed to replace Hofstede's apparently Western-orientated uncertainty avoidance. It contrasted **the importance of**:
   persistence (or perseverance),
   ordering relationships by status (and observing this order),
   thrift,
   having a sense of shame,
with **the relatively lesser importance of:**
   personal steadiness and stability,
   protecting 'face' (i.e. saving face socially),
   respect for tradition,
   reciprocation of greetings, favours and gifts.

Bond called this characteristic Confucian Dynamism, insofar as its most important four values can be taken to imply a forward-looking, thrifty outlook, supported by stable relationships and shame in offending them. The less important values imply a more static preservation of traditional ways.

Hofstede (1991) subsequently preferred to call this 'long-term orientation versus short-term orientation'; since not all the nations which scored high (or 'dynamic') were influenced by Confucian morals. But *all five Dragons* (Japan, Taiwan, South Korea, Hong Kong, Singapore) *and the Giant Dragon* (China) *were high in Confucian Dynamism.*

(from Hofstede and Bond; and Hofstede, 1991, Ch. 7)

The Chinese Han people spread southwards from northern beginnings into shifting areas controlled by changing royal dynasties. By Chinese reckoning, the Ming (1368–1644) and Ching (1644–1911) dynasties are the most recent and last. The Ming followed a period of Mongol conquest, the folk memory of which evokes the same hatred as it does in Russia. As also in Russia, it left an authoritarian imprint on the use of authority. Subsequently, the Manchu Chings assimilated into Chinese society, and under them China became the wealthiest and perhaps most sophisticated nation on earth.

Of momentous significance in the history of management, the dynasties ruled through a semi-'bureaucratic' system of administration. The Chinese are credited with having been the first to devise a form of organization in which appointments are made not by family position, hereditary or otherwise, but by impersonal criteria which could apply equally to anyone. In plain terms, anyone who can meet the requirements has, in principle, a chance of getting the job (the meaning of the term 'bureaucracy' as it is intended here is explained under 'The Anglo Way' in Chapter 3). Of course, in ancient China, aspirant mandarins did not come with what are regarded nowadays as management qualifications; they had to pass examinations in classical (largely Confucian) texts. But the principle was established, reinforced by a 2,000-year-old 'Legalist' school of thought, which advocated imperial rule through strict impartial law and regulation. The bureaucratic division of responsibilities and setting of rules is now so widespread worldwide as the basis of most management that it is easy to take it for granted, and to recognize it only when the word itself is used as an epithet to castigate inefficient bureaucracies.

However, in the China of old this element of impersonal administration functioned within an essentially feudal type of system. That eventually stagnated and its administration became corrupt, so that in 1911 the last of the dynasties, the Ching, was toppled and replaced by a republic. Subsequent Japanese military invasions, and internal dissension and civil wars, led to the ultimate success of the People's Liberation Army after the Second World War and the proclaiming in 1949 of the new People's Republic, led by Communist Party Chairman Mao Zedong (Tse-tung).

Communist management had two fresh resources with which to begin. It had ideals, of a revitalized, egalitarian, self-sufficient society, and it had the PLA 'cadres'; that is, it had dedicated people, experienced in military administration (though not in business), untainted by having held appointments under any previous regime. They were placed in positions of authority as the State gradually took over ownership (the State had owned much of heavy industry anyway).

Experimenting With Management

The Chinese soon encountered the same sorts of management difficulties as the Russians and others in Eastern Europe were then struggling with: plans that failed to fit realities, an inefficient economy, evasion and corruption. So they tried to shift away from the over-centralized Soviet model towards greater mass participation. They tried to mobilize mass effort with huge, ideologically based campaigns, most memorably the **Great Leap Forward** (1958–9) and the **Cultural Revolution** (1966–76). Neither succeeded. The Great Leap Forward, an attempt to use the prolific labour power of the peasantry in small-scale rural industry (the so-called 'backyard furnaces') and in new farming methods, was a step backwards instead of a leap forward. National income fell, though partly this was due to drought.

The Cultural Revolution, which also brought economic growth to a standstill, can be regarded as having the greater import for management the world over. It can be seen as the world's most populous nation undertaking humankind's biggest-ever experiment in management. That was not, as such, its purpose nor its only aim, but it is of foremost concern here.

Chairman Mao, together with some of his Party colleagues from the former days of armed struggle, became more and more critical of the bureaucratic administration of ministry and factory. Their peasant army had had an inherent suspicion of officialdom because of the exploitation of their forebears. Now an even larger bureaucracy, whose bureaucrats too often were over-bureaucratic, haughty and buck-passing, seemed to be arising under the very communism they had fought for. They had inherited an ancient Chinese ideal of the bureaucrat as a broad-minded, benevolent generalist, whereas they saw administrators taking a restricted and rigid approach.

In all organizations there is a potential strain between normative (moral) and utilitarian (economic) aims. In hospitals, for example, the difficult choices between giving the fullest possible health care and containing costs are obvious, and even in manufacturing there are strains between efficiency and pollution, in construction between cheapness and safety, and so on. In China the strain between the Maoist vision of society and the administrative means to it became acute. In a typically Chinese pithy expression, the issue was 'Red versus Expert'.

Mao and his supporters opted for 'Red', that is, for a supreme effort to reaffirm the paramountcy of ideals above administrative expediency. As they saw it, this needed a drastic change in values, a cultural revolution to complete their political revolution.

Those at the top had to be shaken out of themselves by enforced experience of life at the bottom. Hierarchies had to be inverted. Party activists, backed by a mass youth movement of Red Guards, sent managers, professors, doctors, the elite of every kind, to billets in the villages to work the land as the peasants did, or on to the factory floor. In factories, universities, hospitals, all kinds of organizations, management (the administrative leg of dual control, alongside the Party Committee) was taken over by a new revolutionary committee of lower-level personnel (so that in each organization there were now at least two leading committees). Furthermore, moral incentives, a commitment to working for a new society rather than just for material reward, had to come first.

The experience was shattering for many and led to factional conflicts, and sometimes to violence, as is illustrated in a textile factory in Box 7.3. It extended throughout society, though not everywhere to the same degree.

This extraordinary attempt to turn management upside down largely failed. Although old-style deferential attitudes were eroded in that particular generation, the idealism faded and, shortly after Mao's death in 1976, the remnants of the revolutionary committees were abolished and conventional management restored.

Box 7.3 Revolution in the Factory

Speaking subsequently to foreign visitors, the director of a textile factory in Beijing said: 'You ask about the cultural revolution. I'll tell you my own experiences. I was deputy director at that time, a Party member since 1956. When it all began in 1966, I did not understand what was going on. I didn't know how to take it. I could not grasp the issues. Two lines, two headquarters, it did not make sense. When I was criticized by the workers, I was aggrieved. Didn't I work hard, come early and leave late, carry out all my duties conscientiously? The more they attacked me, the less I understood. I became quite bewildered and could not carry on. The workers cried: Stand aside. They made me go to work on the shop floor. I was working as a machine-minder from January to November 1967. I thought to myself: Let's see how you manage the factory. I felt it was just as well to be working on the shop floor, for I knew that I might have made mistakes and as long as I was in a prominent position I should be fired at. The workers criticized my methods of management; they said I was a "boss" . . . I could not understand it, I lost my self-confidence. What was it all about? Hadn't I been a good Party member? I was quite confused.

'There were two factions among the workers called "East is Red" and "Red Rebels". A work team had been sent . . . and had set up a so-called cultural revolution committee. The factions formed in disputing about it, but they very soon forgot all about criticizing revisionism: they were only interested in criticizing each other . . .

'I am glad to say that it did not come to blows with us as it did in many places, but the situation was really absurd. Both groups were working, but they would not speak to each other; one would not pass a tool to another. Each lot said to the others: We can carry on production without your help. There were two factions in every workshop. All the cadres were doing manual work, and the workers were carrying on as they pleased. All rules and regulations were defied. There were rival loudspeakers set up on the premises, blaring away at each other all the time. Some output was produced but of course it fell far below normal.'

(from Robinson, p.29)

Even during the upheaval, the very adulation of Mao, when workers carried in their pockets the Little Red Book of his writings and sayings which was supposed to inform the answers to all questions of management, itself betrayed the persistence of the attitudes it was supposed to demolish; it was itself a continuing dependence on authority from on high.

A small but rare questionnaire study, only four years after Mao, showed that any difference between Chinese workers and their European counterparts in the level of influence they were felt to exert as compared to the greater powers of top management above them was trivial. Despite the attempt to invert hierarchy, Chinese workers had the lesser influence (Box 7.4). Their traditional cultural values had been reasserted. The Communist Party committees did appear to have had more influence on *long-term* decisions than did the weak Employee Councils of European factories with which they were compared (2.5 as against 1.9 on average, in the third column), but that was due to the normal role of the Party, rather than to the Cultural Revolution. Further, despite the factional conflicts engendered by the Cultural Revolution, customary conceptions of harmony survived (see again the telling instance in Box 2.6).

So there was no *revolution* in culture. Core values change slowly, if at all, as Chapter 2 has argued. So, it seems, do forms of organization which are difficult to jerk out of prevailing patterns and trends. The implications of this are considered later, in Chapter 11.

Another Way?

The open question is whether this society, having laid down two landmarks in the history of management by first devising bureaucracy and then demonstrating the difficulty (if not the impossibility) of undoing it, will reach a third landmark by evolving an effective system that is neither wholly centrally planned nor wholly free market. Is there another way? A 'socialist market economy', so-called?

In economic terms, the first decades have been spectacular, even though the bulk of China remains labelled a developing country. Leaving aside the periods of the Great Leap Forward and the Cultural Revolution, growth of the Chinese economy under communist rule had in any case

Box 7.4 Hierarchy Rules OK

Mean scores out of 5 for influence over three grades of decisions, in European enterprises (134 enterprises in 12 nations) and Chinese enterprises (9 enterprises) in 1980 (E = European, C = Chinese).

Decisions	Workers		Top Management		Representative bodies	
	E	C	E	C	E*	C**
Short-Term	2.5	1.4	3.6	3.8	2.5	2.1
Medium	1.6	1.8	4.1	3.9	2.4	2.7
Long-Term	1.3	1.2	4.3	4.2	1.9	2.5
All 16 Decisions	2.0	1.6	3.8	3.9	2.4	2.4

* Employee Councils in each company
** Party Committee in each workplace

(extracted from Laaksonen, Table 2)

outstripped that of the Soviet Union. The post-Mao shift market-wards accelerated this to a level where, by the beginning of the 21st century, the Chinese economy had become third largest in the world after the United States and Japan, and was growing fastest. It was and is a growth greatest in the Special Economic Zones and coastal towns of the south-east and east, where liberalization and consequent investment from 'overseas Chinese' (in Hong Kong, Taiwan and elsewhere), Japan, and the West has gone furthest.

Central planning had never been so complete or so precise as it was in the former Soviet Union. This was partly because of poor transport and a policy of regional self-sufficiency which made a unified economic view futile, partly too because of the Chinese inclination to see a plan or a contract as a beginning from which continually to renegotiate as events unfold rather than as a comprehensive blue-print. So the gradual diminution of planning allowed scope for an initiative that was already to some degree extant. The proportion of production from small private firms and from semi-marketized collectives, under local government and regional control, rapidly increased, whilst the mostly larger, fully State-owned organizations became financially less and less viable. They were and are locked into dependence on national and regional ministries and State agencies for finance, materials, personnel, and disposing of production. Managerial decision-making was more administrative than entrepreneurial. Or if it was entrepreneurial, it was so in devising ways of manipulating the system to its own advantage via networks of personal relationships.

So the Chinese Communist Party, nominally the largest political organization in the world, can be seen as presiding over two economies (Box 7.5). The private one has spurred mass urbanization, the Chinese joining the worldwide movement of population into huge cities. It has brought mass private ownership – of houses and apartments, of cars, of household goods. It has brought a growing middle class. Its growth was such that the 1990s economic reverse suffered elsewhere in Asia was hardly noticed.

Box 7.5 Two Economies?

Today, China . . . has two economies . . . The first continues to shape the managerial practices of the state-owned sector . . . It is an economy in long-term secular decline and kept alive by a continuous drip-feed of state subsidies. The second, building on the revival of a dynamic commercial culture that pre-dates communism, provides a framework for a vigorously growing private sector which now accounts for over 50 per cent of . . . industrial output.

(from Boisot, pp. 925–6)

The other economy continues state-owned or publicly-controlled in various ways. Managements have varying degrees of discretion in procuring materials and personnel, deciding prices and distributing outputs, within the public sector. Fully state-owned enterprises have the least discretion but receive full government support. More flexible, but more at risk, are collectively-owned enterprises, formerly in employee ownership, and thirdly are enterprises owned by townships or villages. All operate under a state-controlled banking system, in markets monitored by state Price Bureaux.

This variation comes from piecemeal relaxation of control, not wholesale privatization. That would grate with the traditional Chinese view of ownership. Capitalism in the West rests on a peculiar notion of firms as legal entities existing separately from the people who run them. The firms in which people work can be bought and sold like goods, over their heads. This notion of impersonal artificial organizations is foreign to the personalistic Chinese outlook and makes it less easy to privatize ownership by a purely financial transaction. Indeed, there is a fundamental notion that ultimately all ownership rests with the ultimate collectivity, the Chinese nation.

Privatization is also restrained by a concept of work organizations which is diffuse. The larger ones, at least, are still regarded as welfare agencies as well as economic providers. As Box 7.6 shows, management was and, in most state-owned organizations still is, responsible for child care, education, healthcare, and also housing, for people live in premises allocated by their 'work units'.

Further, the Communist Party continues omnipresent in the state sector. There is the classic communist 'dual hierarchy' in organizations, just as there was once in Russia and the wider Soviet Union. Alongside the management hierarchy is a Party hierarchy whose ostensible purpose is to see that what management does is in accord with Party policy.

Box 7.6 Welfare Management

In 1985, the Sichuan No. 1 Textile Factory included the following categories of personnel:

	Number
Canteens	218
Kindergarten and child-care centre	106
Teachers in factory primary and high schools	144
Teachers in adult education	82
Medical and other hospital and clinic staff	206
Housing maintenance	76
Tea-house, water tower, and gatekeepers	97
Chronically sick (over 6 months)	487
Attending full time TV University	241
Labour Service Company (finding jobs for employees' children)	23

These are from a total 12,000 personnel.

(extracted from Jackson, Table 9.1)

At each level of an organization there is alongside management an equivalent Party Committee. There is in each factory, for example, a supreme Party Committee and Party Secretary and, below that, committees for each workplace chosen from the Party members there: a drawing office committee, a canteen committee, a committee in each production workshop, and so forth. Under Maoist rule, this leg of the dual hierarchy was dominant. A factory manager did what the Party Secretary told him to do. Nowadays its influence is waning, and its committees are more and more concerned with employee welfare, less and less concerned with management decisions.

An employee's pay may still include allowances for transport or foodstuffs or rent or medical care, but the 'iron rice bowl', which guaranteed pay and a job for everyone, is cracking. Employees are more often free to move if they think they can better themselves, probably in the booming cities. Managements cannot promise indefinite security if they are caught between market forces and a state Planning Bureau which insists on fixing five years ahead how much money each enterprise will make for the state, just as it did before market forces were allowed to intrude.

Not everyone has caught 'business fever', as it is sometimes called. That would be surprising after generations have tried not to fail rather than to strive for success. In a planned system the aim is not to fail to meet the output stipulated, even if that is achieved uneconomically with what would be a financial loss.

Ways that Persist

As the failed attempt at a cultural revolution showed, culture cannot be changed quickly, in everyone, all at once. Box 7.7 summarizes typical differences in outlook between the Chinese and the more individualist, competitive, Americans.

Chinese culture is imbued with the regard for authority that is to be expected in the tradition of an age-old society. It shows both in respect for the head of the family and in respect for officials and those in management positions. Though the effects of a more open economy, and of the emphasis in Western-style management training on participation by subordinates, are beginning to show, **managing authority** is

---

Box 7.7 Contrasting Views of Responsibilities and Rights

American

Chinese

1. Employees try to make maximum contribution in exchange for maximum returns – and have a right to commensurate reward.

1. Employees do what the organization assigns them to do – and have a right to equable reward.

2. Employees should try to sharpen their job skills – and deserve company-sponsored training and education.

2. Employees should help inexperienced co-workers to improve their skills – and can expect help from co-workers more skilful than themselves.

3. Employees should help their organization beat competition – and be supported in doing so.

3. Employees should help their organization gain collaboration from other organizations – and be supported in doing so.

(selected and adapted from Osigweh and Huo, pp. 88–9)

---

predominantly top-down. Even if what is expected of subordinates is sensitively referred to as co-operation rather than as obedience, they 'do what the organization assigns them to do', as Box 7.7 puts it, and that includes the managerial ranks described in Box 7.8. Since tasks are not usually tightly defined, a great deal is open to the personal use of power from above. This is demonstrated by the Chinese of Singapore and Hong Kong who appear in the higher power distance range of Box 2.5 in Chapter 2, with Taiwan in a middle position.

Box 7.8 Authority in the Middle

The role of middle managers in the decision-making process

Chinese middle managers are characterized by their deference to higher-placed authorities: they leave important decisions to a higher management level; they are unwilling to offer individual suggestions or opinions when requested to do so; and they are reluctant to recognize responsibility for enterprise performance. They are in fact trained not to make unilateral decisions. Most wait patiently for the single senior manager to decide on the correct course of action, and then carry out this manager's instructions obediently.

(from Wang, Zhang and Goodfellow, p.77)

Among the collectivistic Chinese, however, authority is not exercised by the individual as such but on behalf of the collective. Documents and contracts are affirmed by the organization's stamp, not an individual's signature.

Managing authority is tied in with **managing relationships** with others. World over, who-knows-who weaves the fabric of society, but nowhere more so than in China. A high value is put on *guanxi* (personal connections or networking), more so than is usual in the West. People draw standing from and are socially positioned by their *guanxi*, and in business deals, more drawn out than in the West, time is spent subtly exploring the other's *guanxi*. In so far as relationships are more up and down the hierarchical administrative system than they would be in a completely market system, good *guanxi* help to get things done. Managers are used to frequent unscheduled and informal meetings. It must be remembered, too, that many have to deal with the other leg of the dual structure,

Box 7.9 Network Capitalism

The Chinese system of 'network capitalism' works through the implicit and fluid dynamic of relationships. On the one hand, this is a process that consumes much time and energy. On the other hand, it is suited to handling complexity and uncertainty. Networks offer greater capacities for generating and transmitting new information, and when they are sustained by trust-based relationships they offer a cushion against the possibility of failure that is a concomitant of uncertainty ... In this last respect, the networks of the emergent Chinese capitalism are qualitatively different from those within the Western market system, for the latter continue to be based on legal contract and ownership rights rather than on long-term trust relationships.

(from Boisot and Child, p 625)

their organization's Party Secretary and committees, though managerial authority nowadays prevails.

The networking in Chinese government, industry and commerce is so striking that the emerging economy has been called 'network capitalism' (Box 7.9). Again, while all forms of capitalism rest on networks, this is nowhere more so than in China.

Networks of relationships, and respect for the other's social situation and saving 'face', mean also that promotion is not solely a matter of individualistic preferment. Rather it is influenced by the collective views of workmates, which include the candidate's moral and political attitudes, and by respect for age and seniority of the candidate and of others who might be affected. Not surprisingly, organizations tend to be overmanned, compared to practice elsewhere.

The personal element means that what is in writing is as good as the relationships on which it rests, and no more. Hence, building mutual confidence in negotiating a plan or contract, for example, is vital. The Chinese participants, probably including representatives of local or national government as well as technical experts, and outnumbering their foreign counterparts when the negotiation is international, will see such a document as covering what is needful at the time. As events unfold it will need to be modified or superseded. Possible problems may be left aside at first to see how things work out. Westerners may then be taken aback when such problems are raised subsequently, as they had thought everything was settled. They may also be surprised to find how many others at higher levels, who never appeared at meetings, are involved in decisions and take time to ultimately decide.

There is a patient, unhurried **managing of time** which allows business discussions to build up gradually. If, as appears probable, the Chinese can be classed as an uncertainty-tolerating people – though perhaps less so in the mainland People's Republic than outside it (again see Chapter 2) – then their capacity to **manage uncertainty** facilitates this. Negotiating both within the system and with foreigners preserves at least the appearances of harmony, and emotional self-expression is restrained so the implicit ambiguities stretch the nerves of all concerned. The Chinese can be persistent bargainers, tenacious if pushed too far.

Banquets are endemic to the Chinese way of doing business. They not only flatter and entertain the other party but give opportunities to mention problems informally which the hosts do not feel ready to put on the table in an arranged meeting. It is difficult for a newcomer to know how to reciprocate, as it is also to know if and to whom and when to bring gifts. Further, a system imbued with state powers and officialdom cannot avoid the touch of corruption. Local contacts with local knowledge can help the outsider.

Despite 'harmonious *guanxi*', to put it that way, it is unlikely that employees are as identified with and loyal to their 'work unit' as are many Japanese, for example. They may well remain there for life, if that is expected of them and there is no alternative, but there is sufficient drive and looking to advantage in **managing oneself** that their Confucian dynamism − if that is what it is − makes it likely that they will look elsewhere in the rapidly developing economy.

This is not an evenly spread impulse. Southerners have long been seen as the more enterprising, and the enterprise they exported to the concentrated Chinese capitalism of Hong Kong is flooding back whence it came. The north may be more cautious. In the Party there have always been factions for and against decentralizing management and opening up to foreigners. There are always those who stand to gain from new opportunities and those whose situation is threatened by changes.

So decentralization is patchy, and it differs from organization to organization. Pronouncements granting greater autonomy to those managements under state control may or may not be followed through in practice. Autonomy is fragile in as much as it remains subject to abrupt reversal by the State for political reasons. Nevertheless despite continuing supply bottlenecks, slow transport, and corruption, the role of management is changing fast, even in the publicly controlled sector.

Nanyang Chinese Capitalism

Chinese businessmen outside China itself, among the Nanyang (Overseas) Chinese, have long been outstandingly successful within the other nations of the Western Pacific rim. The adaptability of the Nanyang Chinese business is based firmly in family control. It does not grow and follow the Western model of increasingly professional and bureaucratic management and structure, nor indeed the Japanese model of linked large conglomerates surrounded by closely bound smaller contractors, and certainly not that of the cumbersome State industries of China. Apart from a handful of notable contemporary exceptions, it remains small. It proliferates rather than grows, spawning a network of small businesses controlled by other family members, friends, or former employees in which firms can readily move in and out of markets or close down or start up.

It is a peculiarity of the overseas Chinese that their part in world production and trade, spreads through the economies of the many societies where they have settled, but substantial were it to be aggregated, is not visible in the brand names and advertising that have made Japanese brands, for example, household words worldwide. The output of any one firm is not large enough for that, and most are engaged in intermediate stages of production rather than in completing final branded goods.

The characteristic Chinese small business is paternalistic and personalistic, as would be expected from a high power distance and collectivistic culture drawn from the ancient traditions of the mainland. Its owner, frequently head of the family, manages it by direct personal involvement in what goes on. He keeps its affairs very much to himself, a benevolent autocrat who relies first and foremost on the personal loyalty to himself of family members and others he has brought in and can trust. In a society of mutually morally binding relationships, benevolence is exchanged for loyalty. It does not mean incompetence. The family members sharing management will be chosen for their abilities and will be supported during their education and training, which may extend to post-graduate degrees. Nor does it have the stigma attaching to paternalism in more individualistic cultures, where employees find irksome what they see as over-dependence.

Given reliance on personal relationships, rather than bureaucratic controls, formalization is low. Written instructions, procedures, reports and the like are minimal, as are the staff departments that generate them.

The owner's personal connections with other businessmen count for a great deal in ensuring good buys and good sales with those in whom trust can be placed. Most links are informal, though they can be signified in the rather larger firms by exchanging directorships, which follow personal networks rather than financial interests as in the West.

The typical management picture is summarized in Box 7.10. It should not be mistakenly thought to typify old-fashioned firms only, as it might

Box 7.10 The Nanyang Firm

The typical overseas Chinese firm has:

a) Centralization of the power of decision-making, usually with a single dominant owner, manager, entrepreneur, founder or father figure.

b) A low level of specialization, with fewer and/or less detailed specialized departments, and with more people responsible for a spread of activities across a number of fields.

c) Less standardization of activities and thus fewer routine procedures.

d) A relative lack of ancillary departments, such as research and development, labour relations, public relations, market research.

e) Reliance on personal relationships for business transactions.

(abbreviated and adapted from Redding and Wong, p. 276)

in other societies. Technically advanced businesses with highly trained personnel can look not so very different.

The typical owner-manager himself is vividly portrayed in Box 7.11.

Box 7.11 The Nanyang Manager

This composite portrait of a typical overseas Chinese, 'each component of which is visible in a real-life instance', is drawn by Redding (pp. 17–18).

Take a hypothetical Mr Lim living in Semarang, an industrial port on the north coast of Java and a base for Chinese power for some centuries past. His family came to Indonesia from China at the turn of the century and in the 1930s adopted the Indonesian name of Hartono. He is Hokkienese by area of origin, and his family and friends still use the dialect among themselves. He has never been to China but members of his family have visited the ancestral village. He has a brother in Singapore, another in Hong Kong, and a sister who is an Australian citizen married to a Hokkien engineer in Sydney. His wife is Hokkienese also, but they met in Semarang through the Protestant Christian church of which they are both members. He owns and manages a factory making plastic household goods. This relies on machinery transferred to second-generation use after its first six years of life in a Hong Kong factory owned by a cousin. He purchases raw materials from a major multinational chemical company, in which two of his nephews are employed, one of them in the pricing department, the other in sales. He sells to three wholesalers in different parts of Java, two of them Hokkienese and one

Cantonese by origin. His banker is a large Indonesian bank owned by an Indonesian Chinese of Hokkien extraction, which employs one of his nephews and two nieces. He is now considering an expansion of his business in partnership with a Singaporean friend of his brother, who would in turn bring in capital raised from a Chinese-owned Singapore bank which has strong connections into Hokkien regional networks. His elder son works for him and has been groomed to succeed him with an engineering degree at California Institute of Technology, followed by a Berkeley MBA. The middle son is a professional accountant, attached locally to a Chinese-owned consultancy company but intending to set up his own practice in time. A third son is in Australia training to be a doctor.

He meets regularly with other members of the Chinese community socially: firstly as a board member of a local hospital funded largely by Chinese business support; secondly through the church which has a large Chinese membership; thirdly with a group of close friends, all businessmen, who play mahjong together weekly; fourthly at a series of social occasions such as weddings, dinners for new-born sons, and various other forms of celebration which bring the Chinese community together, almost always to tables of twelve in a restaurant where the occasion might justify anything from one table to fifty.

Mr Lim travels about twice a year around the region, in each place renewing friendships and acquaintanceships in a round of business-orientated socializing. He normally stays with relatives, travels economy class and spends frugally except in entertaining, when he can be a lavish host. On these trips he accumulates information on new products, new technologies, new market possibilities, alternative sources of finance and of supply, and continues to investigate the possibility of exporting goods from Indonesia. Most of this information is gathered in conversation with his sources rather than via any formal reports, and he keeps most of it in his head.

The advantages of small-scale flexibility and an accessible boss are offset by limitations, of course. All matters big and small go to the top. Middle managers can be frustrated, and their potential contributions may not be taken advantage of. Lower-level employees are unlikely to feel much personal commitment to the firm. So far, however, it has been a successful mix overall.

The prominence of Nanyang Chinese in Indonesian business is described in the section of this chapter on Indonesia, but the prime example has long been Hong Kong. This erstwhile British colony having been returned to China in 1997, its people are no longer 'overseas'. On a strict definition they never were since a large proportion of the six million Hong Kongese live on the mainland side of the narrow strait that separates off Hong Kong island itself. Even so, they fully share the characteristics of Nanyang Chinese.

Though British colonial rule provided a vitally supportive administration, it was not a British achievement to turn this tiny crowded territory into an exporter and trader prominent in the world economy, which claimed to be the financial capital of Asia. It was achieved by the energy and capability of their Nanyang Chinese subjects. The question for the 21st century is whether Hong Kong can continue to flourish as a Special Administrative Zone within the People's Republic.

JAPANESE CULTURE AND MANAGEMENT

The 127 million Japanese (minorities are a tiny proportion of the population) are an island race. They live on four main islands rising from the sea in a crescent-shaped row which, so to speak, lies on its back in the Pacific Ocean. These islands are mostly mountainous so that the population is crowded into only a small part of the total land-surface, predominantly coastal. Japan's industrial revolution of the past century and a half has created a huge urbanized belt 300 miles long, the spine of the crescent's back, running westwards from the enormous sprawl of Tokyo through Osaka to Kobe and beyond. In this belt live 50 million people, two-fifths of all Japanese.

Their island geography has given the Japanese comparative homogeneity and independence for thousands of years. As already mentioned, this is signified by a royal family which claims ancestry going back over two thousand years, and by an exclusive religious practice, Shinto, as well as a historically feudalistic and immobile class-system. For six centuries the emperor played only a nominal role, real power being in the hands of successive shoguns (military overlords) and their samurai warrior underlings. This is the period, evoked in fierce and romantic novels and films, which laid the cultural basis of strong, self-sacrificing group loyalty. It ended with the abdication of the last shogun in 1867.

That also ended over 200 years of self-imposed isolation, during which virtually all contact with foreigners and especially Westerners had been banned for, despite the protection of the seas around them, the Japanese have felt vulnerable first to their giant Chinese neighbour and then to Western incursion. Like the Chinese have sometimes done, they rejected alien influences and felt they had nothing to learn. But when Emperor Meiji came to the throne in 1868, his ministers accelerated the opening-up of Japan to the rest of the world and, with that, its rapid industrialization. From their retreat, the Japanese came out to assert themselves, first in wars with Russia and with China and in the Second World War, and then economically.

As is well known, astonishing economic recovery followed defeat in that last war and foreign occupation, as it did in Germany. The Japanese 'economic miracle' raised Japan to rival the USA in economic performance. It was the first and foremost industrial 'late developer', an exporting and financial dragon to whom all the world owes money for the quality goods they have eagerly bought. Essentially, Japanese industry did what Western industries were already doing but did it better, aided by a readiness to act in concert with agencies of government such as the Ministry of International Trade and Industry, MITI.

The economic reversal of the 1990s did not erase this achievement, but showed that it was not impervious to world conditions nor domestic weaknesses. At the heart of this reversal was an over-extended banking and financial system, which added to the difficulties of production cutbacks, redundancies, and a collapse in property and share values.

Unique Culture

All cultures are unique in as much as no others are quite the same. However, Japanese culture is even more unique, if it is possible to speak of degrees of uniqueness. Of course, every society shares with others characteristics that make it similar in some respects, and this is why it is possible to group together the Latins or the Anglos or, in this chapter, the Asians. So Japanese society fully shares the general Asian inclination to manage relationships harmoniously and to respect authority and seniority. It shares the general 'Oriental Way' described earlier. But it differs, as described earlier in this chapter, in the apparent strength of its assertive drive and its 'uncertainty avoidance'. When its characteristics are taken all together (see Box 7.12), then they appear to be a distinctive, absolutely unique *combination*, probably not matched in any other society.

Worldwide, there are many who look to **authority** and who even verge on authoritarianism more than the Japanese (who are no more than medium in power distance). Nevertheless, there is a respect for seniority in age, status and experience that is typical more of the East than of the West. Implicitly, authority is expected to be used responsibly and paternally. A bust of the founder may stand beside a Shinto shrine at a factory entrance.

Box 7.12 Uniquely Japanese

In Chapter 2, Boxes 2.5, 2.7, 2.9, and 2.10 show Japan ranked by Hofstede on power distance, individualism/collectivism, masculinity femininity, and uncertainty avoidance. According to this researcher, the Japanese cultural profile is:

medium power distance	high masculinity
medium collectivistic	high uncertainty avoidance

Whilst all other profiles are shared by several of the nations covered by Hofstede's research, he found that Japan alone had this particular profile.

(Hofstede)

Likewise, there is a degree of collectivism in **managing relationships** that makes a great impression on any Western visitor, business person or tourist. Courtesy and bowing to one another reflect the effort to sustain social harmony, or *wa* in Japanese (Box 7.13 reflects this). There is a high regard for loyalty within the in-group of family or friends, and this is capable of transference to the work group more than it is in China. As in China, work superiors often act as go-betweens in marriages. There is a comparatively high level of implicit understanding of customary ways and of what is meant when communicating in a 'high-context' language (see Boxes 2.8 and 7.14).

Of course appearances can be misleading. Outward harmony does not always mean that all is harmonious. Within the workplace employees do jockey for position, and in the crowded Tokyo subway strangers can be brusquely shoved aside. Moreover, loyalty has been found to conceal corruption.

The distinctive Japanese drive in **managing oneself** (the masculinity in Box 7.12) gives a drive for achievement, together and through others, allied to an ethic of unremitting hard work. This competitive assertiveness may have derived a fresh impulse from the tremendous shock to national pride given by the Second World War experience.

Box 7.13 Individualistic Top Dog

One of the authors of this book was rising to the occasion brilliantly, in his own estimation. He was indeed holding the attention of his audience very well. What his humble hosts in a Japanese provincial city had indicated need only be an informal chat – or so he had interpreted what they meant – had turned out to be a most magnificent occasion. He found himself on a floodlit, decorated podium giving a special anniversary address to a sell-out audience of businessmen and women.

Caught unprepared, he had resorted to talking about the approaches to management in different societies. Few if any of the large audience could have heard anything of this kind before, so it seemed to be the right thing. Pauses for translation gave him time to think, and all was going smoothly . . .

Until he ventured to comment on the political and economic rise and decline of nations and empires. He used a commonplace English language expression. 'Every dog has its day,' he said.

The translator hesitated. 'Please could you repeat that.'

'Well, er, every dog has its day.'

'I am sorry, but I do not understand. What does this mean?'

Our author hastily tried to find simple words to make explicit an implicit meaning that he had never thought about before. The audience waited whilst he and the translator tried to understand each other. They failed. The flow of his talk disrupted, our author abandoned the point altogether, shifted the topic, and tried to recapture momentum.

Afterwards, he found that the language of collectivistic, respectful, Japan had no exactly equivalent expression. He saw for the first time its Anglo assumption of individualistic striving to be personally on top, in overt competition to become top dog even though each will be ousted when its time is over.

It is complemented by the Japanese way of **managing uncertainty**. A sense that uncertainty is under control can be gained by orderliness and diligent attention to detail, so that instead of 'If anything can go wrong, it will,' as Westerners despairingly say, the Japanese equivalent would be 'If anything might go wrong, it must not.' Future business uncertainty can be forestalled by equalling or bettering competitors, so, whilst change is itself an uncertainty, to make changes can also be a way of thwarting uncertainty by improving performance.

Box 7.14 Feeling One's Way

Ideas of feeling rather than rationalization are basic to Japanese society. People tend to feel empathetically for each other and a genuine relationship is one in which both parties *feel* thoughts and emotions rather than constantly verbalizing them.

A simple example would be *feeling* whether a business visitor desires tea or coffee rather than asking him. In the West, it would be considered too assertive and rude to assume that the host already knows whether the guest wants tea or coffee. In Japan it is rude and insensitive not to feel what the guest wants.

(from Taplin, p. 35)

The Japanese way of **managing time** is apparent to any stranger on a Tokyo railway platform where the trains slide in to the second. Here again is diligent attention to detail, shown also in punctuality in business appointments. Present promptness goes with an Asian patience to await results in due time, comparatively greater weight being given to the growth and future stability of a firm as against short-term profit.

The competitive thrust, combined with loyal orderliness, lies behind the so-called 'Confucian Dynamism' of Japanese society (Box 7.2).

Large and Small in Business

Dynamism has always been most visible internationally in the large business conglomerates whose names and brands flicker in lights in cities across the world. Sony, Toyota, Mitsubishi, and so on. Each encompasses numerous companies engaged in a range of businesses, joined together by ownership, joint directorships, and interests in common.

However, they are only a minute number among Japanese companies (though they create a large share of national output). Most companies are small. These are more likely to take the brunt of market fluctuations, their employees having less security than those in the big groups. Many are closely linked with those groups by contracts and by the understandings that go with the contracts. Whilst this may mean becoming dangerously dependent on purchases by a group, and being first to bear the effects of hard times for the group, it can also mean being treated almost as a group member, with the benefit of mutual loyalties in sharing business. When visitors to Mitsubishi Motors, the largest single unit in the vast Mitsubishi group of companies, are handed the usual leaflet with pictures of robots and statistics of size and output, they may not at first notice anything about it that is different from what is handed out anywhere else in the world. Then their eye is caught by a 'Summary of Sub-Contractors'. At one time this showed 35 supplier companies with 12,000 employees among them. By including 'outsider companies' – as they would be considered in other countries – in the company's own glossy publicity, Mitsubishi signals a strength of (collectivistic) relationship with them that makes them quasi insiders. It is this kind of relationship that makes 'Just In Time' (JIT) operation possible for a plant such as Mitsubishi, which can carry minimal or zero stocks of components because it can rely on its suppliers to deliver the needed quantities just in time to keep work in full swing.

To keep informed, the Japanese manager similarly tends to rely on personal contacts with customer firms or distributors as much as or more than impersonal market research, whereas an American manager is more likely to tilt the other way.

This personal element also imbues business contracts which are seen, much as the Chinese see them, as formal affirmations of a developing relationship, open to continuing discussion and adjustment in the context

Box 7.15 Three to One

(from Moran, p. 136)

of that wider relationship. This may not be understood by negotiators from abroad (Box 7.15 depicts a possible American reaction), nor may the Japanese preference for dealing with matters in groups (the cartoon shows three Japanese to one American). This keeps more people informed, allows on-the-spot consultation together, and diffuses responsibility. Over the wider scene, the Japanese negotiator has also to be sensitive to possible reactions in linked companies and in the industrial or trade association.

Yet neither at home nor abroad is the Japanese negotiator – and certainly not the competitor – an easy touch. Co-operativeness within the group has its converse in vigorous competitiveness outside it.

Identifying and Co-operating

'Who am I?' is the unconscious question that every human being lives with. Individualistic societies tend to answer it in terms of what the individual has achieved and what *occupation* they have held, such as shop assistant, skilled machinist or lecturer. Collectivistic societies tend to answer it more in terms of family and friendship – I am a father/mother, son/daughter, so-and-so's friend – and, in Japan, not occupation but *organization*. The Japanese is likely to answer that he or she works in Hitachi or Nissan, all the more so if the organization does have a famous name such as these.

This degree of identification with the workplace goes together with a set of supporting features of employment, in the same way as there is a contrasting set of compatible features in more individualistic societies.

Japanese firms prefer to recruit members (a term used rather than 'employees') young and untrained, straight from school or university, so they can be trained by the company for the company in the company's methods. There is a well-educated population to choose from, trained from infancy to work well with others. Literacy is high, in a language that uses Chinese ideograms and Japanese phonetics. In other words, the sounds evoked by the written characters are Japanese, but spoken Japanese is no more Chinese than English is French just because both use the same alphabet.

Internal training goes with internal rotation through different jobs to maximize common understanding around the organization. This in turn goes with an assumption of internal promotion rather than of external job-hopping from firm to firm. Typically employees are less interested in pay rises now than in future long-term promotion chances. Job-hopping happens, of course, but as the exception rather than the rule. It carries a greater imputation of disloyalty than it would in, say, North America. Japanese hierarchies tend to be comparatively taller, with enough levels to absorb steady promotions which, within considerations of competence, give weight to age and seniority.

The complementary understanding that employment will be long term keeps the employee's gaze inwards and upwards rather than outwards. As in China, it may well be lifetime employment, especially in the larger organizations. This long-term mutual obligation began as a culture-compatible response to the need to train and retain employees when industrial growth accelerated in the mid-twentieth century. It carries men through to retirement at a comparatively early age (which was fifty-five but is becoming sixty), when some managers keep an association either with their company direct or with its supplier or customer companies. For women, things are different: their jobs more easily come and go with market fluctuations, and it is expected that they will leave upon marriage. Nor ultimately can the security of male employment be sustained through severe economic vagaries. During the Asian economic recession of the nineties, redundancies were forced upon firms which had never before encountered such a crisis. Further, as expansion ceased the customary advancement primarily by seniority was strained as there was no longer an increasing number of higher positions for older personnel to move into. At the same time it became more costly to tie pay to seniority as an ageing population meant an older labour force.

Box 7.16 You Are Funny, We Are Not

In a Japanese electronics firm in Telford, England, the new manager had come to the firm to take over from the general manager who had returned to Japan. The first thing the new general manager did when he arrived was to put the mokuteki outlining the company's goals in all of the offices of the company, including his own and the board room. The company goals, however, seemed odd to the British employees as they stressed pleasantness, harmony and people working together and trying to develop their own personalities to further the goals of the company. The Japanese general manager found it very difficult to come to terms with the fact that the employees tended to make fun of these goals and not take them very seriously.

(from Taplin, p. 76)

Paralleling this *nenko* or seniority-based system, employee stock ownership has been widespread, especially in larger firms. It suits Japanese thriftiness. Furthermore, the majority of employees are not members of unions and, if they are, most unions are company unions, organization-related not occupational. Usually they represent both 'blue collar' and 'white collar' employees on the principle of 'one enterprise, one union'. Thus if the company were to go out of business, so would the union. So the union is committed to the progress of the company, rather than to advancing the interests of an occupation across companies irrespective of the consequences for any particular firm.

Not that there is a marked 'blue collar/white collar' distinction. The emphasis on common purpose is symbolized by all grades of employees, including management, wearing the same or similar uniform and eating in the same canteen. Offices are likely to be open plan, where everyone can see everyone, with fewer individual offices and personal files.

There can be company songs and communal physical exercises, and *mokuteki*, slogans expressing the expected attitudes towards the company and colleagues (which may not go down well in more individualistic cultures (see Box 7.16). Managers work long hours for what is widely referred to as *uchi no kaisha*, '*our* company'. Long hours are no strange thing for managers anywhere, of course, but in Japan they are added to by frequent after-hours recourse to bars and restaurants where reserve can be dropped and camaraderie strengthened. If things go amiss, resignations, emotional TV appearances and, in the (very rare) extreme, suicides signify just how strong the identification and sense of personal responsibility of executives can be.

Taken together, this approach to recruitment, training, employment prospects, pay and promotion, and identification symbols underpins a commitment that minimizes suspicion and resistance to change and fosters hard work. Tasks can be flexible, with less rigid specialization. Quality circles in which workers discuss how to improve their work can succeed, whereas if workers are defensive, as is often so in other societies, they fade away.

Commitment should not be overstated, however. Work groups are not made up of magically identical and equally dedicated people. They are made up of differing individuals with likes and dislikes, who have to learn to co-operate. Loyalty to group and organization is given by most much of the time, but not by everyone all of the time. Rather than given freely, it may be necessitated by the difficulty an employee trained and experienced in only one organization can have in getting a job outside it. Moreover, commitment to workmates and organization is not the same as *job satisfaction*.

Recurrent research findings suggest that the Japanese employee is no more satisfied – probably less so – than others doing equivalent work.

A routine high-pressure job yields no more joy here than anywhere else.

Communicating and Deciding

The same endeavour to ensure general commitment, or at least concurrence, gives managerial decision-making its particular Japanese flavour. The *ringi* practice that is commonplace in larger organizations attempts to bring in all those who are or may in future be concerned.

A proposal emanates from someone – probably in concert with colleagues – in the middle echelons of management. He – it is almost certain to be a male – talks it over with others in relevant departments. He explores the broad feelings of superiors. Differing viewpoints and possible obstacles are substantially ironed out. Given that the proposal is of sufficient significance, which usually means that any financial implications are above a prescribed sum, he then issues a *ringi-sho*. This is a document summarizing what is intended, which spirals its way slowly up the hierarchy. Each of those concerned affixes his personal stamp (an ideogram equivalent to a signature) until finally it is approved at the highest appropriate level. Should anyone along the way still not be able to concur, there is further discussion and, if need be, a revised *ringi-sho* begins the process all over again.

This unifying procedure does not have the connotations of the word 'participation' as that is most often used. Participation implies an effort to consult those who do not participate as a matter of course, in order to cope with potential conflict, whereas *ringi* is set in a constant process of *nemawashi*, that is of perpetual interpersonal discussion that builds trust. By the time a *ringi-sho* appears, assent is usually assured, and much of what has been decided upon may already have been done.

A lengthy process of this nature helps to avoid future uncertainty by making sure that, since everyone has considered the implications beforehand, implementation will be smooth. It spreads influence. But the final decision is not necessarily decentralized, in so far as ultimate authorization is at or near the top, probably in the *jomukai* or senior directors' meeting (see Box 7.17). Box 9.15 in Chapter 9 shows that in Japanese manufacturing firms the degree of centralization of decisions is

> **Box 7.17** All On Board
>
> *The Japanese board of directors is much larger than is typical in the USA. In 1990 the board of Sony consisted of 33 directors and that of Canon had 26. In addition, the board is usually composed entirely of full-time directors and it has many gradations. It is not surprising that it is not the key decision-making body since its large size would inhibit this. In addition various grades of director are often in direct line relationships to one another and deference to seniority applies just as much on the board as elsewhere.*
>
> *Since the board plays a mainly ceremonial role, decision-making devolves to the* jomukai *(senior directors' meeting), or to the* keiei kaigi *(general managers' meeting).*
>
> (from Campbell, p. 21)

much the same as in firms in other market economies. Even so, the no more than middling Japanese power distance referred to earlier is borne out by the way in which those above try not to move until they know that those below will move with them.

The *ringi-sho* is a form of documentation, or formalization, that is typically Japanese. Japanese organizations also have a very full panoply of the documentation familiar in organizations everywhere: the rules, instructions, charts, forms, etc. To the Japanese, a formalized framework for informal co-operation gives a reassuring feel that everything is in order and not left open to uncertainty.

The outstanding achievements of Japanese companies managed Japanese-style lead others to think, 'If only we could manage in a Japanese way, we could do better than we are doing.' As will be pointed out in the final chapter, it is not possible to transfer methods wholesale into other societies with different economies and cultures. In any case, even Japanese methods can have disadvantages as well as advantages. The *ringi* element in decision-making takes a long time, and may not a *ringi-sho* be open to wasting time by people becoming involved just to be seen to be involved? Cannot awkward people delay it needlessly? Might it foster conformity since, the more who signify assent, the more difficult it is not to concur? How far is it collective *ir*responsibility?

Could *wa* foster conformity generally? Could low specialization in tasks mean lack of depth experience in any single area? Could promotion with regard for seniority under-use younger ability?

There are no answers here to such questions. Nor is it clear how quickly, if at all, Japanese management may be shifting towards Western practices as wealth increases with economic success. Or is it the West that is shifting? Or both?

SOUTH KOREAN CULTURE AND MANAGEMENT

Koreans live on a comparatively small peninsula, squeezed between the great mainland bulk of China to which it is attached and the islands of Japan from which it is separated by a narrow strait of sea. Korea enjoyed many centuries of unified independence, despite Mongolian and Chinese incursions, and eventually became known as 'the hermit kingdom' when, like its Chinese and Japanese neighbours both did at times, it closed itself off to foreigners. This isolation could not be sustained. In the nineteenth century it was prised open to Western trade, until at the end of the century Japanese military successes against China and the nearby Russians extended first their influence over Korea and then direct rule when they annexed it in 1910.

The defeat of Japan in 1945, which ended World War II, brought independence again for Korea, but not for long as a single entity. A three year internal war, which broke out as an early flashpoint in the worldwide so-called 'cold war' between communist and capitalist systems, culminated in 1953 with the country sliced in half, West to East. It has stayed divided between communist North Korea and capitalist multi-party South Korea, respectively the People's Democratic Republic of Korea and the Republic of Korea. The North has emulated China, politically and economically, while the South has looked to Japan and the United States. It is South Korea which is described here.

South Korea's 47 million population is a mere tiny fraction of China's immensity and only just a third of Japan's total, but it is a lot in a small space. With industrialization it has become urbanized, being especially densely concentrated in and around the capital Seoul and the second largest city Pusan, in which cities about half the population live.

There are twice as many people in South Korea as in North Korea. Those in the South are extremely homogeneous racially and in language and culture and, like both China and Japan, have their own distinctive script.

They also have their own Shamanist religious tradition, interwoven with Confucian thought and with Buddhism. Further, there are more professing Christians than anywhere else on the Asian continent, except-ing possibly the Russian Federation's easterly extremity, most of them Roman Catholics. This is attributed to that church having been popularly resistant to Japanese domination much as it was in Poland to communist control.

Racing but Stumbling

South Korea's feat of becoming one of the five 'racing dragons' of Asia in just a quarter of a century astounded the world. Its war-shattered economy began from scratch in 1953, the North having inherited any minerals and such industrial base as there was. During the 1970s and 1980s it attained some of the world's highest economic growth rates, by far outstripping the North, and transforming South Korea from a largely rural to a largely urban society. Some of the workforce were drawn in from less successful Asian economies, including Filipinos, Pakistanis, Sri Lankans and Vietnamese.

There can be no firm reasons for this performance, and certainly no single reason. Perhaps the Koreans felt impelled to fight back, after being politically severed, just as the Germans did on the other side of the world after being cut in two. Certainly they resented having been the underdog, under foreign military control. They were shamed by the backwardness of their hermit kingdom when it came up against Western military technology in the hands of the Japanese, just as the Japanese had been galvanized before them. They were, and are, a highly literate and well educated people readily mobilized into a new economy. They had the social discipline inherent in pervasive Confucian ways of thought, as described earlier in the chapter. This may well contain a 'Confucian Dynamism', as it has been dubbed, which could coexist profitably with the unusual Christian element even though that has more of a Roman Catholic than a Protestant ethic.

Then the dragon stumbled. Through the 1990s economic performance flagged. Businesses found they had over-extended themselves with government-backed credit. Costs continued to be pushed up by a labour force more militant than most in Asia, strikes being frequent. As the Japanese economy also faltered and its yen weakened, Korean manufacturers became less competitive. Since Korean industry depended on Japanese industry for many of its components, the falling cost of Japanese items may at the same time have prevented an even worse downturn in Korea.

The *Chaebols*

Most Korean firms are small, but the conspicuous feature of Korean business is the eminence of relatively huge *chaebols*, diversified conglomerates (see Box 2.3). There is a greater concentration of production capacity in these, and a wider gap between them and the small firms, than there is in Japan with its big *kaisha* groups. Their ownership is concentrated, whereas in the Japanese business groupings it is spread through the group. Further, *chaebols* have more widely spread and assorted activities, which are mostly under their direct ownership. Production is, in this sense, mostly in-house, rather than subcontracted out, Japanese fashion.

Like the Japanese, however, they keep ultimate control within the country. They are not the creatures of multinational corporations, though some did originate in businesses set up by the Japanese during their occupation. Korean government-backed financial credit played a large part in their growth as well as giving government a guiding influence, though links with the state are now weakening. The 'familism' of society, a cultural characteristic referred to in Chapter 2, is exemplified in the ownership of most *chaebols* by the founder and his family.

A number of leading *chaebols* bear names that have become recognized brands around the globe. Samsung is sometimes called the grandfather of the *chaebols*, though internationally it is far outweighed in size by the largest Japanese manufacturing group, Mitsubishi. Even so, it is among the largest business corporations in the world outside the United States, and has or has had branches in electronics, semiconductors, hotels, insurance and many other fields, with thousands of products. Hyundai, Daewoo and Lucky-Goldstar are other widely recognizable names. The *chaebols* have been large enough to take risks by diversifying rapidly, though the 1990s was a sharp correction to their over optimism.

Paternalism

Given the predominance of family ownership in the *chaebols* and beyond, and the implicit pervasiveness of the Confucian ethic, a paternalistic style of management is to be expected. Korea being a relatively familistic society where loyalties to family and friends are strong, an owner and his kind are even more likely to see their firm and its employees through a paternal 'fatherly' eye than owner-managers elsewhere, most obviously in the West, may do. There are executives in all countries who like to speak of their organization as one big family, but Korean owners are more than likely to see it that way.

So recruitment into management has drawn heavily on the extended family and its friends (see Box 7.18), and on contacts in the place where the owner himself originated, though this becomes diluted when expansion requires open advertisement for greater numbers of managerial personnel.

Managing authority in a paternalistic way can be benign as far as the sense of obligation to 'one big family' stretches, but beyond that self-defined sphere there may be less consideration. Layoffs are commonplace in the outer constituents of *chaebols*, contributing to the industrial unrest that has been mentioned. Indeed Korean management has been accused of being militaristic. That is far-fetched, but there may be an element of this kind in a society where widespread military training continues, including in-company military training, because of the stand-off with the North which was for a long time not much more than an armed truce.

Box 7.18 Family on the Job

The founder of the Hyundai *chaebol* was said to breakfast at home with those five of his sons who were top managers in the conglomerate, before walking with them to their respective offices in the Hyundai office building.

(from Song, p. 194)

This element, if such there be, and paternalistic ownership, bring a top-down view of authority to a society where it may not be ingrained (see Korea's middle position in Box 2.5). It is typically expressed in a tall, many layered, centralized structure. When this is headed by a controlling family, their actions do not have to stay within the rules and procedures and can be arbitrary or flexible or both, depending on whose viewpoint is taken. Those below accept but do not always feel comfortable with such a system.

They may feel more comfortable if the organization is highly formalized. Written rules, clear procedures, written instructions and job descriptions which make their responsibilities plain, give a reassuring feeling that things are under control. Koreans are inclined to avoid uncertainty (Box 2.10).

Box 7.19 Korean Chairs at the Ready

Ordinary administrative personnel were given a chair without armrests and a desk with a single bank of drawers; section chiefs were given chairs with armrests and slightly larger desks with banks of drawers on both sides; department heads were issued with still larger desks, a separate two drawer file cabinet, and a chair equipped with armrests and a higher backrest than those given the section chiefs. Directors had their own offices . . .

(from Janelli, p. 166)

Status symbols abound. Korea is far from alone in this, of course. The furnishings described in Box 7.19 will be instantly familiar to most readers, though they are likely to appear extreme to some, like those from Japan or from Sweden, for example, countries where such symbols may be less pronounced.

Personal regard and loyalty between those above and those below softens how things work day by day, though it can inhibit subordinates from fully expressing themselves. In a typically Asian way (as described previously) they try to avoid injuring the dignity or 'face' of someone senior to them. Even more so than in the West, communication is better in informal situations than in formal meetings, building up consensus behind the scenes much as the Japanese do through their *nemawashi* discussion. However, the also apparently similar decision-making process whereby those concerned signify their concurrence on a circulated document is regarded by Koreans as being more top-down, a request for consent, rather than gradually developing assent as the Japanese tend to use it. Box 7.20 summarizes a Korean/Japanese comparison as it looks to a British author.

Box 7.20 Authority and Control in *Chaebol* and *Kaisha*

	Korean Chaebol (business conglomerate)	Japanese Kaisha (business corporation)
Importance of personal authority of owners	Higher	Lower
Reliance on family top managers	Higher	Lower
Centralization of decision making	Higher	Medium
Delegation to middle management	Some operational decisions	Greater
Work group task autonomy	Higher	Lower
Managerial involvement in work group	Higher	Lower

(adapted from Whitley, p. 77, Table 3.4)

Facing Up To It

Saving face by **managing relationships** harmoniously shows a collectivistic as against individualistic orientation. With that orientation it can be more important to respect someone else and protect them socially, by not openly expressing doubts let alone contradicting them, than it is to tell the full truth of the matter. Koreans are likely to react to a conflict of views in a less confrontational manner than, say, Americans may do, as is typical of Asians generally. 'No', even 'Yes', may be indicated indirectly, for instance by length of bowing (see Box 7.21), which has much the same meaning as an extra long or vigorous handshake in Western cultures. This may convey more than does a written contract for it is personal integrity that matters rather than what is written, which might be thought of as renegotiable.

Box 7.21 Meaning in Bowing

Koreans bow at the beginning and end of a meeting. An exit bow that is longer than the greeting bow is an indication that the meeting went well.

(from Morrison, Conaway and Borden, p. 345)

Personal relationships being crucial, deserve careful attention. Koreans working in the United States or Britain where this attention is less readily forthcoming find work life cold and isolating. It is, for them, difficult to get through to people, to feel included. Though giving relationships careful attention does not mean rushing things. Outside the network of family and friends, trust has to be built up. A stranger will do well not to go straight in cold but to be introduced by someone already known, be it business agent or bank or acquaintance. 'Getting to know you' conversation comes before getting down to business, as it would in Asian cultures generally. Yet once business is underway, Koreans are not impassive. They can surprise outsiders by becoming emotional, even angry.

Within the organization, loyalty is inclined to be more to the person of the owner or a superior than to an impersonal business. Insofar as this is reciprocated, it limits the effectiveness of Western originated performance appraisal and reward systems. While these suppose that an individual who does well will receive individual recognition in pay and prospects, Korean superiors are reluctant to pick out one more than another from their group of loyal subordinates.

This collectivist standpoint shows too in the company pronouncements. Box 7.22 lists the key sentiments professed by the managements of prominent *chaebols* in their *sahoon* or company ideologies: trust, service, co-operation, even affection are aspired to – until, that is, you reach the last two in the list, LG (Lucky-Goldstar) and Samsung. Here the direction of change in Korean management is revealed. Respect for the individual, empowerment and customers come to the fore in a form that parallels a gradual shift in managing away from rewarding loyalty and seniority to rewarding performance. A hint of individualism creeps in.

Whatever the impulses may have been which spurred Korean economic achievement, they roused a still mainly collectivistic people who have a capacity for hard work. This was not and is not the kind of assertive drive

---

Box 7.22 Collectivistic *Sahoon*

Shared Values or Official *Sahoon* of Some Prominent *Chaebols*

'Traditional cultural values (collectivism and loyalty) are frequently stated in the *sahoon* of Korean firms'.

Chaebol Group	Shared Values or Official *Sahoon*
Hyundai	Diligence, thriftiness, trust and affection
Daewoo	Creativity, challenge and sacrifice
Sunkyong	Humanism, rationalism and realism
Ssangyong	Trust, credibility, innovativeness and harmony
Hanjin	Service, credibility and progressiveness
Hyosung	Service, sincerity, innovativeness and unity
Hanwha	Trust, credibility, modesty and excellence
Lotte	Honesty, integrity, service and passion
LG	Value creation for customers, respect for individual and empowerment
Samsung	Respect for individual, pursuit of technology and empowerment

Source: company brochures

(from Chung, Lee and Jung, pp. 147–8)

---

that distinguishes the Anglo nations, for example, nor in Asia the Japanese, for unlike them the Koreans are notably inclined to the 'feminine' end of Box 2.9 where quality of life and being of service weighs as much or more than ambition to succeed. Rather there was the kind of self-discipline in **managing oneself** that Confucius extolled, together with a Japanese-like need to **manage uncertainty** (in this the two nations are indeed similar: see Box 2.10) by working for an assured, more certain, future. In short, the supposed Confucian Dynamism remarked upon before.

Their geographical and political situation being what it is, South Koreans are forever being compared to and comparing themselves with the Japanese, and with the Americans who led in defending them from invasion by the North. It is noticeable that they are not compared in style of management with the North nor with the Chinese. Successful capitalism does not take its lead from hostile communism.

Box 7.23 Not Like Us, Like Them

The Korean management style . . . appears to lie between the Japanese and American approaches. Most Americans appear to believe that Koreans are very much like the Japanese – and that 'Korea is a second Japan'. But when Koreans talk with Japanese they find that many Japanese consider Koreans to be more like Americans than like themselves.

(from Song, p. 189)

Which way they appear to lean can depend on the vantage point, as Box 7.23 shows. Even so, they do come within the broadly collectivistic Asian way, and not the Western Anglo way. That said, the summary of the Korean pattern in Box 7.24, simplification though it must be, shows that they are not Japanese. The weaker Korean 'flexible commitment' is inclined to rather more top-down decision processes to control it, with more ostensible status distinctions, lower group loyalty, and less lifetime employment than the Japanese. The Korean dragon races in its own colours.

Box 7.24 The (South) Korean Way of Management

- Paternalistic ownership
- Top-down decision making
- Sharp distinctions between owners, managers and other employees
- Emphasis on personal loyalty
- Flexible lifetime employment

(adapted from Min Chen, p. 213)

INDONESIAN CULTURE AND MANAGEMENT

The Indonesian archipelago curves along the Southern edge of the vast number of islands that fill the South Pacific between Asia and Australia. Itself encompassing almost 14,000 islands, though more than half are uninhabited, it stretches three thousand miles from end to end and at its widest is one thousand miles from North to South.

Over 200 million people live in this geographically unique nation, making it the fourth most populous in the world, as has been said earlier. Most are ethnically Malay. Over half live on the densely populated island of Java. Migration from outer islands to its cities, especially the capital Jakarta, continues to increase the pressure of numbers there, though the overall national growth of a young and largely literate population is slowing down.

Indonesia today has a religious and artistic diversity given it by thousands of years of incursions into its great array of islands. Ancient animist pagan ways still persist in mountainous areas and far-flung islands, though the original inhabitants were displaced by Malays. Hinduism came with Indian settlers a millennium or more ago, and is practised now mainly in rice growing areas and the tourist-favoured island of Bali. The Confucian Buddhism, if the two may be referred to together, of Chinese traders is still with their descendants in urban areas. By far the most successful has been Islam, brought by Arab traders more than half a millennium ago. Islam has the allegiance of nine out of ten Indonesians. Christianity first appeared early in the sixteenth century with Portuguese spice merchants, its adherents being now a small and at times contentious minority, mostly Roman Catholics.

The Dutch ousted the Portuguese in 1596, and were the dominant European influence. Some older Indonesians still speak Dutch. Dutch rule was effectively ended by Japanese military occupation from 1942–1945 during the Second World War.

By the time the Dutch had arrived and begun to impose central government, Javanese dominance of the archipelago was already established. This continued when independence came after the war, since when the Jakarta government has striven to build a nation. Independence is a story of two presidents, first Sukarno, and then for over three decades until 1998, Suharto. The latter's paternalistic regime under which authority was concentrated in and flowed from himself, his family and personal associates, brought a stability which, though militarily based, was needful.

It gave time to extend transport links between the islands, to achieve almost universal primary education, and to spread further the common language, Bahasa Indonesian, a Malay dialect. By these means national identity was strengthened.

It gave time for sustained economic development and a marked rise in living standards. In the second half of the twentieth century, although population doubled, the economy expanded several times over. Even if Indonesia was not quite up with the 'racing dragon' economies, this was a marked success. Manufacturing came to count for more than agriculture, and a third of the population became urbanized with a growing middle class.

A crucial contribution was made by the five million or so Indonesians of Chinese origin, who built up and control three out of four privately-owned businesses. Their large family-owned conglomerates have put some of them among the wealthiest businessmen in the land.

The run of economic success was marred at the end of the nineties when Indonesia followed other South-East Asian nations into a reversal which brought unemployment, inflation and a drop in share and property values.

Managing Authority and Relationships on the Job

The State having been described as paternalistic, the **managing of authority** in organizations can be characterized in much the same way. Indonesians respect the authority of their elders and seniors, an authority gained with age and social standing as well as by organizational position. This is so throughout humankind but it is much more so in Asia as the section on 'the Oriental Way' at the start of this chapter says. Whereas in Europe and North America especially, comparatively more weight is given to competence on the job. The feeling that it is right and proper to honour older and higher status people, recognizing their place and one's own place, is known in Indonesia as *bapakism*. Such a person is a *bapak*.

This comes through in Box 7.25, where the Indonesians feel the need for hierarchy at work much more than do the Dutch or the Americans. It shows too in Box 2.5, where Indonesia ranks high on power distance even among the Asian nations. So superiors are expected to act in a fatherly manner, expecting obedience to their instructions yet giving benevolent support when there is need. To get things done their backing is vital, as is that of elders in any walk of life. Western forms of supposedly open participation, in meetings where what higher management does can be questioned, are out of place. As elsewhere in Asia, this could be too personally offensive, too socially crude. Problems and divisive issues are more likely to be communicated indirectly, perhaps by having a quiet word with someone who is in a position to themselves have a quiet word with an appropriate senior person. Likewise, direct performance appraisal is delicate, to be done by nuance or not at all. Just as in South Korea, to take another example, comparatively greater value is put upon loyalty and trustworthiness, as against performance, than is commonly the case in Western management.

Box 7.25 One More Time, Hierarchy Rules OK

	Percentage agree or strongly agree among		
	Indonesians	**Dutch**	**Americans**
The main reason for having a hierarchical structure is so that everyone knows who has authority over whom	82	38	18

Responses to a questionnaire given respectively to 96, 50 and 50 managers from three countries on courses at the INSEAD business school, Fontainebleau, near Paris, by A. Laurent, and quoted by Hofstede, p. 22.

This is the collectivistic way of **managing relationships**. It tries to sustain harmony in personal relationships, as already illustrated in this chapter by the examples of China, Japan and South Korea. As far as possible, the respect due to someone else, and that person's self-respect, are not damaged. 'Face' is saved by mutual consideration.

So work is about relationships with others as much as task achievement. Which is better, to hurt someone else's feelings, and also let yourself down by doing so, or to put up with their inadequacies or mistakes? The Indonesian view is plain in Box 7.1, Managing Harmony, contrasting with that of the Americans. The Japanese view is much the same as theirs. A biblical anecdote from Islamic Indonesia in Box 7.26 makes the same point.

Box 7.26 Biblical Harmony

The need for formal harmony is illustrated by the story of a Dutch missionary in Indonesia who told the following biblical parable: 'A man had two sons. He went to the first and said: "Son, work in the vineyard today". He replied "I will go, sir", but he did not go. The man went to the second and said the same to him. He replied "I will not". But afterwards he changed his mind and did go. Which of the two did the will of the father?' (St Matthew 21: 28–31, Moffatt translation). The biblical answer is 'the last', but this missionary's Indonesian audience chose the first. For this son observed the formal harmony and didn't let his father lose face.

(from Hofstede, p.18)

Since loyalties to family, friends and ethnic compatriots are of prime importance, it is socially proper to take these into account. Not to do so in filling a vacant job, for instance, would be both socially clumsy and store up trouble for the future. Who could work harmoniously with whom, and to whom is there any obligation? Here is the difficulty in Western eyes of what is seen through those eyes as corruption. To honour someone else with a personal favour is praiseworthy, not corrupt, as long as it is within customary limits. It is when those limits, hard for an outsider to discern, are greatly exceeded that the favour becomes an excessive bribe.

Gifts are necessary when a low level of impersonal trust in a society between individuals who do not know each other, requires that such trust be built up. It comes by their getting to know one another and becoming mutually obligated. So in Indonesia business should not be rushed, 'getting to know you' conversations and social engagements are the done thing, and an appropriate level of gifts should be exchanged.

Yet here, as elsewhere in the world, Western influences, especially American ways, are having an effect. The contacts that businessmen, the military and academics have with their Western counterparts bring them up against more open styles of managing, an experience reflected among Indonesians generally in overt political comment, demonstrations, and strikes which would have been unthinkable in the past.

Which is the Right Time?

Engagements are timed by social priorities as well as by the clock. Shifting business and social obligations prevent appointments being kept promptly if they are fixed too far ahead, so just as in Brazil, for example (Chapter 4), appointments are more usually arranged at short notice, or callers walk in without forewarning.

In contrast, to more northerly Asians (the Japanese, South Koreans and Taiwanese, for instance), Indonesians share a South Asian greater tolerance for the uncertainties of life. Indeed, Box 2.10 suggests that South Asians, the Filipinos, Malays, Chinese in Hong Kong and Singapore, and Indians, as well as Indonesians, are similar in this to the Scandinavians and Anglos on the other side of the world. Where the Indonesians are not similar is in their much more flexible, casual, less clock-bound **managing of time**, 'rubber time' as it has been called in nearby Malaya (see Box 2.12). They live at ease with the apparent uncertainties this creates inside and outside work. Finishing properly the niceties of a previous meeting, business or social, can be more important than cutting it short and hastening to keep a subsequent appointment to the minute. That is especially so if the first meeting is with persons of higher social standing. The person who is kept waiting will understand, and why should life be hurried?

As in the Islamic Middle East, no undue effort may be given to planning ahead. A somewhat fatalistic attitude to the long term means, for example, that while attention is paid to immediate industrial injuries little thought is given to future deterioration of eyes or lungs from poor working conditions, a failing shared with many other newly industrializing countries.

The Chinese Indonesians

When the word Indonesians has been used here it has implicitly meant the great bulk of the population who are racially of Malay extraction, and among them primarily the Javanese who predominate in the larger commercial and industrial organizations. But the economic prominence of the tiny minority of Indonesians of Chinese extraction has been pointed out.

They have been typified already in the section in this chapter on the Nanyang Chinese (see Box 7.11 The Nanyang Manager), which applies to 'overseas Chinese' everywhere in Asia, Indonesia included. They have brought to Indonesia over the centuries something of the so-called Confucian Dynamism that gives a capacity for frugal hard work, together with a patience to await its long-term fruits. They have a longer view of future time and a prompter use of present time.

Box 7.27 Javanese and Chinese Businesses in Indonesia

The market organisation of the Indonesian jamu (herbal medicine) industry corresponds, to a large extent, with the characteristics of Chinese family business systems . . . However, Javanese owners/managers express their social responsibility for highly dependent suppliers and customers by taking care of them in a (paternalistic) way . . . referred to as bapakism . . . In contrast, the Confucian-based paternalistic behaviour in the family business of the Overseas Chinese does not [go beyond] the borders of the firm.

(Rademakers, p. 1022)

Chinese and Javanese Indonesians share a similar paternalistic and collectivistic approach to life but, each to their own, as the British say. Box 7.27 describes how the family and friendship networks which link Nanyang Chinese family businesses with one another also limit their sense of responsibility, compared to a wider Javanese care for suppliers and customers, for example by sharing orders around in the far larger Javanese society.

   *   *   *

A particular combination of collectivism and competitiveness has played an influential part in the astounding Asian business success of recent times. It has demonstrated that a basis in 'harmony' can be as effective managerially as comparatively abrasive individualism was in much of the West. Not that Asians are all the same – far from it. This chapter has shown that the Chinese and Japanese each have distinctive ways of managing, for example.

Nevertheless, they are on the same side as the Arabs in the 'culture cake' because they have in common with the Middle Eastern peoples a respect for personal loyalties beyond the workplace. The Arab approach to management is very different in other ways, as soon becomes clear in the next chapter.

Further Reading

GENERAL

Harris, Philip R. and Robert T. Moran. 1991. *Managing Cultural Differences* (3rd edn, Ch. 15), Gulf Publishing.

Hofstede, Geert. 1991. *Cultures and Organizations: Software of the Mind*. McGraw-Hill.

Hofstede, Geert. 2001, 2nd edn. *Culture's Consequences: Comparing Values, Behaviors, Institutions and Organizations Across Nations*. Sage.

Hofstede, Geert and Michael Harris Bond. 1988. 'The Confucius Connection: from Cultural Roots to Economic Growth'. *Organizational Dynamics*, 16, 4, 4–21 (reproduced in P. Blunt and D. Richards (eds.), *Readings in Management, Organization and Culture in East and South-East Asia*. Northern Territory University Press, Australia, 1993).

Kao, Henry S. R., Durganand Sinha and Bernhard Wilpert (eds.). 1999. *Management and Cultural Values: the Indigenization of Organizations in Asia*. Sage.

Maruyama, Magoroh. 1984. 'Alternative Concepts of Management: Insights from Asia and Africa'. *Asia Pacific Journal of Management*, 1, 2, 100–11.

Redding, S. G., A. Norman and A. Schlander. 1994. 'The Nature of Individual Attachment to the Organization: a Review of East Asian Variations', Ch. 13 in Harry C. Triandis, Marvin D. Dunnette and Leatta M. Hough (eds.), *Handbook of Industrial and Organizational Psychology* (2nd edn, Vol. 4). Consulting Psychologists Press.

Whitley, Richard. 1992. *Business Systems in East Asia: Firms, Markets, and Societies*. Sage.

Wilkinson, Barry. 1994. *Labour and Industry in the Asia-Pacific*. De Gruyter.

CHINA

Chen, Min. 1995. *Asian Management Systems: Chinese, Japanese and Korean Styles of Business*. Routledge.

Child, John and Martin Lockett (eds.). 1990. 'Advances in Chinese Industrial Studies: Vol. 1 (Part A)' – *Reform Policy and the Chinese Enterprise*. JAI Press.

Child, John. 1994. *Management in China During the Age of Reform*. Cambridge University Press.

Jackson, Sukhan. 1992. *Chinese Enterprise Management Reforms in Economic Perspective*. De Gruyter.

Kelley, Lane and Oded Shenkar. 1993. *International Business in China*. Routledge.

Laaksonen, Oiva. 1988. *Management in China During and After Mao*. De Gruyter.

Wang, Yuan, Xin Sheng Zhang and Rob Goodfellow. 1998. *Business Culture in China*. Butterworth–Heinemann Asia.

(HONG KONG)

Redding, S. Gordon. 1990. *The Spirit of Chinese Capitalism*. De Gruyter.

JAPAN

Chen, Min. 1995. *Asian Management Systems: Chinese, Japanese and Korean Styles of Business*. Routledge.

McMillan, Charles J. 1985. *The Japanese Industrial System* (2nd edn). De Gruyter.

Moran, Robert T. 1985. *Getting Your Yen's Worth*. Gulf Publishing.

Ohmae, Kenichi. 1982. *The Mind of the Strategist* (Ch. 15). Penguin and McGraw-Hill.

Ouchi, William C. 1981. *Theory Z: How American Business Can Meet the Japanese Challenge*. Addison-Wesley.

Smith, Peter B. and Jyuji Misumi. 1994. 'Japanese Management – A Sun Rising in the West?', in Cary L. Cooper and Ivan T. Robertson (eds.), *Key Reviews in Managerial Psychology*. Wiley.

Taplin, Ruth. 1995. *Decision-Making and Japan: A Study of Corporate Japanese Decision-Making and its Relevance to Western Companies*. Japan Library.

Whitehill, Arthur M. 1991. *Japanese Management: Tradition and Transition*. Routledge.

Whitley, Richard. 1992. *Business Systems in East Asia: Firms, Markets, and Societies*. Sage.

Woronoff, Jon. 1991. *The 'No-Nonsense' Guide to Doing Business in Japan*. Macmillan.

SOUTH KOREA

Bello, Walden and Stephanie Rosenfeld. 1990. *Dragons in Distress: Asia's Miracle Economies in Crisis*. Penguin Books.

Chen, Min. 1995. *Asian Management Systems: Chinese, Japanese and Korean Styles of Business*. Routledge.

Chung, Kae H., Hak Chong Lee and Ku Hyun Jung. 1997. *Korean Management: Global Strategy and Cultural Transformation*. De Gruyter.

Janelli, Roger L. with Dawnhee Yim. 1993. *Making Capitalism: the Social and Cultural Construction of a South Korean Conglomerate*. Stanford University Press.

Song, Byung Nak. 1990. *The Rise of the Korean Economy*. Oxford University Press.

Whitley, Richard. 1992. *Business Systems in East Asia*. Sage.

INDONESIA

Hill, Hal (ed.). 1994. *Indonesia's New Order: The Dynamics of Socio-Economic Transformation.* University of Hawaii Press.

Morrison, Terri, Wayne A. Conaway and George A. Borden. 1994. *Kiss, Bow or Shake Hands: How to do Business in Sixty Countries.* Adams Media Corporation.

Munander, Ashar Sunyoto. 1995. 'Indonesian Managers Today and Tomorrow', in Henry S. R. Kao and Ng Sek-Hong (eds.), *Effective Organisations and Social Values.* Sage.

Rademakers, Martijn F. L. 1998. 'Market Organization in Indonesia: Javanese and Chinese Family Business in the Jamu Industry'. *Organization Studies*, 19,6, 1005–27.

Other Sources

GENERAL

Hamilton, Gary G. and Cheng-Shu Kao. 1987. 'Max Weber and the Analysis of East Asian Industrialization'. *International Sociology*, 2, 3, 289–300.

Weber, Max. 1930. *The Protestant Ethic and the Spirit of Capitalism.* Allen & Unwin (revised edn Peter Smith, 1984).

CHINA

Boisot, Max. 1996. 'Institutionalizing the Labour Theory of Value: Some Obstacles to the Reform of State-Owned Enterprises in China and Vietnam'. *Organization Studies*, 17, 6, 909–28.

Boisot, Max and John Child. 1996. 'From Fiefs to Clans and Network Capitalism: Explaining China's Emerging Economic Order'. *Administrative Science Quarterly*, 41, 600–28.

Derong, Chen and Guy Olivier Faure. 1995. 'When Chinese Companies Negotiate with their Government'. *Organization Studies*, 16, 1, 27–54.

Laaksonen, Oiva. 1984. 'The Managerial and Power Structure of Chinese Enterprises During and After the Cultural Revolution'. *Organization Studies*, 5, 1, 1–21.

Ng, S. H. and M. Warner. 1998. *China's Trade Unions and Management.* Macmillan.

Osigweh Yg, Chimezie A. B. and Y. Paul Huo. 1993. 'Conceptions of Employee Responsibilities and Rights in the United States and the People's Republic of China'. *International Journal of Human Resource Management*, 4, 1, 85–112.

Robinson, Joan. 1973. *Economic Management: China 1972.* Anglo-Chinese Educational Institute.

Shenkar, Oded. 1984. 'Is Bureaucracy Inevitable? The Chinese Experience'. *Organization Studies*, 5, 4, 289–306; together with: Clegg, S. R. and W. Higgins, 1987.

'Against the Current: Organizational Sociology and Socialism'. *Organization Studies*, 8, 3, especially 210–12.

Shenkar, O. 1989. 'The Chinese Case and the Radical School in Organization Studies'. *Organization Studies*, 10, 1, 117–22.

Westwood, Robert. 1997. 'Harmony and Patriarchy: the Cultural Basis for "Paternal Headship" Among the Overseas Chinese'. *Organization Studies*, 18, 3, 445–81.

(HONG KONG)

Ng, Sek-Hong. 1990. 'The Ethos of Chinese at Work: Collectivism or Individualism?', in J. Child and M. Lockett (eds.), Advances in Chinese Industrial Studies, Vol. 1 (Part A) – *Reform Policy and the Chinese Enterprise*. JAI Press.

Redding, Gordon and Gilbert Y. Y. Wong. 1986. 'The Psychology of Chinese Organizational Behaviour', pp. 267–95 in M. H. Bond (ed.), *The Psychology of the Chinese People*. Oxford University Press (Hong Kong).

JAPAN

Campbell, Nigel. 1994. 'The Role of Japan's Top Managers'. *Journal of General Management*, 20, 2, 20–28.

SOUTH KOREA

Dunung, Sanjyot, P. 1995. *Doing Business in Asia*. Lexington Books

Lee, Chang-Won. 1996. 'Referent Roles and Conflict Management styles: A Empirical Study with Korean Central Government Employees'. *Korean Review of Public Administration*, 1/1, 237–52.

McLeod, Ross H. and Ross Garnaut (eds.). 1998. *East Asia in Crisis: From Being a Miracle to Needing One?* Routledge.

Sommer, Steven M,. Seung-Hyan Bae, and Fred Luthans. 1996. *The Structure–Climate Relationships in Korean Organizations. Asia Pacific Journal of Management*, 12/2, 23–36

Whitehill, Arthur M. (ed.). 1987. *Doing Business in East Asia*. Croom Helm.

INDONESIA

Hofstede. Geert. 1982. *Cultural Pitfalls for Dutch Expatriates in Indonesia*. Twijnstra Gudde International b.v.

MacIntyre, Andrew. 1992. *Business and Politics in Indonesia*. Allen and Unwin.

Munander, Asher Sunyoto. 2000. 'Management in Indonesia', in M. Warner (ed.), *Regional Encyclopedia of Business and Management: Management in Asia Pacific*. Thomson.

Vroom, C. W. 1981. 'Indonesia and the West: An Essay on Cultural Differences in Organization and Management'. *Management and Usahawan Indonesia*, November–December, 25–31.

| # The Arabs of the Middle East

Highlighting
Saudi Arabia
Egypt

Arab lands and influence stretch right across North Africa to the Atlantic Ocean, claiming the entire southern shore of the Mediterranean Sea. They originated in – and for religious purposes still look to – the largely desert Arabia of the Middle East, from the River Nile and the Red Sea to the oil-fringed Gulf. This chapter focuses on that heartland.

At its centre is the desert bulk of Saudi Arabia (with a population of 20 million or so), ringed by Egypt (by far the most populous, approaching 70 million), Jordan (5 million), Lebanon (perhaps 4 million), Syria (16 million), Iraq (22 million), the tiny but rich Gulf States of Kuwait, Bahrein, Qatar and the United Arab Emirates (6 million altogether) and finally, at its southern extent, Oman (2 million) and Yemen (North and South, together about 16 million). This population is in total something like two-thirds of all the Arabs, though the exact numbers are unreliable, principally because it is a youthful, rapidly increasing population, so that figures quickly become out of date. Partly, too, this is because the figures can be inaccurate, and partly because people are on the move from labour-surplus poor States to labour-shortage rich States on the Gulf, in several of which the nationals have been greatly outnumbered by expatriates, especially by North Africans (including Egyptians), with Palestinians and Pakistanis as well as others from far-flung sources such as the Philippines.

The population is very unevenly distributed, hemmed by the deserts into coastal areas and along the rivers and their marshes and deltas: since there are few continuously flowing rivers, this generally means just three: the Nile in Egypt and the Euphrates and Tigris in Iraq. It could be said that oil flows more freely than water, at least in those States where the oil gushes, for, as population grows, finding enough water becomes a greater and greater problem.

THE INFLUENCES OF HISTORY

For thousands of years Arabia has contained nomadic Bedouin tribes roaming the deserts, as well as its ancient civilizations settled along the great rivers. The cultural influence of stern Bedouin tribal codes of loyalty and honour in a strongly patriarchal family system has been profound.

So, too, has been that of Islam, and far more conspicuously. Though centuries old, it is the most recent of humankind's major religions. The Prophet Muhammad was born in Mecca (also spelt Makkah), in what is now Saudi Arabia, in AD 570 and died there in 632. He began his religious revelations and mission in middle age. Islam, a word meaning 'peace found in submission to the will of God (Allah) and his law', therefore originated in settled trading communities near the Red Sea – Muhammad himself was a merchant – but spread into the desert as it succeeded in overcoming tribal divisions and tribal gods.

It gave an enormous impulse to everything Arab. In not much more than 100 years after the Prophet's death, zealous Arab armies with a new sense of common identity and purpose swept westwards as far as the Pyrenees mountains dividing Spain from France and attempted one foray deep into France itself. Eastwards and northwards, they reached what are now Afghanistan, Pakistan and adjacent republics of the one-time Soviet Union. They began the golden age of Islamic achievements in science, architectural design and mathematics (all humanity now counts in the decimal system of Arabic numerals). They created an extraordinary Islamic world, linked as no other has been by a single, highly definitive religion and a single 'high-context' language, Arabic, known for its out-standingly colourful, imaginative and idealistic character. Although there are significant Christian minorities in the Arab Middle East, it continues today to be overwhelmingly Muslim.

This Arab empire did not last as a political entity, any more than any other empire has done. The mainly twelfth-century Christian crusades to attempt to recapture 'the Holy Land', notably Jerusalem, expressed

European hostility. They overlapped with the intrusion of the Mongols from the opposite direction. The onrush of the Mongol conquerors carried them not only into eastern Europe and China (as mentioned in Chapters 6 and 7) but to Baghdad, which had become the largest city in the world, and in 1260 almost into Jerusalem and Egypt. Who knows how far they left an authoritarian imprint here, as they are said to have done elsewhere? Not long after, there followed 500 years of rule by the empire of the Ottoman Turk dynasty, which did not finally end until their defeat, allied to Germany, in the First World War. As the Ottomans had begun to weaken, the West, mainly France and Britain, had encroached, and so after 1918 it was the victorious Allies who arranged a somewhat artificial pattern of national boundaries for the peoples freed from Ottoman domination. In an area with no recollection of popular self-government, those in control ever since have based their rule on traditional respect for military power, rather than on multi-party voting.

Then came oil. Or, rather, since the oil had been there all along, there came the ubiquitous internal combustion engine. Suddenly, in the second half of the twentieth century, this caused the consumer wealth of populations far and wide who used cars and trucks and planes to cascade into a handful of Arabian States with tiny populations in a way unprecedented in human history. Suddenly they found that other nations, especially in Western Europe, had become dependent upon them and their oil-distorted economies.

FOUR INFLUENCES UPON ARAB MANAGEMENT

This curious history exerts four primary influences over Arabs in general and over Arab management. They are the Bedouin and wider tribal inheritance, Islam, foreign rule, and the oil-thirsty West.

The Bedouin tradition, which still carries a romantic image of the camel-mounted tribesman, impregnates Arab culture everywhere, as already mentioned, though it is strongest in and around the deserts. This is most visibly symbolized by the traditional costume worn by many city-dwelling politicians and businessmen. The tradition centres on a patriarchal family in which authority runs from father to eldest son and downwards, and also on the tribal sheikh. The authority of the sheikh was paramount but, significantly for future management ideals, it was seen as resting on tribal opinion.

Pride in the honour of each and the honour of all was supreme. Honour required generous hospitality to friend and to stranger. An affront to honour demanded revenge (often violent), and this was one reason why attitudes could swing quickly from friendship to hostility and back again. Shame in the eyes of others was to be avoided by almost any means.

Overall, this cultural heritage inclines to a style of organizing that has been called a 'Bedo-aucracy' or sometimes 'Sheikocracy' (Box 8.1). It inclines to top-down (if consultative) authority, and its members use it as much for their own interests and those of family and friends as to pursue impersonal organizational goals. In societies where consideration for others, and personal considerations, are highly valued, it can be both strange and a strain to be expected to give undivided commitment to abstractions such as goals and projects.

Box 8.1 Bedo-aucracy

Just as it was natural for Max Weber, the German sociologist who expounded the nature of bureaucracy as a form of organization, to discover bureaucracy . . . so it was for Arab students of public administration to discover 'bedo-aucracy'. [they] . . . developed the theme that Arabia is a traditional society. Despite the introduction of modern organizations and methods, administrative behavior is still highly traditional.

(Kassem and Habib, p. 16)

With the coming of the Prophet Muhammad, Islam enhanced the Arab tradition, making moral guidance more explicit in the Quran and in the Shari'a law accompanying it. Nowhere else in writings on management is there such a recurring exposition of an ethical framework for business and administration. In the predominantly Judaeo-Christian West there are periodic spasms of concern about the ethics of management, which could be seen cynically as passing fashions; but within the Islamic world a more overt awareness has always been with the devout and the secular alike. Maltreatment of employees, for example, is likely to be regarded as sinful rather than only bad practice. Whilst the Arab nations differ in how far they are specifically constituted on a religious basis (Egypt, for instance, is formally constituted as a secular State, in contrast to Saudi Arabia, which takes the Quran to be its constitution), the realm of Islam does not separate religion and State in the way that the West has come to do.

Islam takes up the consultative aspect of authority in the tribal tradition. Wise consultation by those in authority (as distinct from 'power sharing') and obedience to a responsively wielded authority are both stressed (Box 8.2).

Whilst successful and profitable business is encouraged, provided it is not seen as exploitative nor harmful to society, there are some particular limits on what business should do; there should be no trade in intoxicants, wine, blood or dead animals, idols or statues, for example. Most intriguing to non-Muslims, there should be no usury (a doctrine which Christianity once shared). *Usury* is prohibited in so far as charging for the loan of money is regarded as potentially exploiting those who borrow it if a fixed price is exacted from them, irrespective of their circumstances – that is, fixed interest.

This does not prohibit the sharing of profits (or losses), of course. Hence depositors in a bank run on Islamic principles do not expect or receive a fixed return; rather, they expect a share of the profit which the

---

Box 8.2 An Islamic View of Authority

The objectives of leadership in Islam are the application of the Sheri'ah and the creation of an atmosphere conducive to generating the prerequisites for the Islamic Order. This sublime goal should be the objective of the Muslim leader if he is to enjoy the support, obedience, and loyalty of the group . . .

[and]

The Quran emphatically orders the Prophet in this way:

> 'It was by the mercy of Allah that thou wast lenient with
> them (O Muhammad), for if thou hadst been stern
> and fierce of heart they would have dispersed from round
> about thee. So pardon them and ask forgiveness for
> them and consult with them upon the conduct of affairs.
> And when thou art resolved, then put thy trust in Allah.'

(Quran, III. 159)

(Al-Buraey, pp. 347 and 348)

bank makes by lending the money (or a proportionate reduction in their funds if there is a loss). In turn, the bank does this on the same terms. It lends money to business on 'PLS', a profit-and-loss-sharing basis. Justice is in the sharing of risk and the fair division of gains and losses, as against the borrower bearing the primary burden.

Therefore Islamic banks have less risk in total because they do not have large fixed interest obligations, and because their depositors share the risk. This has two effects: first, banks can lend a greater proportion of their reserves; secondly, they can take more commercial risks by becoming comparatively closely involved with their borrowers' businesses. Since they and their depositors have a direct stake in the profit or loss, they have an immediate interest in how those businesses are managed.

Conversely, firms which are financed by numbers of short-term PLS loans, some of them direct as well as via banks, in addition to equity capital, assume bank-like functions. They may have a special accounting department to accept loans and administer numerous calculations of payments and repayments.

The difference between what banks do and what other business organiz-ations do therefore becomes less sharp in an Islamic system than other-wise. They overlap. Further, such banks may lend capital long term, and indeed set up other businesses of their own. They also actually buy goods on behalf of clients, who pay a mark-up for the service and in return get two benefits: better deals obtained by the bank as a more powerful buyer, and the paperwork done for them. More details of this kind of bank as well as of a retail firm are in Box 8.21.

Islam also promotes *Zakat*, either a specific tax by the State in the more constitutionally Islamic nations, or a voluntary set-aside contribution by firms and by individual citizens, for religious, medical and general charitable purposes.

This unique financial system is compatible with either private or State ownership of business organizations. However, it is not universal. Its extent varies from State to State. Again as a contrast, Saudi Arabia operates wholly on Islamic law and in principle does not approve fixed-interest charges even by foreign banks with branches there, whereas Egypt allows a mixture of domestic and externally based Islamic banks, and non-Islamic banks, all of which conduct their affairs in their differing ways.

Nor do all firms choose to abide by full Islamic principles, of course, and that is not the intended implication here. Furthermore, these principles are ideals and Arabs are idealists. Not all Muslims live up to ideals – and not all Arabs are devout Muslims. Furthermore, things do not always work out as intended, any more than in the rest of the world. Corruption and bribery take their toll to a degree not unconnected with centuries of extraneous rule when the aim was to cheat the system.

This prolonged foreign rule is the third influence upon what happens nowadays. Whereas south-eastern Europe was colonized by the Ottoman Turks, and Asia, Africa and South America by Europeans, the Arabs had both, though the Europeans held sway comparatively briefly and usually not by full colonization. The centuries of Ottoman rule demanded obedience to absolute authority, instilling not only corruption as a means of survival but also outward submissiveness, though local ways of life were left undisturbed.

Fourthly, the impact of the West may well be less from its former imperialism than in the consequences of its demand for oil and of its models of management. As in so much of the world, the struggle to reconcile these models of specialist departmentalization, forward planning, smooth information-flow, impersonal control systems and committed human resources, with traditional ways, and in the Middle East with Islamic codes, is acute. For oil wealth has forced the pace of change, especially in the oil-rich States, but also spreading out from these, so that modern forms of organization were erected almost before they could be managed, and expatriate managers had to be brought in.

So history has bequeathed a people proud of their heritage, but a society pulled in different directions (Box 8.3).

MANAGING UPWARDS AND DOWNWARDS

If Arab culture can be said to have an abiding duality, then Arab management has many paradoxes. Two fundamental paradoxes are already apparent in this chapter.

They run right through **managing authority** and **managing relationships**. First, Arabs are disposed to handle authority centrally with high power distance (see Chapter 2), yet at the same time they aspire to an 'open door' for all comers, high or low, and to consultation (Box 8.2) in the manner of the sheikhs. Secondly, they pursue their own individual

Box 8.3 Arab Duality

. . . the Arab individual is suffering, in general, from a problem of duality in thinking and practice . . . [the Arab] takes pride in front of strangers in being liberal and not religious, but manifests a traditional attitude in front of others and recites verses from the Quran or the Prophet's sayings . . . Likewise, the Arabs display an infatuation with ideal forms, even when they know these forms to be contradicted by reality. To Western observers, it is incomprehensible, but for the Arab it is a normal way of life. The simultaneously contradictory patterns of behaviour Arab individuals display (love–hate, pride–self condemnation, individualism–conformism, friendship–hostility) are judged in the Arab environment as natural and healthy.

. . . the influence of these forces is exemplified by (1) establishing a huge number of administrative laws and regulations while no attempt is made to implement them – they are just signs of modernity; (2) designing systems for selection and promotion according to qualification and merit, but hiring and rewarding according to social ties and personal relations; (3) setting up organizational structures and designs that remain as decoration, while abiding by them only on an exceptional basis.

(Ali, pp. 20–21)

interests, yet do so by collectivistic means through personal relationships.

Great prestige attaches to positions at the pinnacle of organization, which wield great authority. This authority, as this chapter has shown, is exercised as a personal property, even paternalistically, intuitively as much as by detached assessment. The power to decide is centralized and rarely delegated. Since organizations are open to personal feelings and obligations, those in authority can readily shape them by creating posts and departments to suit whomever they esteem. From one point of view this is flexibility, from another it may be playing favourites. Box 8.4 gives two examples from Jordan.

As these examples imply, the opportunities for lower-level managers to bear responsibility and use initiative can be restricted. So too can the opportunities for those at the top to appreciate what is happening below. And in as much as both those below and those above have a personalized concept of power, failures are blamed on the head of the organization

---

Box 8.4 Banking on Organization

Interviews with Arab managers in Jordanian, other Arab, and Western banks in Jordan elicited the following experiences:

Autonomy at . . . bank [Western] was very strong. At the moment you join the bank they make you feel that you are important, that you are able to make decisions, that you should not fear making decisions. Of course they give you the proper training and the proper example, they make collective decisions, and if you make a mistake, but not serious, they try to help you. From the first moment they let you feel that you are a responsible person, an officer of the bank who makes decisions, who supposes to lead not to be led. At Arab banks, it is the other way around, you do not do anything without referring to the boss, even as a manager, even if you are senior. It is highly centralized, no set up, autonomy is very minimal and they [senior top-level management] do not give you the benefit of having confidence, and if you make a mistake it is against you.

And from a second manager:

In foreign [Western] banks, the structure is stable and the chart is fixed based on the requirements of the job, and they fill positions in the organization chart according to each job requirement. In Arab banks, the organization chart is made to fit people and usually changes. It is easier with foreign banks, you know where they are going, it is more relating to your job and what is expected from you in the job and what is next. In Arab organizations, no, you come to work in darkness, despite the organization chart. Because you know it is there to be changed again and again. So it is really not important, but it is not clear for you where you are going. You might be somewhere on the organization chart, and then all of a sudden they change it and you end somewhere else.

(from Rasheed pp. 506 and 510)

---

personally and the solution is seen in his removal as much as in an analysis of what is wrong.

With Quranic encouragement, managers aspire to overcome the problem, as Box 8.5 shows. It gives what executives believe they would do when taking a decision. Of course, what people say they would do when they are reflectively weighing up a hypothetical situation and what they would actually do under the circumstances and pressures of the moment are not necessarily the same. Even if there is consultation, it may not range far and, as everywhere, committees may be mere 'talking shops'.

Nevertheless, the emphasis on consultation by these executives is striking and it does indicate their inclination and the reality of the 'open door' tradition.

Remarkably, the book from which the material in Box 8.5 is taken itself symbolizes the Arab sense of personal obligation and of drawing status from personal connections. It is the only research publication recalled by

---

Box 8.5 Consultation Aspiration

Fifty-two Arab executives were interviewed from organizations of different sizes. These were engaged in a variety of services and manufacturing, in three non-oil-exporting countries (Egypt, Jordan and Lebanon), and three oil-exporting countries (Kuwait, Saudi Arabia and the United Arab Emirates).

The executives were asked what they would 'normally' do if making decisions to promote, discipline or terminate the services of an employee supervised by one of their own subordinates, or increase or reorganize the workforce under that subordinate; or to reduce the total workforce by 20 per cent; or to introduce a new product or project or enter a new market (seven decisions in all). Would they (1) make the decision without consultation; (2) consult subordinate(s); (3) analyse the problem together with subordinate(s) who have 'as much influence as you have on the final decision'; (4) 'ask subordinate(s) to make the decision on his/their own'?

They answered:

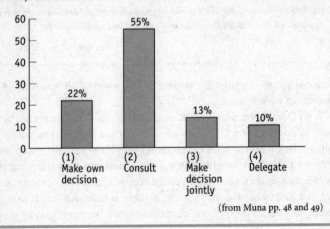

(from Muna pp. 48 and 49)

the authors of this book that lists in its opening Acknowledgements the full names of all the executives who were interviewed (except for thirteen who did not consent to be named). This contrasts with the universal practice established by Anglo writers of impersonally preserving the anonymity and confidentiality of research subjects.

Returning to the authority to make decisions, in the Middle East as everywhere, a centrally planned economy and state ownership of organizations each raise the level at which decisions can be taken. The autonomy of each management is reduced, and those decisions which are permitted to them become more centralized within each organization (Box 8.6).

On the other hand, those higher up can be accessible through their 'open door'. Executives are on call from those closer to them among employees, clients or government officials, not only at work but even at home and over the weekend, because these are not just employees, clients and officials, but persons with whom there is a relationship. Conversely, friends and family members can drop in at the office for chats over coffee. Even overburdened contemporary executives can find it difficult not to live up to the ancient norm of hospitality in this respect.

Box 8.6 The State and Managerial Decision Making

Using the method of measuring centralization described in Box 9.15 on India, Egyptian and British researchers Mohamed Badran and Bob Hinings showed that in thirty-one (mostly manufacturing) organizations in Egypt, ownership by the State limited the decisions their management could take, and centralized them. Comparing Poland at a time when both it and Egypt had planned economies (see again Box 9.15, on Poland), they wrote:

In Egypt and Poland with their planned economies, almost all decisions are approved at a very high level in the organization. It is only decisions that can be clearly seen as having no policy connotations that are decentralized below departmental heads.

(Badran and Hinings p. 15)

Conversation builds relationships. Managers rely on informal means to get things done. As they are using a high context language (see Chapter 2), their meaning is dependent very much on when, where and how it is spoken, with 'body language' in expression and posture. Arabic has been said to be a language of persuasion rather than of cold reasoning, a language of the moment, where what is said for effect may not apply subsequently in other settings.

When people first meet, identities are conveyed in the manner typical of traditional developing societies, as indicated in Box 8.7. Where action may depend on personal ties, trust and loyalty are vital (Box 8.8). With business affairs and personal life interwoven, managers do what they can to care for those they know and to help them with their personal problems. Loyalty is more precious than cold, hard efficiency (Box 8.9). The result can be comparatively high levels of staffing, and such Western management devices as job descriptions, personnel appraisals and manpower planning are not found necessary. The way in which expatriate Westerners tend to treat their Arab subordinates is seen by comparison as ruthless and inhumane, betraying a harsh 'business is business' approach.

Box 8.7 Introductions

It is interesting . . . that when Arabs meet their countrymen for the first time, they usually attempt to establish each other's family identity. In the West, on the other hand, it appears that the initial conversation revolves around a person's occupation or profession. In Japan, introductions are made with reference to one's organization or company.

(Muna, p. 36)

Box 8.8 Who to Trust

Another manager among those interviewed as described in Box 8.4 said: *In local banks there could be trust but it is a personal matter, not a procedural one. There are no procedures. The teamwork is not there. The manager in an Arab organization relies on 'watch dogs' everywhere in order to bring him information. While at the Western bank you can manage a big institution by basically having openness.*

(Rasheed, p. 510)

Box 8.9 Loyalty above Efficiency

Executives were asked in the research described in Box 8.5: 'The ideal employee would be, among other things, both loyal and efficient. But unfortunately this does not always occur. In such cases, would you prefer your immediate subordinate to be (a) more loyal to you, or (b) more efficient in his work?'

The executives replied:

● Prefer loyalty: 37 (71 per cent)
● Prefer efficiency: 15 (29 per cent)

(Muna, p. 79)

Whereas in the Western management model the aim is to fit the right person into the rightly designed job, Arab management is more concerned with finding a job for a highly regarded individual. So job titles may have little to do with functions.

Some advice to foreigners, especially Westerners, in the Middle East appears in Box 8.10.

MANAGING THE UNCERTAIN FUTURE

The advice to clock-watching foreigners is to be 'flexible with time'. Arabs do not see time and events in the same way as do Americans (the most obvious comparison), to whom the future should be as plannable and controllable as possible. In the Middle East, time is not a containable quantity that can be controlled in detail. It has long been debated to what extent there may be implicit in Islam an assumption that the future is best left to Allah, which, unawares (as core culture is unawares to those whose culture it is), colours the outlook of managers. How far this may be so for the contemporary (Western) educated Arab manager is a moot point. If there is less explicit managerial planning for the future than the precepts of Western-type management education urge, then may this not be due as much or more to political and economic instability, which renders it superfluous, as to latent fatalism? Nor are Arab organizations

Box 8.10 Advice to Outsiders

Guidelines for Managing Business Negotiations in the Middle East:

● *Do not rush to the heart of the problem at the first meeting, try to strengthen your social relationship first, sometimes you must meet your counterpart several times before you talk business.*

● *In this part of the world space and sitting position have important meaning: people breathe on each other, and sitting close to the other party is a sign of personal closeness and a friendly manner.*

● *Do not get confused by other people interrupting, it is an inevitable element of the Middle Eastern business culture.*

● *Be flexible with time. Time in the Middle East means something different, to be late for 20–30 minutes is usual, do not get upset, and be patient.*

● *In this part of the world 'a man's word is his bond', avoid giving a [verbal] promise unless you are sure of its implications.*

● *Finally, once you reach agreement, your counterpart may kiss you! Do not be afraid, this is a sign of friendship and brotherhood.*

(selected from recommendations by Hossein Dadfar
of the Department of Management, Linköping University, Sweden)

Box 8.11 How Long is the Arab Manager's Future?

The same executives as in Box 8.5, when asked about payback on capital investment, corporate planning and management development, mostly said they took a three-to-five-year view.

(Muna, p. 92)

the only ones worldwide which do not conform to such precepts. Moreover, executives do claim to take some view of the future (Box 8.11).

Yet in **managing time**, the clock is valued less than other, more human, considerations. We have seen how social obligations often take precedence – which means that honouring such obligations may throw out the timetable of a senior manager who is already overloaded with matters referred upwards. So at the top, appointments may not be kept. Lower down, there may be tardiness and absenteeism. Moreover, time can be expended over business negotiations in a way that exasperates those to whom the clock is more important, as is shown by the experience of the European businessmen described in Box 8.12.

Box 8.12 The Englishman, the Frenchman, the German, the Italian – and the Egyptians

The Englishman, the Frenchman, the German and the Italian sweated in the sticky heat of Cairo. They had come to compete on behalf of their companies for an order for catering equipment from the Egyptian Ministry of Defence. They sat in an ante-room of the ministry, each waiting to deliver his company's tender and negotiate possible details. They had arrived punctually, and were uncomfortable not only in the heat but at being kept waiting, and in each other's presence at that. They eyed one another uneasily.

One by one they were called in to sit before a row of beribboned officers. They were asked for their credentials, which were scrutinized officiously, and told to return in four days' time. Each felt irritated. Though cheered by the prospect of an unexpected holiday viewing Egypt's historical treasures, each was frustrated by the delay. They could see no reason for it. Indeed, they had expected to walk in and present their tenders there and then, at the first meeting. They were being trifled with, they felt.

They met again four days later, fresh from the pyramids and bazaars. This time they did present their tenders, but these were just brusquely taken without discussion and they were asked to return at the end of the week. They had expected full discussion of what the ministry wanted and what their companies could do. They felt affronted. Indeed they began to suspect, from what they took to be hints, that the ministry was changing what it wanted without informing them.

The Englishman, the Frenchman and the German became furious. They had already spent a whole week getting nowhere, and the only prospect was more wasted days and another inconclusive meeting. Making it clear that their offers stood, take it or leave it, they left Cairo and returned home.

The Italian realized that he had the field to himself. He was beginning to comprehend the Arab way of going about things, move by move testing commitment and building a personal relationship. It was not so different from what he took for granted in Italy, with its manoeuvrings and political shrewdness. He began to think, too, that it would not be a bad idea to invite the Egyptian officials to Italy, to be entertained by his company, as the next step in the negotiations. There was no need to be hasty about actually concluding the deal. The formalities of the contract would be just the final stage in the process.

(from the experience of a business contact of the authors)

If the view of the future that may be inherent in Islam is much debated, so too the influence of its framework of rules for living is debatable. Does a deep sense of living within divinely inspired regulation inspire caution, a feeling that, if the right way of following the rules can be found, all will be well? There are signs of a preference for structured situations, and of the false formalism alluded to in Example 8.3 which uses rules to shelter the individual from having to take responsibility. At a more strategic level, managements in the oil states are seen by one researcher, at any rate, to be cautious rather than venturesome in their strategic outlook (Box 8.13).

Box 8.13 Strategic Caution

After interviewing the 'top management' of a total of eighteen banks, airlines, hospitals, hotels, consulting and computer software firms, and a private school, and forty-nine family-owned firms, in the Gulf States, Kassem (together with his Arab students) classified about two-thirds as 'reactive' or 'defensive' in strategy. Those that were 'innovators' were usually *long-established, medium-sized, single-business entrepreneurial firms operating . . . with the help of a foreign partner who provides the management know how.* However, Kassem stresses that strategies change, and that more firms seemed to have been 'proactive' in an earlier phase of the economic cycle.

(summarized from Kassem and Habib pp. 116–181)

On the other hand, here are people grappling with the management of oil-wells and petrochemical plants, airlines and financial institutions, where not so long ago there were none of these and, in some States, just fishing villages and desert nomads. They have had to cope with a phenomenal pace of change.

Paradoxically, then, individuals working in centralized organizations which breed an avoidance of responsibility by shifting problems upwards, and who shelter behind the rules when it suits, try also to move things along through informal personal relations and retaining their own scope for manoeuvre. Paradoxically again, that same scope which is maintained by a less than specific definition of posts and a less than complete specialization (akin in this to the Japanese approach more than the Western) is accompanied by a high regard for the foreign specialist 'expert'.

Box 8.14 An Arab on Arab Management

The Arab culture has certain distinctive characteristics which dominate managerial thinking and behaviour. The author's experience as an Arab himself, working in an Arab culture, together with the literature and his own research, all suggest the following observations about the distinctive nature of Arab management:

- Within an organization, status, position and seniority significantly outweigh ability and performance in importance.
- Organizations are centrally controlled with a low level of delegation.
- Subordinates act with deference and obedience in the formal hierarchy of authority.
- Authoritarian management style is predominant.
- Decision-making is constantly pushed upwards in the organization.
- Most decisions and commitments are renegotiable at a later time.
- The decision-making process is influenced by the prevalence of paternalistic and familial patterns. There is an absence of Western-style democratic systems.
- Consultative styles of decision-making are pervasive and dominant. This consultation is usually carried out on a person-to-person basis, thus avoiding group meetings. Moreover, decisions are often made in an informal and unstructured manner.
- Management is reactive and crisis-orientated.
- Organization members are motivated by affiliation and power needs rather than by performance objectives.
- Social formalities are extremely important.
- Innovation and risk-taking are activities which seem to be more often punished than rewarded.
- A low-trust atmosphere and political gamesmanship characterize organizations, together with closed information systems and low levels of disclosure to organization members.
- Constant change and high levels of uncertainty at work.
- There is little opposition and resistance from subordinates.
- There is a strong preference for a person-orientated approach rather than a task-orientated approach in managerial activities.
- In group affiliation and group interaction, kinship ties are important.
- Nepotism is regarded as natural and acceptable. Arab managers view their organizations as family units and often assume a paternal role in them. They value loyalty over efficiency.

- There is a strong adherence to the open-door tradition. It is an integral part of the 'undwritten' or 'informal' organizational structure.
- Punctuality and time constraints are of much less concern than in Western cultures.
- Managers rely upon family and friendship ties for getting things done within an organization and in society in general.

(from Al-Faleh, pp. 20 and 21)

An encompassing verbal portrait of Arab management by an Arab writer is reproduced in Box 8.14. Has it something of caricature as well as portraiture?

However that may be, the few writings in Arabic on Arab management accord closely with the much greater volume written in English, though that itself is sparse relative to what is available on management in Western societies or in Japan. Box 8.15 summarizes a summary of what could be found in Arabic, together with that author's warnings against an over-cultural explanation.

Box 8.15 Arabs on Arab Management, in Arabic

Attiyah summarizes in English the findings of research which at or just before his review in 1992 had been published in Arabic and were not available in English. Management was found to be formalistic, especially in State organizations with 'excessive emphasis on control and compliance with rules and regulations'. Planning was minimal. An authoritarian style was commonplace, together with a personalistic handling of decisions relying on personal judgement.

Attiyah warns against attributing too much to an Islamic culture. Lack of planning could instead be due to a shortage of planning specialists and of usable data. The combination of both authoritarian and consultative styles alternately may be due to switching from one to the other to suit different situations.

(summarized from Attiyah,)

The puzzlement of non-Arabs is well illustrated by the experience of an expatriate described in Box 8.16. This also shows that those to whom this style of management 'comes naturally' can handle it well.

Box 8.16 Expatriate Bewilderment

[An] expatriate who joined a large Arab organization at the vice-presidential level described his initial experience as follows:

After the first three months I was convinced that the company was run in the most chaotic way imaginable; nothing like I ever experienced in my twenty years of work experience in the United States. But now, after nine months, I must admit these fellows are sharp, shrewd, and efficient . . . What they have is organized chaos and if you can adjust to that, it's a great place to work.

(Muna, p. 84)

Two illustrative nations have already been mentioned more than once in this chapter because they make such an informative contrast. The one is the largest in area, the other in population; one is an Islamic kingdom and guardian of the Muslim holy places, the other a republic; the one originates in desert tribal society, the other in an ancient riverside civilization; the one is oil-rich, the other is not. They are:

Saudi Arabia

and Egypt.

SAUDI ARABIAN CULTURE AND MANAGEMENT

This desert State, which has no permanently flowing streams or rivers, is constructed around a family, a religion, and an oil company.

Saudi Arabia takes its name from its royal family, the Al-Sauds. It is a hereditary monarchy in which the king is prime minister and the crown prince is first deputy prime minister, and members of the extensive royal family dominate public appointments. Family connections, royal or otherwise, are crucial throughout society, though not to the exclusion of merit and competence which can be found from among the numerous members of large and widespread kinship networks. Although Saudi Arabia is an independent State originating no longer ago than the aftermath of the First World War and the demise of the Ottoman empire, the age-old Bedouin tribal loyalties to family and sheikh are clearly continued in the way it is constituted. Politically it has been notably stable.

Islam was born here, and it was from here that Islamic Arabia erupted in the seventh century, to spread so far and so wide west and east. The Ka'aba shrine in the city of Mecca, towards which the faithful pray five times each day, and the city of Medina, where the Prophet Muhammad established the new faith whilst exiled from his home town, are near the Saudi Red Sea coast. Not surprisingly, therefore, Saudi Arabia has no constitution other than the Quran, and Islamic Shari'a law is fully observed. Work stops everywhere and shops cease trading at least three times in the working day for orthodox Muslims to pray at their place of work (the two other times of prayer are likely to occur outside working hours). Most are Sunni in allegiance, a minority Shia. There are no churches, synagogues, temples or shrines of any other religions, and no proselytizing is permitted.

The third element after the royal family and Islam is the Aramco oil company. Managed at one time by a consortium of American oil companies, Aramco is now State owned. It is responsible for virtually all oil production, the largest single supplier to the Western world. Beneath the sands and seas of Saudi Arabia lie perhaps a quarter of the world's proven oil reserves, and substantial natural gas and precious metals. More than any other institution, Aramco has been responsible for change in Saudi Arabia. Its revenues have paid for a modern infrastructure and modern cities, to transform society from a tribal, semi-nomadic way of life in less than half a century. Employment by Aramco has created a sub-culture of Aramco personnel living in company housing or in their own homes around company installations.

Many of the company's employees are expatriates. At a managerial level they support Saudi Arabian managers by what might be termed a 'shadow structure' of deputies and specialists (a personal experience of this is reported in Box 8.17).

As with the other Arab Gulf States, Saudi Arabia is in exactly the reverse situation to the usual predicament of developing countries. Usually such countries have many people but little money. Saudi Arabia has untold oil wealth, but few people. Hence the need for expatriates both to provide labour in less skilled jobs and to provide managerial expertise – though, in that respect, the situation is changing to a glut of over-qualified Saudi graduates who are unwilling to take on what in their eyes are jobs beneath their competence.

Box 8.17 Inside Aramco

During the 1980s a Briton, William Mullens, worked in Aramco for four years, the last two in what he calls the 'shadow structure' as a staff adviser to a Saudi General Manager. This General Manager had an expatriate staff group of five. Beneath him were department managers, each having an expatriate business analyst; beneath them division heads, each having an expatriate planning analyst; and beneath them section-heads, most of whom were expatriates.

Expatriates were treated in accordance with their grade and position. For instance, they were expected to make appointments in advance to see senior Saudi managers, whereas Saudi employees were treated on a more personal basis, and older Saudis especially would be seen automatically out of respect for age if they called in or, even if doing a low-grade job, they had a grievance.

(summarized from Mullens, pp. 86–8)

It is questionable whether Saudi Arabia can still be referred to as a developing country, given its advanced roads, air transport, medical and educational provision, and cities. Yet it has a one-sided economy, trying to find the best balance between investment of oil revenues at home in expensive agricultural irrigation and diversifying industries, and investment abroad. A symptom of its one-sidedness is that it has one of the world's highest import bills per head of population.

Not everything is oil extraction and refining. In addition to petrochemicals of many kinds, there is some manufacture of textiles, paper products, pottery, building materials, metal items, etc. Few of the manufacturing companies have limited liability and few are public companies. Control usually remains with a family or is shared with a foreign joint-venture partner. There are also numerous small family-owned trading businesses. The State plays the leading role, another symbol of this, in addition to Aramco, being its ownership of Saudi Arabian Airlines. Though Saudi Arabia is small in population, this is one of the world's largest airlines, and it dominates among Arab carriers. More than half its personnel are now Saudis.

The abrupt arrival of Western forms of organization, from Aramco onwards, pitched Saudi Arabians into trying to comprehend and work with Western management models, in a society which aims to sustain traditional ways, as befits the cradle of Islam. There is no evidence that in this they differ in any particular respect from the raw stereotype of Arab management shown in Box 8.14. That does not mean that all Saudi managers do everything listed there all the time, but that enough appear to do so enough of the time for that stereotype to be a useful start to understanding, together with the broad picture of the Arab approach drawn in this Chapter so far.

It suggests a tendency for managers to be cautious, to be reactive, not to act until a crisis looms, not to encourage independent initiative. Other personal experiences of the author cited in Box 8.17 bore this out in Aramco, and it has also seemed to be so across the middle levels of the hierarchy in government ministries (Box 8.18).

Box 8.18 Avoiding Uncertainty

Three hundred questionnaires were completed by 'middle range bureaucrats in the ministries of agriculture, education, finance, petroleum, social welfare, information, health and municipal affairs' in Saudi Arabia. Asked how they saw their fellow officials, they saw them as conservative and protecting good relationships. 'Few . . . were perceived as looking for new ideas, and an even smaller number were perceived as willing to take risks. The prevailing concerns appeared to be the avoidance of conflict and the maintenance of job security.'

For example, in answer to a question about how far 'Saudi bureaucrats are receptive to new ideas',

    12 respondents said 'all of them'
    70 said 'most of them'
    181 said 'few of them'
    and 16 said 'none of them'
    (making a total of 279 replies to that particular question).

In general, Saudi bureaucrats 'process routine paperwork, avoiding decisions or policies that might rock the boat or cause them undue stress . . . Risk-taking, to the extent that it occurs, is a function of the endless succession of committees that characterizes the Saudi bureaucracy.'

(Al-Nimir and Palmer pp. 95/96 and 101)

Again, Saudis share the tendency to the centralized, even authoritarian, use of authority which draws decision-making upwards; but here again this is ameliorated by the emphasis put upon consultation as desirable and laudable. As elsewhere in Arabia the open-door tradition is still valued.

Relationships are comparatively personalistic, managers relying on personal connections to get things done and giving preference to those they know, as Box 8.19 says and as was experienced by the expatriates in Aramco (Box 8.17). Knowing the right people, or knowing people who know the right people, whilst helpful everywhere in the world, is here vital to successful business. Especially, time must be spent in personally negotiating and bargaining over any commercial deal.

Box 8.19 Practising Personalism

Comparing Saudi Arabian with American 'governmental and business managers', researchers found that the Saudis were, predictably, more likely to depart from the rules for personal reasons, and more inclined to use criteria other than merit in making personnel-type decisions. Saudi officials in ministries were even more so inclined than were the Saudis working in business where, it was suggested, commercial pressures forced a more impersonal (Western) approach.

These findings came from 201 questionnaires completed by Saudis, 153 in the ministries of agriculture, health, finance, posts and telecommunication, and education, and 48 in firms in agricultural products, basic industries, real estate, and hospital, resort and financial services; and from 44 questionnaires completed by Americans.

(Al-Aiban and Pearce)

The dedication to a book which is reproduced in Box 8.20, unusual though it is, conveys much that is distinctively Saudi Arabian. Through it run Islamic commitment, loyalty to and adulation of the leader as in the Bedouin tradition, and Arab idealism. The cultures of societies are inherent in their languages and, though this dedication was written in English, the English language must surely be inadequate here for a style and a content better suited to Arabic which is more elaborate, more emotive and more flattering.

Box 8.20 Saudi Dedication

The dedication of the book *Modernity and Tradition: the Saudi Equation* (1990) by Fouad Al-Farsey, on the economic and social development of the kingdom, is reproduced here. The author was Deputy Minister of Information, and the book was supported by the Ministry.

In the Name of Allah, the Compassionate, the Merciful

DEDICATION

To King Fahd bin Abdul Aziz Al Sa'ud, the patron of the Saudi revival and leader of the Kingdom's progress and development.

If a man (whether he be a national leader, a military commander, a social reformer, or a scientific researcher) performed a single act in the national interest which secured the defence of his homeland, or assured for his country a prominent place amongst the nations of the world, or improved living conditions for the citizens, or ensured the prosperity of his people, or established security, stability and social justice, then such a man would, from the national viewpoint, deserve for this single act the highest degree of admiration and respect.

What then would history say of a man who has achieved all this for his country, many times over!

Any attempt to comprehend the scope and scale of the achievements of King Fahd bin Abdul Aziz can be only partially successful, for his unique personality and outstanding abilities are not limited to the material benefits he has brought to the Kingdom of Saudi Arabia, but extend to issues of morality and humanity in the world at large. King Fahd has been recognized as a 'powerful statesman, skilful, talented and experienced politician; leader of his country's march to development; a powerful voice for Arab and Islamic solidarity; and a moderate international politician who works tirelessly to achieve peace based upon justice for all nations'.

This book is dedicated with the deepest respect, appreciation and gratitude to the Custodian of the two Holy Mosques, King Fahd bin Abdul Aziz. His acceptance of this dedication will do me the greatest honour, for this modest book is but one of the fruits of his flourishing and auspicious reign.

(Fouad Al-Farsey)

EGYPTIAN CULTURE AND MANAGEMENT

Egypt is a nation created by a river. Its ancient civilization, symbolized to the rest of the world by its pyramids and almost legendary pharaohs, grew up along the River Nile. The relatively narrow settled and cultivated strip on either side of the river and in its delta is still only a tiny fraction of the total area bounded by the Egyptian State. Most is desert.

For over two millennia, following the passing of the pharaohs, the Egyptians were subjected to foreign rulers, among whom were the Persians, Greeks, Romans, the Byzantine empire and the Ottoman Turks. Not until recently, after the Second World War, did they regain full independence. They did not regain their own historic language, long overtaken by the Arabic brought by the Islamic Arab conquerors.

Unlike Saudi Arabia in its present constitution as well as in origin and history, Egypt is not an Islamic-based monarchy but a secular republic, though Islam is the State religion and nine-tenths of the people are Sunni Muslims. The remainder are mainly Christian. The Egyptian's ethnic origins are more mixed than those of the more purely Arab Saudis. In number of the order of 70 millions, they dwarf the populations of any of the other Arab States. Cairo has become the metropolis of the Arab world with perhaps 20 million inhabitants. Despite economic growth in recent times, most Egyptians are still poor and illiterate.

Also unlike Saudi Arabia, Egypt's is not an oil economy. Oil output is comparatively small; there is a greater variety of industry, notably textiles, and from the earliest times there has been substantial agriculture, especially cotton crops.

Most large-scale enterprises continue to be State-owned or -controlled, following a period of 'Arab socialism' in the 1950s and 1960s, when there was complete nationalization. As the research reported in Box 8.6 showed, the consequence is centralization of decisions in the hands of government, in particular the officials and agencies of the Ministry of Industry. Efforts to devolve responsibility have been less than successful. Managers of public-sector enterprises are in a position analogous to that of civil servants (State officials). Their autonomy is limited, and they have little discretion in practice over employment and pay. Overmanning is commonplace. Employment is sustained by subsidies. Investment is controlled.

Yet the economy is a mixed economy in two senses of that term. First, in the more usual meaning, it has a private sector as well as a public sector. Not everything is under the aegis of the State – far from it. There are numerous, mostly small, private businesses and traders in the expanding private sector, as well as foreign-owned companies and joint ventures between foreign and Egyptian owners.

Second, in the less usual meaning, there are both Islamic and non-Islamic businesses. Firms may operate in a secular way under secular law, or under the Islamic law described earlier in this chapter, as they choose. Examples of a bank and a chain of furnishing stores working on Islamic principles appear in Box 8.21.

There is no evidence that the Egyptian approach to management differs markedly from that in other Arab societies, any more than the Saudi Arabian approach does. The study described in Box 8.5, in which the general ideal of **managing authority consultatively** is plain, included both Egyptian and Saudi managers. It therefore enabled a rare direct comparison of the two, which is given in Box 8.22. Both emphasize consultation in making a decision, but, if there is any difference between them, the Egyptians are inclined more often to keep a decision in their own hands whilst the Saudis (more highly trained? more Western-trained?) see themselves as delegating now and then. Unfortunately the numbers of executives are so small that, whilst this can be noted, no firm conclusions can be drawn from this alone. However, generally speaking, Egyptian managers in an upward-looking, high power distance, Arab culture are unlikely to find it easy to delegate authority, or to be flexible in executing decisions or to respond well to criticism (Box 8.23). This does place a question mark over how far consultative aspirations are realized in practice.

Box 8.21 Organizations under Islamic Law

The *Faisal Islamic Bank of Egypt* is Saudi instigated. It and similar banks elsewhere in the Islamic world aim to use Saudi oil wealth to assist non-oil economies. It is backed both by the Saudi royal family (and named after the former King Faisal) and by the Egyptian government, which guarantees Saudi investment against nationalization. Share ownership is restricted to

Muslims who accept the principle of Islamic banking. The bank operates in the way described earlier in the chapter, avoiding usury; that is, no fixed interest is charged, and borrowing and lending are on PLS (profit-and-loss-sharing) terms. Most account-holders deposit money for fixed short periods.

The bank has a Religious Supervisory Board of Islamic jurists and scholars to ensure that it is managed in keeping with Shari'a law. This also administers the bank's *Zakat* fund for social and religious purposes, which is contributed to by the bank itself and by individual donors. All employees must be Muslims, and work stops for prayers. Male and female customers are separated, women going to counters where they are attended to only by women. There are both genders among the employees, the women specializing in office administration.

The *Fatteh Company* runs a chain of furnishing stores in Egypt. It is typical of commercial firms working in accord with Islamic principles in being financed by a combination of equity capital and relatively short-term PLS loans. There are no preference shares or loan stock or equivalents carrying fixed interest. Trading risks are therefore shared with all shareholders and lenders. Insofar as the company is administering and turning over short-term loans, it has bank-like functions. As mentioned earlier, the difference between banks and other businesses is less sharp under Islamic practice.

The owners and managers of the firm are ideally regarded as trustees of what Allah has made available, balancing the interests of society at large, of investors, and of employees, to achieve a reasonable but not excessive profit. As in the bank, all employees must be Muslims, and work stops for prayers.

(from El-Ashker)

Box 8.22 Egyptians and Saudis

What managers said they would 'normally' do if making decisions (fuller details in Box 8.5):

	Make own decision:	Consult:	Make decision jointly:	Delegate:
9 Egyptian executives:	3	5	1	0
10 Saudi executives:	2	4	3	1

(extracted from percentages given by Muna p. 50)

Box 8.23 How Egyptian Managers See One Another

Questionnaires were completed during interviews with 156 senior, 321 middle, and 319 lower-level Egyptian administrators and managers from the Ministries of Social Affairs and of Industry, and the State-owned aluminium corporation. Asked about the characteristics of 'the individuals you work with', those questioned saw them as unlikely to 'delegate authority frequently', be 'flexible in executing decisions', be 'responsive to constructive criticism', or be 'willing to take risks'.

(Leila *et al.*, p. 348)

As elsewhere in the Middle East, in **managing relationships** the personal touch is valued. It is crucial to have good relationships with equals and superiors on the job, partly for the satisfaction this brings of itself and partly because links inside and outside work can be vital to survival and success. Who you know matters. Although there is a tendency to what many see as excessively formalistic bureaucracy, when personal relationships are right things can actually be done in a much more informal and direct manner. Job responsibilities are less precisely defined than in organizations in the more clearly structured of Western societies, and this allows superiors to act in a more personal, arbitrary way. For good or ill, it also leaves the way open to the pursuit of personal aims rather than abstract organizational goals.

Appointments are likely to be treated more personally than a Westerner expects. They may be interrupted by 'phone calls, and visits by friends and family. Westerners can also find it discomforting when Egyptians sit or stand closer to them than is usual in their own cultures.

Managing uncertainty means caution, not rushing into things, and not being disposed to take needless risks (as, for instance, in Box 8.23). For **managing time** means a slower pace than most Western managers are used to. It may take a week or longer in Egypt to do what they expect to do in a day or two. A graphic instance of this in Cairo has already been described in Box 8.12, which bears out the advice in Box 8.10 to Western businessmen to 'be flexible with time. Time in the Middle East means something different.'

By their criteria, Western managers frequently feel that Egyptian management falls short. In State-owned industry, incentives are lacking. Pay

Box 8.24 An Egyptian on Egyptians

Egypt shares many behavioural characteristics with other developing nations. Western sources characterize these nations with short-term time orientation, preference for centralization of authority, and rigid social structures among others. In Hofstede's terminology, Egyptian management would score high on power distance and uncertainty avoidance and low on individualism, where loyalty is encouraged and initiative is not rewarded. This is expected because Egypt has a hierarchical structure due to its well established bureaucracy.

While these behavioural tendencies can be traced back to historical roots during pharaonic times or more recently to colonial administrations, other cultural, educational, political and economic factors are also important. A hierarchical family structure, an educational system based on memorization, and a dominant one-party ruling for many years are certainly conditions conducive to a hierarchical structure . . .

However . . . the Egyptian experience shows examples of success such as the building of Aswan High Dam, managing the Suez Canal and the successful crossing of the Suez Canal in the October War of 1973. Prior to the 1952 revolution, which opted for the Socialist path, Egypt had a prosperous free enterprise system.

(from Youssef, pp. 17, 18, 19)

is low, especially so in public administration, and earnings follow seniority rather than performance. Managers have neither the rewards nor the sanctions with which to spur worker productivity. In public administration, central to a State-led system, low pay results in most officials having second jobs. This reduces their energy and commitment for their primary employment, in which they are also distracted by responsibilities owed to family and friends. Government service is seen as security rather than opportunity. Box 8.24 gives an appraisal by an Egyptian.

*   *   *

Arab management in the Middle East functions in societies more overtly conscious than are most of the religious dimension. Furthermore, some of them are also directly affected, and all are indirectly affected, more than any societies have ever been, by a sudden influx of windfall wealth on a colossal scale. Just as the societies to which they belong strive to reconcile traditions, including religious edicts, with the resultant economic and social change, so managers juggle opposing requirements.

On the one hand is immemorial personalism, giving others their due as persons with particular statuses and needs that transcend the work situation, and wielding authority by personal decree; on the other hand are Western ideals of impersonal rules and dispersed decision-making.

It is plain in the following chapter that these strains typify developing countries, and in some respects the Arab nations fall into that category.

Further Reading

GENERAL

Al-Buraey, Muhammad A. 1985. *Administrative Development: An Islamic Perspective*. Kegan Paul International with Routledge.

Al-Faleh, Mahmoud. 1987. 'Cultural Influences on Arab Management Development: A Case Study of Jordan'. *The Journal of Management Development*, 6, 3, 19–33.

Ali, Abbas, J. 1990. 'Management Theory in a Transitional Society: The Arab's Experience'. *International Studies of Management and Organization*, 20, 3, 7–35.

Almaney, A. J. 1981/3. 'Cultural Traits of the Arabs: Growing Interest for International Management'. *Management International Review*, 21, 10–18.

Atiyyah, Hamid, S. 1992. 'Research in Arab Countries Published in Arabic'. *Organization Studies*, 13, 1, 105–10.

El-Ashker, Ahmed Abdel-Fattah. 1987. *The Islamic Business Enterprise*. Croom Helm.

Harris, Philip R. and Robert T. Moran. 1991. *Managing Cultural Differences* (3rd edn, Ch. 17). Gulf Publishing.

Muna, Farid A. 1980. *The Arab Executive*. Macmillan.

Wright, P. 1981/2. 'Organizational Behavior in Islamic Firms'. *Management International Review*, 21, 86–94.

SAUDI ARABIA

Al-Buraey, Muhammad A. 1985. *Administrative Development: An Islamic Perspective*. Kegan Paul International with Routledge.

Al-Farsey, Fouad. 1990. *Modernity and Tradition – The Saudi Equation*. Kegan Paul International.

Al-Nimir, Saud and Monte Palmer. 1982. 'Bureaucracy and Development in Saudi Arabia: a Behavioural Analysis'. *Public Administration and Development*, 2, 93–104.

Kassem, M. Sami. 1989. 'Strategy Formulation: Arabian Gulf Style'. *International Studies of Management and Organization*, 19, 2, 6–21.

Kassem, M. Sami and Ghazi M. Habib. 1989. *Strategic Management of Services in the Arab Gulf States*. De Gruyter.

Khalid, M., Al-Aiban and Jone L. Pearce. 1993. 'The Influence of Values on Management Practices: A Test in Saudi Arabia and the United States'. *International Studies of Management and Organization*, 23, 3, 35–52.

EGYPT

Badran, Mohamed and Bob Hinings. 1981. 'Strategies of Administrative Control and Contextual Constraints in a Less Developed Country: The Case of Egyptian Public Enterprise'. *Organization Studies*, 2, 1, 3–21. Reprinted in D. J. Hickson and C. J. McMillan (eds.), *Organization and Nation: the Aston Programme IV*. Gower, 1981.

El-Ashker, Ahmed Abdel-Fattah. 1987. *The Islamic Business Enterprise*. Croom Helm.

Leila, Ali, El Sayed Yassin and Monte Palmer. 1985. 'Apathy, Values, Incentives and Development: the Case of the Egyptian Bureaucracy'. *The Middle East Journal*, 39, 3 (Summer 1985), 341–61.

Youssef, Samir. 1994. 'Egyptian State Owned Enterprises: A Sector in Transition'. *International Journal of Commerce and Management*, 4, 4, 5–25.

Zahra, S. A. 1980/3. 'Egyptian Management at the Crossroads'. *Management International Review*, 20, 118–24.

Other Sources

GENERAL

Dadfar, Hossein. 1990. 'Industrial Buying Behavior in the Middle East: a Cross National Study'. *PhD Dissertation*. Department of Management. Linköping University, Sweden.

Kaynak, Erdener (ed.). 1986. *International Business in the Middle East*. De Gruyter.

Laffin, John. 1975. *The Arab Mind Considered*.* Taplinger.

Rasheed, Adel M. 1993. 'Managerial Practices and Organization Systems Relevant to Manager's Motivation and Job Satisfaction: A Comparison Between Western and Jordanian/Arab Banks'. *Proceedings of the Arab Management Conference*. University of Bradford Management Centre, England.

Roukis, G. and P. J. Montana (eds.). 1986. *Workforce Management in the Arabian Peninsular*. Greenwood Press.

* A critical Anglo view

SAUDI ARABIA

Al-Aiban, Khalid M. and Jone L. Pearce. 1993. 'The Influence of Values on Management Practices: A Test in Saudi Arabia and the United States'. *International Studies of Management and Organization*, 23, 3, 35–52.

Ali, Abbas, J. 1993. 'Decision-Making Style, Individualism, and Attitudes Toward Risk of Arab Executives'. *International Studies of Management and Organization*, 23, 3, 53–73.

Ali, Abbas and Mohammed Al-Shakhis. 1989. 'Managerial Beliefs About Work in Two Arab States'. *Organization Studies*, 10, 2, 169–86.

At-Twaijri, Mohammed I., Abdelaziz A. Al-Dukhayyil, and Ibrahim A. Al-Muhaiza. 1994. 'Saudi Arabian and US Supervisors as Perceived by Their Subordinates: an Intercultural Comparative Field Study'. *International Journal of Commerce and Management*, 4, 4, 60–70

Mullens, W. J. G. 1987. 'National Culture: a Comparative Case Study of Ethiopia and Saudi Arabia'. MBA Dissertation. University of Bradford Management Centre, England.

EGYPT

Doig, Alan. 1993. 'Policing the Consequences of Economic Change: Political Climate and Controls', in *Proceedings of the Arab Management Conference*. University of Bradford Management Centre, England.

Henley, John S. and Mohamed M. Ereisha. 1987. 'State Control and the Labor Productivity Crisis: The Egyptian Textile Industry at Work'. *Economic Development and Cultural Change*, 35, 3, 491–521.

Parnell, John A., and Tarek Hatem. 1999. 'Cultural Antecedents of Behavioural Differences Between American and Egyptian Managers'. *Journal of Management Studies*, 36, 3, 399–418.

Price, Gillian and Essam Mahmoud. 1986. 'The Prospects for Export Marketing to Egypt', in Erdener Kaynak (ed.), *International Business in the Middle East*. De Gruyter.

9

Developing Countries

highlighting:
Africa (below the Sahara)
India

All societies are developing, but some need developing more than others. Or, to put it another way, these latter have a greater need for economic growth and the building up of health, education and other services. Theirs are the poorest peoples on earth; during the sterile 'Cold War' between the so-called 'East' and the so-called 'West' they were often known as the Third World. Most of their forebears were the colonial subjects of European States in the days of overseas empires. They live in much of Africa, the Middle East, China, India and South-East Asia, and Central and South America (though, since the Arab lands, China and the Americas are grouped culturally in other chapters in this book, this chapter has primarily Africa and India in mind, and it is these which will be described later in more detail).

In these countries a minority may be wealthy, but most people live in sparsely furnished, crowded huts or small houses, and many in the cities on the streets under boxes and plastic sheets. They have an inadequate infrastructure – which is a coldly technical way of saying that they have just footpaths and tracks, or rutted roads (unless they squat in shanties on the edge of a roaring highway), meagre or polluted water and no sewage system, and either no electricity or electricity for just a few hours each day, and even that unpredictably switched on and off. In India, for example, it is a common sight to see men climbing with great agility up the poles that carry power wires so as to connect into and pirate the current, a risky practice which makes the legal supply that much more unreliable.

Managing and administering industry or services in this situation holds problems long forgotten or never encountered in what are now the better-off lands. Although there are richer districts in the urban areas of all the poorer societies in cities such as Lagos (Nigeria), Nairobi (Kenya), Bombay (India), and Jakarta (Indonesia), for example, where the wealth of the wealthy is in the starkest contrast to the poverty of the poor, the educated middle class is relatively small. Moreover, those with what is often regarded as the best education, the intelligentsia educated Western-style, can be cut off by that very education from their fellow citizens whose outlook and lifestyle they no longer share. As many people (and most women) are illiterate, it is difficult to find appropriately trained candidates for the supervisory and clerical posts required to sustain effective management. Little wonder that frustrating failures happen all too often (see Box 9.1).

Box 9.1 Administering Frustration

When I was growing up in Butambala, a small county in southern Uganda, I was constantly confronted by the dualities and contradictions of development and underdevelopment side by side.

I grew up in a business family and started several of my own businesses at a relatively early age. As a teenager, I served as a consultant by reading, writing and translating for the local 'progressive farmers' who, with assistance from the government, were supposed to eliminate traditional farming practices and usher in a new era of modern commercial farming. No matter how hard they worked, and no matter how much the government agencies promised, the results were always well below expectations.

I was always struck by the gaps and inconsistencies between official government strategic plans and the hard realities of my clients' and family businesses. Official explanations, whenever attempted, were often incomplete and inadequate. At the university I soon realized that my clients were not alone. Working with more complex development organizations, I came to realize that the problems of implementation and sustainability of development initiatives are pervasive and persistent.

(Moses N. Kiggundu)

PERSONAL AND IMPERSONAL ORGANIZATION

We have suggested before that some of the explanation for this situation lies in trying to graft on to such societies impersonal forms of organization. The impersonal bureaucratization which diffused the way of life of Western societies during the nineteenth and twentieth centuries gave them comparatively effective administration and became the mainstay of their economic standard of living. Although this has had a cost in the anonymous and materialist 'facelessness' of large organizations, it is a contemporary model for poorer societies. Whereas the West in its time did not have any particular example to copy, its forms of management and organization are now constantly there in front of societies which are still developing their own. So that what was introduced at the beginning of this book as the tension between the impersonal and the personalistic reappears here at its most acute.

It is worth being reminded once more what 'impersonal bureaucratization' means. It means that kind of organization where in principle it does not matter who is doing the job or who the customer or client is; the job will be done in the same way and they will be given the same service reliably and consistently. No favouritism, even-handed, fair to all. That is generally speaking, of course; for Westerners, too, know that things do not work quite like this. But the principle is clear, and it is difficult for Western minds reading these words to conceive differently.

Whereas in developing countries in economic transition, who you are and who you know matters more, as we have seen in management in developing Latin, Asian and Arab societies. Especially relationships with family and friends matter. So as larger-scale organizations are developed, the hard edges of working impersonally, which Western managements strive to soften with human-relations policies and training in synthetic politeness to customers, are here softened by personal connections.

Not surprisingly, impersonal organization creaks under the strain. Whilst there are many who act without fear or favour as it supposes them to do, it is susceptible to nepotism, bribery and misappropriation more than in already bureaucratized societies. This may not always appear as culpable as it sounds. True, the family and friends of those at the top may indeed get the best jobs, but that is because they offer a loyalty that is indispensable. True, a firm whose owners are from the same tribe may indeed be awarded a contract on favourable terms, but then the work will get the necessary priority. Further, it is hard to say where a handsome commission or expensive gifts in a society where generous presents are customary niceties slide into bribery. However, it is clear that extra payments for public services (Box 9.2 gives some instances) can go beyond what is tolerable. So does the emergence of what is virtually a market in the obtaining of public appointments, such that side-payments for the chance of getting a post increase with its rank and with the opportunities it offers for making money out of such payments. Also, the more the State dominates the economy and itself owns service and business organizations, the more the opportunities for corruption multiply. A disturbing list of possible forms of corruption by officials is given in Box 9.3. But since, in the poorest nations, public administration (including military administration) is often the most advanced instrument available, and since those in power have to use the most readily available means to try to accelerate economic progress, State control – and therefore its weaknesses – tends to be widespread. The weaknesses are worldwide, but it is in the poorest lands that they are most ubiquitous.

Box 9.2 Illegal India

An Indian governmental report found: *pervasive tax evasion on legal economic activities and widespread corruption and abuse of all forms of public discretionary authority.* It went on: *The use of discretionary authority to extract or levy illegal tolls has spread far beyond the area of economic controls. Particularly at the lower levels of the state apparatus it has become quite common for illegal payments to be demanded in return for regular public services such as the registration of a document, the repair of a telephone, the issue of a tax-assessment order, the admission of a student in an educational institution or decisions on postings and transfers in the public services.*

(from *The Economist*, 'India Supplement', 4 May 1991, p. 16)

Box 9.3 Some Forms of Corruption in the Public Sector

- Misappropriation; forgery and embezzlement; padding of accounts; diverted funds; misuse of funds; unaudited revenues; skimming
- Deceit and fraud; misrepresentation; cheating and swindling
- Bribery and graft; extortion; illegal levies; kick-backs
- Misuse of inside knowledge and confidential information; falsification of records
- Unauthorized sale of public offices, loans, monopolies, contracts, licences and public property
- Manipulation of regulations, purchases and supplies; bias and favouritism
- Tax evasion; profiteering
- Acceptance of improper gifts and entertainments; 'speed' money; blackmail
- Misuse of official seals, stationery, residences and perquisites

(selected from Caiden, Table 1)

GOVERNMENT AND BUSINESS

Though widespread, real control by the State is incomplete. In part this is due to the problems already mentioned; in part it is due to the State not being integral to the daily lives of many people. The State is irrelevant to subsistence farmers who work to feed their family, who exchange crops or animals with other families or at small local markets, and who help one another in the fields or with tending animals, just as it is to childbirth and to domestic crises. These are hardly, if at all, part of the money economy. But they are part of an extensive 'personal economy', made up of many small networks of personal relationships based on family, clan and religion, which is beyond the reach of impersonal administration.

That administration serves governments which are normally single-party, or an oligarchy around a strong leader, or military. They struggle to hold together a State where any consensus on how things should properly be done, on the 'rules' of public life, is as yet patchy and weak, so that governments are often changed by assassination or coup. Like those in all nations who have been out of office, those who take over are unduly optimistic about what they can do once in office, and when there they tend to disappoint.

They govern through a public service (or civil service) in which the colonial legacy can still linger. Whilst, on the one hand, colonial times may have set a standard of work to aim at, on the other hand colonial administrators were there to rule, not to serve. They ruled on behalf of a single power, a single source of authority. Nowadays this suits the needs of one-party power, but it can also mean officious officials insisting that regulations be complied with. The colonial legacy left no tradition of officials being competent to engender economic growth and efficiency in the way post-colonial governments hoped they would. Staying safely within past precedents was more likely than being entrepreneurial, and preserving status and promotability more likely than taking risks. Despite this, and despite also having to act on unreliable information and statistics, governments have tried to boost economic development by direct intervention. Full or partial State ownership of factories, mines, irrigation schemes, tea estates, development banks and so on is common. Since this has not been very successful (see Box 9.4), developing countries have joined in the worldwide shift towards privatization.

State-owned organizations are among the larger organizations in developing countries, as are the branches of multinational corporations. Depending on how far the State has allowed the multinationals to move in and on how far they see a promising market, they form a distinctively modern and high pay sector of the economy. They are frequently front runners in management practice, the implications of which are explored in Chapter 11. Always open to the suspicion that they take much more out of the economy than they put in, they may be required to indigenize management or they may do so themselves without direct compulsion. The number of expatriates may be limited, and sometimes there is what is in effect a dual hierarchy, as in some Middle Eastern organizations (Box 8.17). Host country citizens may double up alongside expatriates in managerial positions, holding the senior appointments, with the expatriates being their deputies.

The larger organizations of the State-owned and foreign-owned sectors co-exist with a vastly more numerous third sector of small-scale, locally owned businesses, usually family firms. Fruit exporters, saw-mills, tanneries, furniture-makers, local breweries, craft souvenir workshops, lorry and taxi firms and many more dominate numerically, even though they may in total be a lesser part of the money economy. In Africa and India, small producer co-operatives also are common.

Box 9.4 Organizational Ambivalence

State-owned airlines, railways, and post and telecommunications organizations in East Africa showed 'an overall pattern of weak and disappointing performance'. In Ethiopia, Kenya, Tanzania and Uganda they were beset by a range of problems, but one difficulty in particular was singled out. It is not peculiar to developing countries; State-owned organizations everywhere are prone to it. But it is intense in developing countries where resources are scarcer. Managements had to juggle both social and financial objectives. The organizations were seen to go through three phases: *co-operative, adversarial* and *autonomous*. When first set up, or nationalized, State or societal objectives predominated during a phase when government and managements co-operated. In Uganda, for instance, as long as trains could carry vital coffee exports and petroleum imports, the government was not worried about profitability or productivity. But as the organization matured and management became aware of technical and commercial standards elsewhere, sharp conflicts occurred with government objectives. So relations generally between governments and the managements of State-owned organizations become less co-operative and more adversarial. In Tanzania Railways, managers struggled to bring in new diesel locomotives and to reorganize appropriately whilst still pressed to increase employment. Finally, some organizations can break through into an autonomous phase in which market criteria predominate, as Ethiopian Airlines did at one time.

(summarized from Jorgensen, Ch. 4, in Jaeger & Kanungo, eds.)

Management in this sector of small firms can be described as traditionalistic. It does not live up to what is taught in Western business schools, nor does it match practice in the branches of the foreign multinationals. Nor does management in the similar small businesses in the Western world, of course – but then small businesses are even more crucial to less-developed economies. Are they therefore to be regarded as backward? Whether they are so, and to what degree, can be debatable (see Box 9.5).

Box 9.5 Backing the So-called 'Backward'

Local firms in developing countries lack the trappings of modern management, so recruitment to positions with managerial prerogatives is not at all impersonal; rather, it is confined to relatives and friends, and to their relatives and friends. The performance of those so recruited is not seriously evaluated. Authority is not delegated beyond this coterie, who keep information about the firm to themselves. There is no planning, no formal production control, quality control or cost control, only rudimentary accounting and no market analysis.

But why take risks recruiting strangers when their credentials cannot be checked? Why incur the administrative costs of sophisticated control systems when the local market is a seller's market? Why plan, when political and economic conditions are unstable?

Is it so backward to adjust to circumstances?

(summarized from Negandhi)

THE APPROACH TO MANAGEMENT

The multi-national corporations, mostly American or European or Japanese in origin, make a variety of compromises with the cultures of the societies in which they operate, as will be discussed in the next chapter. It is the State-owned organizations and the locally owned private businesses which typify the indigenous approach.

In broad terms, cultures are likely to be both collectivistic, which shapes **managing relationships**, and to be less competitively assertive than the Anglos or Japanese in **managing oneself**. Therefore, as already mentioned, personal relationships intrude into management. The entertainment of family members who have arrived from afar may be held to be more important than getting on with work that is probably late anyway for uncontrollable reasons. So why not take some unannounced days off work? Certainly everyone will expect this for family '*rites de passage*' such as puberty ceremonies, marriages and funerals, which may extend over several days. Preference may be given in appointments or in contracts, as has already been said. Indeed, those who hold office can be judged by how much they can do for others as much as by whether they progress in their own careers, a less selfish moral stance than that which is usual in the West.

The **managing of authority** throughout the developing countries is done in a centralized fashion, sometimes verging into authoritarianism. Power distance is on the high side (Box 2.5). The control exercised by the male patriarch of a family is duplicated within the organization, especially in the family firm, and full due respect is required and given, step by step, down the hierarchy. Accelerating matters by bypassing a superior to get to higher authority more quickly would be an insult (though that does not stop it happening), and in any case **managing time** is not an urgent problem. Tasks can wait whilst personal affairs are settled, and people can come back later. The right of signature is a highly regarded symbol of authority, and its careful use guards against abuse. When the wielder of signature power is away, there may be no provision for a substitute to sign in his place, for such a discretion could be taken advantage of. Queues patiently await a required signature or official stamp, and in public administration it is usual for people to have to trek from office to office around the ministries to obtain multiple permissions for the same thing. Lower officials, fearing reprimands, can find it tempting to refer questions upwards as often as possible, for to do the minimum carries less risk of doing something that incurs displeasure.

In fluctuating political and economic circumstances, **managing uncertainty** (Box 2.10) can be vital. Culturally, the peoples of the poorer lands have learnt how to live with it. Accountants have learnt how to keep dual sets of accounts which cope with inflation in different ways, sellers have learnt how to build personal links which will survive abrupt changes in State-owned enterprises or sudden new government regulations. A kind of protection is afforded by applying rules and documentation seemingly for the sake of rules and documentation, giving the appearance of control and stability but at the same time creating the unwelcome formalistic face of bureaucracy (for instance Box 9.6).

Box 9.6 Steaming Away

In a hurry to catch the train, the foreign businessman on his first visit to India arrived at New Delhi railway station. He wanted a first-class ticket. As he beheld the jostling, sweating crowd in the ticket office he realized why the driver of his hired Mercedes had come to help him.

They pushed through to a table where he found that people were filling in forms to apply for tickets. There were no forms left, and no pens to fill them in with. Luckily, his driver rescued a crumpled grey form from the floor. He filled in his name and destination and, surprisingly for him, also his home address and his age. His driver chose a queue for him at the ticket counter, others smarter and better versed than he having pushed ahead of him. After what seemed to him a very long time in a long slow line, he arrived at the ticket window. Here there was an up-to-date, computerized ticket machine, into which the details on his application were typed. His age was queried since it was not legible on the grubby form. Eventually out came his ticket. It had taken twenty-five sticky minutes to get it.

The driver pushed a way for him out of the ticket office and towards the platform. For him it was a puzzling experience, an unfamiliar combination of slow formalism with modern technology. And who wanted to know how old he was?

(from the authors' experience)

Since people in less-developed countries tend to think in a more visual, situation-linked manner than those in more economically developed lands (see Chapter 2), they may make decisions in a way that to the latter seems *ad hoc*, even inconsistent. They respond more intuitively to the circumstances of the moment, less to the abstract logic which western cultures see as the ideal.

Taken all in all, then, there is a risk that when on the job in a system imitating impersonal organizations elsewhere, people will too often be mere 'performers' of roles. They will be going through the motions the system asks of them, but the jobs they do are less genuinely a part of themselves than might be so in a developed economy, and their heart is not in it. They are more likely to do it mechanically, poorly motivated. They fail to confront problems openly, they lack trust in others in the organization beyond those with whom they have a personal relationship, and they feel helpless to improve matters.

Managements do manage, and organizations do work, but often they depart from – or is it 'fall short of – the model of impersonal organization in ways that are summed up in Box 9.7.

The businessman or woman from a wealthier economy must weigh up the situation carefully, distinguishing what is similar and what is different. This takes time. So do business negotiations. Therefore they should not expect to fly in and out and clinch a deal in a day or two. Negotiations

Box 9.7 General Profile of a Developing Country Organization

Top Management

- Overworked
- Authoritarian, paternalistic
- Centralized control and decision-making
- No clear mission or sense of direction
- Extensive extra-organization activities
- Politicized
- Weak executive support systems
- Learned, articulate, travelled

Middle Management

- Weak management systems and controls
- Inadequate management and administrative skills
- Lack of specific industry knowledge and experience
- Understaffed
- Risk-averse, unwilling to take independent action or initiative
- Exercise close supervision, little delegation
- Low levels of motivation

Operating Levels

- Inefficient, high-cost operations
- Low productivity
- Overstaffed, underutilized
- Low pay
- Poor morale
- Weak boundaries and unprotected vital technical core

(reproduced from Kiggundu, p. 10)

over major State-financed projects can take a long time in all nations, but what takes months in the West may take years in developing countries (once more the example in Box 8.12 is apt). Since the State is so widely involved, a good knowledge is needed of regulations or currencies, importing and exporting, taxation, foreign ownership, prices and subsidies, and so on. This is where a local agent who 'knows the ropes' in every sense, including local customs, can be useful. One way or another, familiarity with how things work 'on the ground' is indispensable.

As was said earlier, it is

Africa (sub-Saharan)

and India

that have been chosen as examples of the difficulties that face managers in less-developed countries. Each is a continent rather than a country. Whilst Africa is a continent of many nations, India is a single nation of many peoples.

MANAGEMENT IN (SUB-SAHARAN) AFRICA

The Sahara desert runs in a broad belt right across the top of Africa, extending from the Mediterranean Sea southwards. Below it, the variously called sub-Saharan or (mainly) black or (mainly) non-Arab bulk of the continent is split up into more than forty nation-states. On the map they look like political 'crazy paving', a paving of irregular, broken flagstones, pushed together anyhow. This is what European colonialism left behind: a nonsensical chopping-up of territory that has now become set in that unreal form by the 'realpolitik' of the national sovereignties created when Britain, France, Portugal and Belgium departed (Germany had been forced out earlier). The resulting States are among the youngest in the world, most having been created since 1955.

There being no lasting liberal democracies, other than what has been arrived at in South Africa, governments are single-party, often military or militarily supported. The usual means of changing those in charge is therefore a coup or civil war. These kinds of changes bring instability – or at least the fear of instability – which hinders management. In the public sector, abrupt changes of policy may leave projects unfinished and buildings half built, whilst private business has to contend with switches in tariffs and monetary controls, permits required, etc.

In this least industrialized of continents, only three million or so people are employed in industry out of something over 400 million in total in sub-Saharan Africa (besides the employment in the mines and manufacturing of South Africa, that is). So the picture of management, unlike that in the industrialized Western nations or Japan, is heavily coloured by the experience of the prominent public sector both in administering the State services and in such State-owned industry as there may be.

Since gaining independence from colonial rule, rapidly increasing populations have eaten up much of what has been achieved economically, and most Africans are virtually as poor today as their predecessors were before. Whatever the intended economic or political system, left or right in its professed ideology, the same patterns of economic crisis have occurred. Attempts to give aid from outside, whether well intentioned or an attempt to gain influence (or frequently both), have often been misdirected (Box 9.8).

Box 9.8 Road to Nowhere

One of the authors was being driven at high speed along a shiny new road cut straight through the central African jungle. He did not feel as scared as he usually did when his Polish-born driver, a United Nations official, was at the wheel, since there were no other vehicles on the road.

For this was a road to nowhere, used by almost nobody. It was only the third surfaced main road across the small state of Burundi. This one had been built by China, which had been competing for spheres of influence with the one-time Soviet Union. It did not begin in a town of any size nor end at one, since there were no settlements that large. It was a vehicle highway in a land where most people walked. They walked between widely separated houses along footpaths that followed the contours of a hilly terrain inappropriate to the growth of centres of population.

The advanced road-building equipment used by the Chinese, the bull-dozers and diggers and tarmac spreaders, stood in clearings in the vegetation at intervals along the roadside. Given fuel, spares, mechanical know-how and construction know-how, and the vital managerial capacity, it could have made more roads. But there were none of these necessities. So it rotted and rusted, never to be used again, millions of dollars' worth awaiting envelopment by the fast-encroaching jungle.

How long would the road itself last?

Managers and the Managed

Too often, employees in the cities consider themselves fortunate to have any job at all. They work long hours for meagre wages at a low level of productivity, following instructions the purpose of which they do not see. In many ways they seem to be re-enacting the early Industrial Revolution in Britain.

Typically, they work beneath a centralized and hierarchical authority system, the common pattern of managing authority in developing countries, that was described earlier. They are in no position to question why. The chain of command is sustained by downward instructions and communication, so to get action, those fortunate enough to be able to do so may have to go to the highest level, as shown by the instances in Box 9.9. The last example there also shows the high status of the military, who can ignore regulations that everyone else must comply with.

Box 9.9 Roads to the Top

I took a proposal to the Finance Ministry, fully justified by facts and figures, for a loan for a road service . . . The officer flatly refused . . . I then went straight to the Finance Minister and got the loan sanctioned.

I wrote a memo to the accounts department asking them to make a payment. They refused, saying I had misinterpreted the rules, and I appealed to the Minister of Manpower Development to get the payment made.

We were charged with the task of collecting money from all the departments for damage caused by their vehicles. Those of the Defence Department frequently are at fault, but they do not bother to pay the accounts due.

(three examples from Blunt and Jones, pp. 34–5)

Overmuch of this both overloads those at the top and misallocates resources. Top managers may or may not have the experience and training to cope with the pressures, for people with the appropriate competence and qualifications can be even more scarce than money. Hence candidates ill-equipped for high office may be promoted, and this problem can be exacerbated if training is regarded as a source of status as much as of competence, so that the qualifications of those promoted do not fit the jobs they do. Having the right mentor or patron can also have something to do with it.

It is often noted that in this kind of hierarchy the 'social distance' between those above and those below exceeds the gap between expatriate managers and their African subordinates.

The strain on the higher echelons contributes to the lack of success in managing large-scale, complex projects and organizations, which are beyond the capacity of those at the top to oversee and control personally in the way which they themselves expect and which others expect of them. Their in-trays overflow and they cannot attend to it all (Box 9.10 has an instance of this).

Box 9.10 Paper Mountain

An examination of two files among the mountain on a senior assistant secretary's table showed that the files had moved to him from an assistant executive officer's table through the higher executive officer (the executive officer was skipped because there was no incumbent), then through an assistant secretary, before reaching the senior assistant secretary who . . . [passed them to] . . . the permanent secretary whose stamp of decision was just the word 'Approved' . . . the right answer had been known by the originating assistant executive officer, who could have taken the decision . . . if he had been given the authority.

(Akpan p. 113)

The authoritarian inheritance from colonial days, left behind in societies with no experience of doing differently – or, at least, no memory of any such experience – is compounded by the tendency inherent in organizations everywhere for those in charge to centralize, to try to get a grip on things as they see them, at times of crisis. As African organizations are often faced with crises, they are constantly subject to this tendency.

Employees are both linked to others and divided from others by ethnicity, tribe, family, and language and religion. Among tribes best known outside Africa are the three largest tribes in Nigeria: the Hausa, the Ibo and the Yoruba, for example. These kinds of connections are not absent from organizations elsewhere in the world, of course. The British 'old school tie' network is well known. They are just more numerous and pronounced in Africa (Box 9.11 has an instance). Indeed, whilst a tie can stay in the cupboard, tribal facial markings and other physical features cannot be left at home.

Box 9.11 The 'Old Tribe Tie'

I did not like the foreman because he did not treat me well. All the time I was working there he was always looking at me and trying to find fault with me . . . Then one day he was very rude to me and told me that people of my tribe should go back to the country and grow food because that is all we are good for. He was always comparing me to . . . better workers . . . of a different tribe . . . Then one day the foreman complained that I had not washed my hands properly . . . We had a quarrel and he told me that he despised people of my tribe. So I left.

(Blunt and Jones, p. 190; from Gutkind, p. 157)

Divided Loyalties

Not that people are unaware of universalistic criteria, the impersonal criteria which universally apply to all in an organization and which are intended to give fair chances of promotion, to ensure that all clients or customers are treated in the same way, and so on. But they also apply personalistic criteria which recognize the particular claims of particular people; Box 9.12 contains some research evidence of this. So there are simultaneously two codes of proper behaviour in the work situation. Whereas in the industrialized nations personalistic considerations are generally secondary, notwithstanding some illicit use of the office photocopier for family purposes or a few mechanical repairs 'on the side' for a friend, in Africa they are frequently uppermost.

So African employees are comparatively more likely to take an instrumental view of their work. They are more likely to see it less as an end in itself, and rather as a way of showing what they can do for family and friends, drawing their own feelings of pride and accomplishment from the regard in which they are held outside the organization as a result. The giving and receiving of favours and gifts is a social obligation more than bribery, though it still has to be talked of in an unofficial jargon, like the word *dash*, which has been used to describe it in Ghana and other English-speaking west African nations.

Officials have been criticized as being content to follow the rules rather than taking an initiative. For taking an initiative heightens the uncertainty,

---

Box 9.12 Universal or Particular

Views of the behaviour proper to a civil servant in Ghana were obtained from 434 civil servants themselves. They were to 'suppose a civil servant arrives at his office one morning and finds several people waiting to see him about routine business. One of these people is a relative of his.' They were then asked: 'Would it be *proper* to keep this relative waiting because others have come before him?' and whether the civil servant would *actually* see his relative before the others, and what the relative would *expect* him to do.

The percentage answers were:

	Believe proper legitimate *thing to do* is:	Think likely *actual action* is:	Think his relative *will expect*:
Universalistic: (to see people in impersonal order of arrival)	75.3	19.4	5.1
Particularistic: (to see particular person, his relative, first)	23.7	80.0	92.6
No answer:	0.9	1.6	2.3

So, whilst being aware that the legitimate action formally required by the organization would be to see everyone in order of arrival (75.3 per cent), most people (80.0 per cent) thought that a civil servant would actually give preference to his relative, and (92.6 per cent) that the relative would expect to be so favoured.

The civil servants who replied were inclined to feel that in such situations their relatives would not understand the formal requirements of their job and would be likely to see them as bad, hard-hearted and generally selfish and uncaring if they did not help their family.

(adapted from Price, p. 64)

both of making a mistake and of incurring the displeasure of superiors. But then, generally speaking, Africans are not as competitive or eager to 'stand out' among their peers as are the individually assertive Anglos, for example (see Chapter 2 and Box 2.9).

Nor are they in such a hurry. There is more to be got from the moment at hand, even from the pleasantries incidental to the job, so why rush on prematurely? Other matters can wait. Whilst to an American the day is neatly arranged in advance into time-slots with little to spare in between, the African view of time is more flexible and fluid. The day can flow around people, who come first, rather than be divided up by punctual adherence to the clock. Sometimes the problem for foreigners is not so much getting a 'no' decision as getting no decision.

It has been said that Africa has been confronted with the difficulties of running twentieth-century forms of organization before its people have had time to adjust to what management requires of them. Small wonder that appraisals of the workings of the prevalent public sector have repeatedly found weak financial controls, waste, over-staffing, and failure to meet targets (see Box 9.13).

However, these problems are not peculiarly African problems. They exist elsewhere among developing countries – and indeed in the richer nations, too. It is a matter of degree. Even so, the future of management in Africa has to improve upon the past. The question is: in which direction, and how? Some advocate clarifying organization structures, defining more clearly what each job is to do and who is responsible for whom and for what. This tries to fit the people to the organization. Others push the other way, seeking a more communal, perhaps paternalistic, kind of organization better suited to the ways of the people who will work in it. This would fit organization to people. Africa is still making its choice.

INDIAN CULTURE AND MANAGEMENT

Though it has similar management problems, India is not Africa. Most obviously, control for over 200 years by a single colonial power (Britain), rather than division among several, left it as a single nation-state covering an entire subcontinent. This is despite the splitting-off of Pakistan and what became Bangladesh at the time of independence (which was declared in 1947). Since then India has maintained the framework of a liberal democracy which, although for long dominated by the Congress Party, has been able to change the party in power without force.

Box 9.13 Management in Malawi

Malawian senior and middle-level managers, in both the public and private sectors, held the following view of their situation, summed up from answers on 105 questionnaires and in 47 interviews:

1. Malawian organizations function in an environment of acute resource scarcity, economic uncertainty, and highly centralized political power
2. These organizations tend to retain the major characteristics of structures developed in the colonial era, namely rather rigid bureaucratic, rule-bound hierarchies.
3. Organizations tend to be viewed by society as a whole as having a wider mission than is generally understood in the West, being expected to provide socially desirable benefits such as employment, housing, transport, and assistance with important social rituals and ceremonies; considerations of profit maximization and efficiency may be viewed as secondary or incidental.
4. There is among Malawian workers a generally instrumental orientation towards work, involving high expectations of the benefits, to the worker and his extended family, that employment brings, but less in the way of loyalty and commitment to the organization (or profession) that is said to typify the employer–employee relationship in the West.
5. There is in Malawian society an emphasis on prestige and status differences, creating relationships of dependency, which in organizations finds expression in wide differentials between organizational levels, particularly between managers and workers, extreme deference to and dependence upon one's boss, and a paternal, concerned, but strict style of management.
6. The collectivist values of Malawian society are reflected in organizations in the high regard managers have for their subordinates as people; in a view of workers as a network of people rather than as human resources . . . and in a reluctance by managers either to accept individual blame for mistakes or to criticize individual subordinates in a direct manner.

(Jones, p. 208)

India is much more than twice the size of Africa in population. Its total of about 1,000 million makes it the second most populous State on earth, after China. The population is made up of numerous peoples who speak numerous languages, though English is the common language of politics and administration. Fewer than half of this population is literate.

India is particularly distinctive in having one of the oldest civilizations, with its own ancient religion. In its popular forms, this has a uniquely Hindu hierarchical pantheon of families of gods. More than 80 per cent of the population are Hindu

India has been economically much more successful than sub-Saharan Africa, especially since controls on buying and selling abroad were relaxed in the 1980s. On the other hand, it has lagged far behind the outstanding Asian economic successes: Singapore, Hong Kong, Taiwan, South Korea and, of course Japan. It has attained only what some Indians have ironically termed 'the Hindu rate of growth'. Even so, India has sustained an economic stability that was almost untouched by the 1990s setback in East Asia. Moreover, it has built up a large industrial sector, both private and State controlled, which places it in the front rank of the world's nations in sheer scale of production, albeit not always in quality and competitiveness. This has accentuated the contrast between those who benefit most from industry and commerce and the bulk of the population who continue poverty-stricken.

Paternalistic Centralization

An outline of typical Indian characteristics as seen by one researcher appears in Box 9.14. The list includes fear of, obedience to and dependence upon those in positions of power. So not surprisingly, as in Africa, the tendency is for industry as well as public administration and services to **manage authority** in a centralized manner. India comes high in power distance in Box 2.5, as do the other Asian nations which were colonized. The British stepped into the authoritarian shoes of the Moghul rulers who preceded them, and then transferred this usage of power into industry and commerce as it grew. There were British bosses, and Indian clerks and workers. So Indian management inherits a long history of aloof, imperious rule. It is inclined to maintain tight control at the top and to minimize delegation, even in larger organizations at a size which usually prompts Western managements to decentralize. Managers value status and power comparatively highly, in a patriarchal tradition where this is naturally so. J.R.D. Tata, for example, was chairman of the great Tata group of companies well into his eighties.

Box 9.14 What Indians Are Like

The counterpart of Tayeb's list of English characteristics that is reproduced in Box 3.4 is her list of Indian characteristics given below. It, too, was synthesized from history, literature, contemporary mass media, and 100 questionnaires completed by (Indian) people chosen at random. Compared to the English, Tayeb saw Indians as:

- more emotional
- fearful of people in positions of power
- more obedient to seniors
- more dependent on others
- more fatalistic
- submissive
- more open to bribery
- less able to cope with new and uncertain situations
- less concerned for others outside own community
- accepting responsibility less
- less disciplined
- more modest
- less reserved
- more collectivistic
- caste-conscious
- law-abiding
- opposed to change
- less self-controlled
- less trustworthy
- more friendly
- less tenacious
- more clan-orientated
- less willing to take account of other people's views

Tayeb is well placed to compare the two societies since, as has been said before, she herself is neither English nor Indian in origin but Iranian.

This is a tendency reinforced from both directions, above and below. From above, the extensive State regulation of business has meant that, since relations with government are vital, they need to be dealt with at the top. From below, an ill-educated workforce, often illiterate, possibly even submissive and untrustworthy, waits upon direct, personal instructions from higher levels. Box 9.15 gives a startling comparison with other nations, though the much greater Indian centralization score is to some extent due to differences in the way centralization was counted.

Yet the picture is not as clear-cut as that. The wielding of authority at the top is offset by the self-image typical to the Indian manager. He is likely to see his style as more caring and more considerate of others than is usual in the West. If he is, then those below him will not object if he is also authoritarian and patronizing. Likewise, Indian managers are inclined to value loyalty from others more, and to judge what is done in a more moralistic fashion, in terms of right and wrong, as much as by efficiency. This may be paternalistic, but it is attuned with the values in Indian society generally.

For each employee's notion of 'self', or sense of what he or she is and where they are in society, is rooted in a male-led family (where the senior male – grandfather, father, elder brother, etc. – bears ultimate responsibility for everyone in the extended family) and in the caste ascribed by it (though it is formally illegal to discriminate on grounds of caste). Many of the parables of the Bhagavad Gita, one of the ancient Hindu scriptures, stress duty and loyalty in the family and upholding family honour.

So, as was said earlier in this chapter, an impersonal job in an organization may be seen as a duty done in the service of the family as much as, or more than, for its own sake. It can enhance family pride, and get a better match for a daughter. The work organization is likely to be a place to earn a livelihood rather than a place to belong. And whilst managers may talk in the same ostensibly rational managerial language as is spoken by managers worldwide, they may act in a more emotive manner which goes deeper.

Yet here in the **managing of relationships** is another offsetting contrast, if not contradiction, in the complexity that is Indian. For although management can be caring and paternalistic, the manager can also treat those beyond his own circle distantly and cursorily, and even be overtly aggressive on the job in a way that he cannot be at home (Box 9.14 lists

Box 9.15 Indian Centralization

A comparison of the centralization of eleven manufacturing organizations in each of five countries shows startlingly high centralization in the Indian firms:

	Mean Centralization	Standard Deviation	Range (lowest to highest)
Poland	173	16	139–180
Britain	120	13	104–141
Japan	120	26	66–162
Sweden	125	10	111–142
India	401	173	183–696

The Indian researcher, Shenoy, comments: *This would not be the first time that it has been suggested that Indian management is relatively centralized, either lacking confidence in lower-level staff or lacking staff with training adequate to the taking of decisions at lower levels.*

Centralization is here measured by what is known as the Aston method. This is, in effect, a count of how many from a tested list of managerial decisions are authorized at which level, scoring higher those that are taken higher up. The greater the number of decisions authorized at higher levels, the greater the centralization.

Two cautions must be observed: (a) whilst these counts can be relied upon as a broad comparison, the exact figures should not be made too much of; (b) *the Indian total has been inflated*, to an unknown extent, by counting for a committee decision every manager on it, whereas for the other nations only the highest level manager was counted.

Poland's score reflected the centralizing effects of State planning when it had a communist-controlled command economy.

(Shenoy, p. 143. The data for countries other than India were reproduced from Kuc, B., D. J. Hickson and C. J. McMillan, 'Centrally Planned Development', Ch. 5 in Hickson, D. J. and C. J. McMillan (eds.), *Organization and Nation: the Aston Programme IV*.)

being more emotional and less reserved and self-controlled as Indian characteristics). Employee loyalty does not transfer from the family situation to him and to workmates, in a quasi-familistic way, as readily as it seems to in Japan (Box 9.16). Loyalties to family and, in India, to caste, can be strong, and patronage – personal support and preferment – follows loyalty. So communication up and down the organization is likely to be comparatively poor.

Box 9.16 Aggression at Work

Contrasted with the Japanese, Indians have very little identification with the work organization and the work group therein. While the American, being an individualist, would draw meaning from his own work and the Japanese from his belonging to his work group and his contribution to it, the Indian would much more largely draw meaning from the state of his familial relationships. The problem gets compounded because, while the Indian contains his aggression when in familial settings, he may displace that suppressed aggression into the work setting to which he has less allegiance. At work the Japanese contains aggression, and the American puts it in the service of his individual achievement, but the Indian does less of either. Hence there is a greater potential for sub-optimal performance, malingering, sabotage, and even outright violence . . .

(Gupta, p. 75)

The underlying potential of Indian management may be in its ability to **cope with uncertainty,** and the value it gives to creativity. Even though this capacity may too often in the past have been devoted to finding ways around and through the regulations of the State, as the report in Box 9.2 showed, it lies behind the growth of industry and it augurs well for economic development. The evidence, such as it is, is scanty and not all one way, as is demonstrated by the contrary assertion in Box 9.14, but nevertheless there have been recurrent research findings showing Indian managers to be able to take risks and to innovate, and to overcome setbacks. Not all do so and not all firms innovate, but some can and do (see Box 9.17). Indeed, Indian business acumen is conspicuous in eastern and southern Africa where Indians are, or have been, to the fore in business.

Box 9.17 Pioneering Innovative Management

Questionnaires answered by senior and middle managers in seventy-five Indian manufacturing and service organizations, both private and public sector, showed how far management policy was seen as emphasizing novel or pioneering products or services, innovation, high quality, high returns even if at high risk, and readiness to adapt to changing circumstances. Whilst only some managements showed a strong 'pioneering innovative' pattern, that they did so indicated that Indian managements are capable of taking a vigorous approach whatever the organization and even if it is government-owned. *The way may be open, therefore, to most organizations in the developing world to choose to be proactive, risk-taking, innovative, and pioneering, despite pervasive governmental control, weak transport and communication and energy infrastructure, and weak work ethic.*

(Khandwalla, 1985, pp. 170 and 175)

So although an element of fatalism in Hinduism is often alluded to, this does not unavoidably stifle enterprise. Furthermore, there are signs of change, especially in the more modern, urban businesses, towards less emphasis on hierarchy, more trust and more initiative.

*   *   *

The difficulties of the developing countries in managing economic growth are extreme. They struggle to adapt contemporary ideas of good management with traditional ways of their own that can clash with those ideas. They do so in a situation where managerial skills are in short supply and poverty is endemic. A tendency to over-centralization, to over-formalism and to poor morale is not surprising. As a result, management aims are often unfulfilled.

This chapter is the last of those which have examined culture and management in particular kinds of societies west to east, north to south. It has described societies which face the greatest challenge and, most likely, the greatest cultural conundrums. The final two chapters consider the demands made upon the individual manager who moves between cultures, and how far managements in all societies, developing countries included, may be drawing together in a common approach.

Further Reading

GENERAL

Cavusgil, S. Tamer and Pervez N. Ghauri. 1990. *Doing Business in Developing Countries: Entry and Negotiation Strategies.* Routledge.

Jaeger, Alfred M. and Rabindra N. Kanungo (eds.). 1990. *Management in Developing Countries.* Routledge.

Kiggundu, Moses N. 1989. *Managing Organizations in Developing Countries: An Operational and Strategic Approach*. Kumarian Press.

Negandhi, Anant R. 1985. 'Management in the Third World', in P. Joynt and M. Warner (eds.), *Managing in Different Cultures*. Universitetsforlaget.

AFRICA

Blunt, Peter and Merrick L. Jones. 1992. *Managing Organizations in Africa*. De Gruyter.

Harris, Philip R. and Robert T. Moran. 1991. *Managing Cultural Differences* (3rd edn, Ch. 18). Gulf Publishing.

Hyden, Goran. 1983. *No Shortcuts to Progress: African Development Management in Perspective*. Heinemann.

Onyemelukwe, C.C. 1973. *Men and Management in Contemporary Africa*. Longman.

INDIA

Gupta, Rajen K. 1999. 'The Truly Familial Work Organization: Extending the Organizational Boundary to Include Employees' Families in the Indian Context', Ch. 6 in Henry S.R. Kao, Durganand Sinha, and Bernhard Wilpert (eds.), *Management and Cultural Values: the Indigenization of Organization in Asia*. Sage.

Kalra, Satish Kumar and Rajen K. Gupta. 1999. 'Some Behavioural Dimensions of Effective Managerial Style in the Indian Context', Ch. 17 in Henry S.R. Kao, Durganand Sinha, and Bernhard Wilpert (eds.), *Management and Cultural Values: the Indigenization of Organization in Asia*. Sage.

Kemp, Tom. 1983. *Industrialization in the Non-Western World*. Longman.

Parikh, Indira J. and Pulin K. Garg. 1990. 'Indian Organizations: Value Dilemmas in Managerial Roles', Ch. 10 in Alfred M. Jaeger and Rabindra N. Kanungo (eds.), *Management in Developing Countries*. Routledge.

Tayeb, Monir. 1988. *Organizations and National Culture: A Comparative Analysis*. Sage.

Other Sources

AFRICA

Akpan, Ntieyong U. 1982. *Public Administration in Nigeria*. Longman, Nigeria.

Ghartey J.B. 1987. *Crisis, Accountability, and Development in the Third World: The Case of Africa*. Avebury/Gower.

Gutkind, P.C.W. 1968. 'African Responses to Urban Wage Employment'. *International Labour Review*, 97, 135–66.

Jones, Merrick L. 1986. 'Management Development: an African Focus'. *Management Education and Development*, 17, 3, 202–16 (reproduced in *International Studies of Management and Organization*, 19, 1, 74–90, 1989).

Price, R.M. 1975. *Society and Bureaucracy in Contemporary Ghana*. University of California Press.

INDIA

Caiden, Gerald E. 1988. 'Toward a General Theory of Official Corruption'. *Asian Journal of Public Administration*, 10, 1, 3–26.

Gupta, Rajen K. 1991. 'Employees and Organisation in India: Need to Move Beyond American and Japanese Models'. *Economic and Political Weekly*, XXVI, 21, May 25.

Khandwalla, Pradip N. 1985. 'Pioneering Innovative Management: An Indian Excellence'. *Organization Studies*, 6, 2, 161–84.

Shenoy S. 1981. 'Organization Structure and Context: a Replication of the Aston Study in India'. Ch. 8 in David J. Hickson and Charles J. McMillan (eds.), *Organization and Nation: The Aston Programme IV*. Gower Publishing and also Pugh, Derek S., The Aston Programme, Vol. II. 1998. Dartmouth/Ashgate.

Singh, Joginder P. 1990. 'Managerial Culture and Work-related Values in India'. *Organization Studies*, 11, 1, 75–106.

Tayeb, Monir. 1987. 'Contingency Theory and Culture: A Study of Matched English and Indian Manufacturing Firms'. *Organization Studies*, 8, 3, 241–62.

The previous chapters in this book have highlighted the considerable differences in management processes across the globe. Managers who have to negotiate deals with those from other countries have the cultural dimension to take into account. Similarly, for managers taking a job abroad in a new culture, work can be more difficult than for those remaining in their home culture. Yet international business activity is continually increasing. Indeed the activities of more and more organizations – not only businesses, but also voluntary and inter-governmental agencies – encompass a worldwide scale of operation.

From a business point of view, the multinational corporation in particular is an efficient vehicle for resource allocation around the world. In a global free market, importing and exporting could ensure economically efficient international trade. But many barriers to free trade exist: tariffs, exchange controls, governmental development policies, and so on. For a company to compete it is therefore often necessary to invest and manufacture abroad, inside such barriers. So during the second half of the twentieth century there was an explosion in international business operation through multinational companies which shows no sign of diminishing. American and Japanese corporations predominate, followed closely by those from Britain and other European Union countries. There are a number from Hong Kong, Canada and Australia, and a scattering from elsewhere.

For example, the countries of the European Union have established an internal open market. This could well lead in the future to tariff barriers being raised against imports from non-member countries. This prediction was indeed made by American and Japanese companies. One of the first results, therefore, of the agreement to establish a full European internal market was investment by firms from those countries in founding or taking over firms inside the EU. In this way the multinational corporations get free access from within to what might otherwise be a difficult or closed market.

A popular form of multinational enterprise is that of the joint venture when two, or more, firms from different countries have joint equity ownership of an operating company. Such a company might be set up because one partner has access to capital or know-how, and the other to new markets. Government regulations which have restricted foreign ownership in many countries of the world (e.g. Sweden, India, Russia) have acted as a spur to the setting up of joint ventures, linking a foreign company with an indigenous firm.

These developments continue apace because there is now something approximating to a global market for most manufactured goods as well as for finance. Indeed, competition is worldwide. As they cope with this global situation, multinational corporations (MNCs) have to take account of existing national and cultural differences as described above. It is no good their trying to treat employees in a participative, open, way if they are not used to it, any more than it is to treat them in an authoritarian manner if they are not used to that, as Box 10.1 points out. They have to strike a balance between extreme 'ethnocentrism' (requiring each subsidiary to conform precisely to parent company ways, regardless of the country in which it is operating) and extreme 'polycentrism' (allowing each subsidiary to be managed in its own way regardless of new ideas and parent company global policy). Both of these extremes will be inefficient, the former by not taking account of local factors which affect performance, and the latter by not gaining the benefits of the integration of global operations. But even without being at the extremes, there is still a wide range of points along this dimension at which an effective balance may be struck for an organization's international structure and operations. Box 10.2 describes the common development phases of MNCs, while Box 10.3 gives a classification of types of business structure.

Box 10.1 Do It My Way!

American researchers Newman and Nollen compared the financial perform-ance (return on assets, return on sales, and managers' performance bonus) of 176 work units in an American MNC. These were 'sales, service and support' departments or sections such as marketing or systems engineering, supplying computers and office products, spread across eighteen West European and Asian countries. They had between ten and one hundred employees (mean 55), who were given regular questionnaires by the corporation to indicate their views of its management practices.

When the researchers analysed how management practices were seen, they found that financial results were better when management acted in a way that fitted a country's culture. Using Hofstede's concepts (including power distance, individualism/collectivism and masculinity/femininity, as described in Chapter 2, and long-term/short-term orientation or Confucian Dynamism, as described in Chapter 7) they showed that a participative management style worked best in low power distance cultures, as might be expected, but was not similarly successful if it was tried in high power distance cultures, and so on.

In their words:

Management practices should be adapted to the local culture to be most effective. Managers' efforts to encourage employee participation might improve the profitability of work units in countries with a culture of low power distance, such as the US, but more employee participation is likely to worsen profitability, not improve it, in countries with high power distance, such as Latin European and East Asian countries. An emphasis on individual employee contributions is likely to improve profitability in individualistic countries, such as the US, but to worsen profitability in collective countries, including those in East Asia. Substantial use of merit-based pay and promotion should improve profitability in masculine countries, such as Anglo and Germanic countries, but worsen it in feminine countries, such as Nordic countries. A short-term approach to problem-solving and a small sense of employment security apparently are good for profitability in short-term oriented countries, such as the US, while long-term approaches work better in long-term oriented countries, such as those in East Asia.

Corporate initiatives that are created at headquarters and promoted world-wide run the risk of conflicting with unreceptive national cultures.

(from Newman and Nollen, pp. 773–4)

Box 10.2 Three Phases of MNC Development

1. MNCs start by being *ethnocentric*; that is, the corporation conducts its activities abroad for the benefit of the home organization in the home country, and the ways of working in the foreign culture are imposed from the home base.

2. As it penetrates into more and more countries, the MNC has to take less and less account of the home country's interests and become *polycentric*. Operations in the host countries are then left more and more to the local management, who are more affected by the host government and the host culture than are the expatriates, but who are nevertheless absorbing the main corporation's culture. All managers are now beginning to take a supra-national approach to objectives, inclined to pay less attention to national interests.

3. As this trend proceeds, the corporation becomes *geocentric*; that is, all considerations relating to growth and survival are based wholly on the interests of the corporation itself – national pressures in any country (including the mother country) being regarded as a constraint like any other and not having any prior status. By then it is more important to identify the manager as a member of the corporation than as of any particular nationality, and position in the global organization can be reached by anyone on the basis of merit, regardless of nationality. A corporation culture emerges and managers do not carry any constraints, including national cultural constraints, from one country to another.

(adapted from Perlmutter)

The move from ethnocentric to geocentric approaches to management is a developmental process that is taking place in many MNCs. There are, in addition, intermediate stages. In the mixed form between ethnocentric and polycentric approaches, certain aspects of management are decentralized from the home country while others are tightly controlled centrally. Very typically, policies and practices in marketing and human resource management are decentralized while policies and practices in regard to finance, technical and product know-how are controlled centrally. A mixed form between polycentric and geocentric approaches is 'regiocentric', where considerable international integration across subsidiaries in each world region is developed, while retaining home country control from head office.

Box 10.3 Types of International Business Structure

1. The Global Organization is the closest to extreme ethnocentrism. These firms build world-scale facilities to distribute standard products to markets everywhere. It is a form pioneered in the motor industry by Ford, and is the approach taken by many of the Japanese international companies such as Matsushita and Toyota. The centre retains strong control in decision-making, and the foreign operations are seen as a delivery mechanism to global markets. The aim is to get the maximum benefits from worldwide integration.

2. The Multinational Organization is the closest to extreme polycentrism. These firms respond to local market opportunities and are prepared to vary their products or even businesses as necessary. Firms such as ITT and Unilever were pioneers in creating the conglomerate – a relatively decentralized confederation with distributed resources and responsibilities. The control exercised may be limited to little more than the supervision of financial results.

3. The International Organization is an intermediate type. While some autonomy is given to the subsidiaries, there are many control mechanisms operating. Firms such as IBM and General Electric run a 'co-ordinated federation' in which particular functions such as R&D, product development and market development, as well as finance, are kept close to the centre. So there is a degree of benefit in both responsiveness to local markets and integrated global development.

4. The Transnational Organization is an integrated network of highly interactive units. Its decentralization allows subsidiaries to acquire the flexibility to adapt to local markets, but the network allows all parts of the organization to benefit from the knowledge of each. Thus the organization gets the benefits of both local flexibility and global innovative integration. It is postulated as an ideal type towards which MNCs will need to develop to obtain maximum efficiency.

(adapted from Bartlett and Ghoshal)

There are many international firms travelling this path on the way to being geocentric. Some consider that the big American-initiated multinationals such as General Motors, ITT and IBM have reached the geocentric stage. They were the ones that led the way in international expansion in the twenty years after the Second World War. Their geocentrism is demonstrated by the fact that these large corporations have at least as many (and probably more) problems of violating national constraints of the USA (their 'home' country) as they do in the other countries in which they operate. As against this, it should be pointed out that there have been very few, if any, non-Americans on the main boards of these corporations. If they were truly geocentric in their management approach, there would be many more.

Every type of multinational organization must have inputs from its home country head office (finance, technical know-how, etc.) which go to its subsidiaries in host countries to aid their performance. The head office must also obtain from each subsidiary information for strategy formulation and managerial control. The usual method of attempting to co-ordinate parent–subsidiary relations is through the use of cross-cultural managers. These can be given assignments to foreign subsidiaries and so gain insights into the local operation and the culture in which it is based. At the same time they develop and propagate the benefits of corporate knowledge. They are thus the key managers on whom the functioning of multinationals depend. Box 10.4 describes four typical members of this group.

The cultural flexibility required to manage effectively in an international situation is not easy to achieve because we are all subject in our thinking – at least to some degree – to 'ethnocentrism'. This term has already been used to characterize some of the corporations themselves. It is the implicit assumption, often unawares, that our culture is the best, our way of doing things is normal, the right way, as discussed in Chapter 2. So the British talk of 'keeping Britain great', the French of 'Paris – capitale du monde', and the Chinese ideograph for China means 'the country at the centre of the world'. We all overestimate the importance of our country and our culture in the scheme of things. When we see something different in another culture, we are liable to view it as abnormal and inferior to our comfortable ways of thinking and ways of doing things.

Box 10.4 Four Cross-cultural Managers

Three men and a woman, who might be seen chatting in the executive lounge of an international airport, represent the commonest types of cross-cultural manager found by British researcher Torrington.

Willem is the fully *international manager*. Fluently speaking English and

German as well as his native Dutch, he travels continually throughout the world, making deals and opening up opportunities for his company. He is constantly on the move and his mind travels easily across languages and cultures. But he is seldom away from his base for more than a week at a time and he deals only with representatives of the companies he visits; there is little or no involvement with their internal structures or management.

Charles is the *expatriate*. He had two years in the Middle East a little while ago and is now on the way to a three-year assignment in South-East Asia. This time he will be joined by his wife, who has had to give up her own career, and by a small son. He has been assured that his next position in the firm will be an important one in the head office, and that then his globe-trotting days will be over. His wife would never have agreed to this posting otherwise.

Chow Hou is the *technical specialist*. He will be away for three months, installing the equipment and training the local staff. He has moderate technical English, but he can usually carry out the training by using diagrams, and by showing and doing. He is often away for various lengths of time, but expects to spend at least half the year back at head office, keeping up to date and giving advice and assistance.

Inge is the '*occasional parachutist*'. She usually makes two or three short trips abroad each year for the company because of her highly specialized expertise; lasting a week or less, they typically involve going in to sort out a systems problem that is troubling the local management, and returning immediately.

(adapted from Torrington)

The development of this belief in our own culture is an important part of our ability to function effectively in it. But it is a feature of human nature which does lead to problems when we come to operate in other cultures. It is the basis of what was called in Chapter 2 'culture shock'. This is the confusion which results from the feeling that you are 'out of your depth' in what is going on around you; what people do and what they say is strange and puzzling and even offensive. All you know is that you are not coping as you do at home, and you resent this. It is an experience which all those working in a different culture go through.

Underlining the problem is a current estimate that over one-third of expatriate managers return home prematurely, not having completed their assignments successfully. In addition to ineffectiveness in the job, alcohol problems and divorce are common results of not coping with

Box 10.5 Responses to Shocking Cultures

1. Spectator phase

2. First **culture shock**:
likely responses: a) flight
                             b) going native
                             c) fight
                             d) primary adaptation

3. Surface adjustment

4. Second **culture shock**

5. Adaptation

(adapted from Gullick)

the new culture. Culture shock needs to be expected, understood and managed.

In Box 10.5 is a series of phases which anyone, managers included, is likely to go through when coming to stay and work in a different culture for any length of time. Learning a new language is generally recognized to be a considerable achievement, and learning to function effectively in a new culture has many similarities. But doing a good job in another country is often thought to flow directly from technical, financial or managerial knowledge and experience alone. Those who know their jobs well and are capable in their accustomed surroundings are assumed to be equally capable elsewhere. It may therefore come as quite a shock for managers to discover that often this is not the case.

The first phase after arrival in a new country has been called the 'spectator phase', where everything in the different culture adds to the excitement. Even mistakes are regarded as interesting – though, since many mistakes are made through ignorance, the new arrival is often seen by the host country nationals as difficult or uncaring. But spectator-expatriates will regard these problems as minor because they will not be able to see the difficulties from the locals' point of view. Box 10.6 gives an instance of how this can happen even between two relatively similar cultures.

Box 10.6 An American in London

An American manager was appointed to take charge of the company's British office in London. Generally things went well, but one thing annoyed him. Visitors were never sent directly to his office. A visitor was first greeted by the receptionist, then handed over to the secretary and then on to the office manager, before being brought to him. The new manager decided to tell his subordinates to send visitors directly to him.

This caused a degree of upset among them. After a while the manager became aware of this feeling. Following a number of delicate conversations, he began to realize the greater stress on formality and hierarchy in Britain compared with America. People did not feel comfortable about the proper channels being bypassed. He then allowed the procedure to revert to the original one.

(adapted from Adler)

Those who look after the domestic arrangements (usually the female partner) cannot stay in the spectator phase for long since they have to shop, cook, organize the household and, in some societies, communicate with servants. But it is possible for senior managers to stay in it longer by working entirely within the local organization, which they continue to see in the same way as they did their organization back home. This is a danger because they will make decisions without regard to cultural differences. They will then be less effective than in their home country and, if this goes on, will lose the confidence of their subordinates.

With increasing participation, expatriates discover enough to avoid the more simple mistakes. They learn, for example, that there are different practices in the promptness of meetings and in the amount of general 'small talk' necessary before getting down to business. They have a greater sense of being able to communicate and being understood, and their own confidence increases. Major cultural differences are more readily recognized and attempts made to bridge them. Firms can assist here by providing 'cultural gatekeepers' who are more knowledgeable and can help to overcome differences. These might be locals who can act as 'interpreters', or a particular manager who is more experienced in, and attuned to, the new culture. Gatekeepers would be called in to help smooth over any difficulties which arise.

This early confidence of the new manager soon wears thin, however, and is followed by the 'first culture shock', in the form of a large attack of discouragement. In this phase the overload of new information on what is going on around is very oppressive. Managers feel that every contact is hard work, new ideas are always resisted, the same work problem is always much harder to solve abroad than at home. The manager learns the hard way that often what sounds like 'Yes' to a foreigner is in fact a polite way of saying 'No'. Problems of living conditions, lack of social life and homesickness crowd in. Expatriates tend to be driven back into themselves and their fellow expatriates and feel unable to rely on local help.

There are four likely ways of responding to this first culture shock:

a) *Flight*: some managers leave the different culture, shaking their heads at the impossibility of it all.

b) *Going native*: a few may fly in the other direction – into the host culture and an over-identification with it. They may even marry into the host culture, bring up their children to be monolingual in it, and make no attempt to bridge the cultures. They are often searching for a Utopia in their adopted land and, if and when they fail to discover it, their second culture shock can be even greater than their first.

c) *Fight*: that is, attempt to run the operation as though it were in the home country by trying to force work procedures towards parent company ways of doing things. The resultant conflict is normally disastrous, if for no other reason than that the host country will be able to impose political and legal constraints in addition to cultural ones. There is rarely sufficient support to defend an expatriate who directly challenges host country attitudes and practices (as Box 10.7 illustrates). Home country ways cannot be transplanted by compulsion, and managers have to find other methods to proceed.

d) *Primary adaptation*: the managers survive the first culture shock, which can last from a few days to several weeks, and, by working hard to understand the society in which they find themselves, can continue to function tolerably well and thus move on into the next phase.

This is the 'surface adjustment phase' in Box 10.5 when the expatriate can operate fairly well in a limited range of activities and with a small group of friends. The newcomer will have discovered differences in polite

Box 10.7 Come to the Party

Bob was a manager who worked in the Saudi Arabian office of a North American international construction company. He was proud that the company was American and he always wanted to do things 'the American way'. When one of his colleagues was leaving to return home, he wanted to organize a coffee party one afternoon to say farewell. He had great difficulty in getting his Arab subordinates to agree to come to the party although he pressed them hard. Eventually they complained to the higher management that Bob was trying to make them break the Ramadan fast. Bob was repatriated within a week for trying to impose home ways on the host culture.

(adapted from Gullick)

conventions, notions of privacy, of giving and receiving gifts, and so on. Crucially managers will have begun to discover differences in attitudes to work and will believe that they are getting a grip on them.

Typically, managers then feel a need for a deeper level of understanding and more effective means of communicating in order to improve their operational efficiency. Since this is very difficult to bring about, they are thus led to continual personal analysis of the culture and of their performance in it, in the hope of reaching their own home country levels of performance. They are also aware that they continue to make mistakes, even though these are now less obvious ones. As they come to realize that they know far less about the culture than they suppose, the second culture shock sets in.

The 'second culture shock' phase is at a more sophisticated level than the first. It may be associated with some necessary hard thinking on the part of the manager about ethical issues. Managers are normally reasonably comfortable about what is immoral behaviour in their own countries – they may not even have felt it necessary to think about such issues before. But in the new culture what to them is bribery (as in Nigeria), child labour (as in China) or the ruthless jettisoning of faithful employees (as in Britain) will be more overtly challenging. Will they attempt to apply their own personal values and practices, which will cause trouble locally? Or will they do what is done where they now find themselves and risk problems with their home country management, who do not want their people to be accused, back home, of malpractice? Or will they make some uneasy compromise between the two? And their position is not helped by the fact that most head offices have an official policy that nothing should be done in subsidiaries which is regarded as illegal or improper in the home country, while at the same time privately requiring the manager to 'fit in and make it work on the ground'. Managers will have to forge an ethical position on such issues, as much for themselves as for their organizations. The second culture shock also leads to a degree of withdrawal and thought. Either flight or adaptation is again likely.

Those who stick it out and attempt further adaptation have by now developed a working knowledge of the culture. They set themselves more realistic levels of communication and achievement. Expectations of what is possible are, in home country terms, changed and perhaps lowered. An important development is the use of host country body language. In the Arab culture, for example, Western managers are regarded as 'shifty' until they learn to look directly into a colleague's eyes for the culturally appropriate longer amount of time than in the West. The ability to 'read' what is communicated by silence is a key skill. It is possible now for the expatriates to relax a little, as they begin to realize that some cross-cultural 'problems' have to be lived with because they can be explained but not solved. It should be noted that this phase does not necessarily require expatriates to like the host culture. It does require, though, that they be realistic about what can be achieved by a manager in a cross-cultural situation.

Clearly it is important to their own futures, to their organizations and to international business for cross-cultural managers to adapt after both the first and second culture shocks. It is not possible to be very specific about how long this will take – quite likely a year or two.

What are the characteristics of managers who can successfully adapt to another culture and function effectively in it? There are two immediate prerequisite conditions for this, without which success is unlikely.

First, the manager must want to operate well in another culture and be excited by the challenge. Unwilling allocation to a posting abroad is a recipe for poor performance. And the same condition applies to the manager's spouse or partner. There are always tough decisions and adjustments to be made about family issues, and the family as a whole must be interested in the benefits which this inevitably dislocating experience will bring to them. The job and career of the spouse or partner may have to change. The nature of housework and family caring will inevitably change considerably if the family accompanies the expatriate. And family relationships will equally change if the family splits, with the manager being able to spend only limited periods at home when on leave.

Secondly, the manager must be prepared to make some attempt to learn the language beyond the purely touristic phrases, for use in work. It is true that for many, if not most, multinational corporations the language of operation is English, and senior managers will be able to function in this language. But host country nationals do not use English when talking among themselves, nor under conditions of stress. Expatriates who make no attempt to understand and contribute in the local language inevitably cut themselves off from anything more than the surface adjustment phase. Except in quasi-colonial situations, they are unlikely to survive the second culture shock to reach the adaptation phase.

With the two prerequisites of commitment to international experience and active fluency in another language in place, what further characterizes a successful international manager? The research described in Box 10.8 brought out the characteristics of those chosen as most international. Box 10.9 describes the approach which made them what they were, compared to the others.

Box 10.8 The Most International Managers

Ratiu studied 250 younger international managers of thirty-five different nationalities who were attending two leading European business schools: INSEAD at Fontainebleau, France, and the London Business School, England. Their average age was twenty-seven years, and most had at least three years' overseas experience. All spoke at least two languages and all wished to continue international careers. They had thus had opportunities to go through the phases of adjustment described in Box 10.5, and seemed to satisfy the prerequisites given above.

What kind of person was the most international, even among this very international selection? The 10 per cent of those on the courses who were considered by their peers to be 'most international' were described as 'flexible', 'open-minded', 'has many friends of different nationalities' and 'speaks with others in their own language'. Not all the descriptions were complimentary, though; terms like 'chameleon-like' and 'unplaceable' were also used.

When the researcher discussed with the managers the question of which

key learning experiences were associated with becoming more internationally minded, some very interesting differences arose between those
who were 'most international' and the others. The differences are summarized in Box 10.9.

(adapted from Ratiu)

The 'most international', open, managers are seen to be very flexible
and subjective in their thinking. They treat each person or each occurrence
on its own merits, trying intuitively to feel what approach is required.
They are always ready to try something else if the current approach
fails. Everybody inevitably uses stereotypes, but the 'most open minded
international' do so only tentatively at the beginning of an experience,
and privately. They avoid giving blanket characterizations and 'public
stereotyping'. They try to be descriptive of the actual situation and to
avoid being over-analytical. They therefore, rather paradoxically, do not
characterize themselves as most international – they don't believe in such
types – but merely talk about the need to describe new experiences and
to think what can be done about them.

Box 10.9 Becoming the Most International

The 'Most Open Minded International' manager:	'Other International' managers:
aims to be able to adapt to individual people within a culture	aim to be able to adapt to the culture
asks questions about what is happening. Looks for descriptions, meanings	ask questions about why is this happening. Looks too soon for explanations, reasons
uses feelings and impressions as relevant information	use only facts as relevant information
differentiates cultures qualitatively without comparing them	compare and evaluate cultures quantitatively
uses impressions to modify and clarify private stereotypes	use impressions to confirm theories and public stereotypes

(summarized from Ratiu)

This forward orientation contrasts with the 'other international' managers, who often take a view that is too immediately analytical and superficial in trying to explain the new situations. It is a view which can stem from a backward orientation. Box 10.10 illustrates the two approaches.

A distinguishing characteristic of the 'most open-minded international' managers is the ease and readiness with which they can recall and discuss the stress symptoms they experienced as part of the culture shock. They regard culture shock as a positive learning experience. The 'other international' managers, on the other hand, refer to it only obliquely and with discomfort as an example of failure. The 'most internationals' deal with the stress involved by having 'stability zones' to which they can temporarily withdraw. These include personal pastimes such as playing chess, writing up a diary, or meditation. Religious practice can also serve as such a zone. These temporary withdrawals allow a rhythm of high participation alternating with short withdrawal periods to absorb and reintegrate mentally, which enables the manager to carry on working effectively in the new environment. This contrasts with the 'other' managers who seek to cope by restricting generally their level of involvement in the new culture, so spending much more time with fellow expatriates out of touch with it.

These distinctions between the most international managers and the

---

Box 10.10 The Obvious and Beyond It

For the 'most open-minded international' managers in the Ratiu study, things are assumed to be not what they seem. Experiences are continually being labelled and relabelled, since the labelling is assumed to be unreliable and must be constantly checked against the new information of unfolding events. Speaking of Britain, one such manager said: 'I've been finding out more and more . . . Arabs absolutely abound in this country, much more than I thought possible. And I mean a Bristol man, is not a Sheffield man, is not a Darlington man, is not a . . . you know . . . it's incredible.'

The 'other international' managers of Box 10.9 have a more analytical approach. Their emphasis is less on information collection and more on early explanation and rapid conclusions. Speaking of Arabs, one of them said: 'Why was it that every time there was a technical hitch on site, a breakdown of some kind, I was quite unable to get it across to the operators, both Yemenis, that there was a perfectly straightforward technical reason? For them it was always God's will: "Nothing can be done about it because God willed it so." At first I just couldn't understand it. But having lived out in the desert for centuries as these people have, subject to the kind of harsh climate they are used to, and with little or no control over its effects, you would expect them to adopt this kind of attitude. To us it seems very passive, but it's really quite understandable. Later I moved to Saudi Arabia. And, sure enough, people there behaved in exactly the same way. I wonder if this sort of passivity isn't typical of the Arabs generally.'

Compared with the 'most international' manager, the approach here is very ambitious, in fact looking for a theory to explain the events. This leads to the overgeneralized 'public stereotyping' shown.

(adapted from Ratiu)

others have been presented in a very polarized way. Many people are likely to be in between in their attitudes: aiming for maximum flexibility and multi-cultural effectiveness but often resorting to being more rigid. The polarization does point, though, to those behaviours to aim for in order to achieve greater cross-cultural effectiveness.

Does training help to produce effective cross-cultural managers? Probably yes, when supported by reading books like the present one which highlight the key issues. But it has got to be appropriate training. There is evidence to show that some training programmes actually reduce the effectiveness of the participants when they move to their new postings. This is probably because the training is too superficial and succeeds only in giving the managers a false sense of confidence in their ability to cope effectively with cultural differences. So they are less open to what they encounter, believing that they know it all. An example of one international organization's training programme is given in Box 10.11.

Is it easier for international managers in a culture closer to their own than in one that is very different? Possibly. There is no clear answer to this. It would seem plausible that the stranger the culture, the more difficult the adjustment. But there are two cross-cutting factors. First, there are the requirements of task and organization. These limit practical differences in the way a job is done, even between very different cultures, as the problems with the Venezuelan manager in Box 11.10 show. Second, ostensibly similar cultures may be taken to be more alike than they are, as the Canadian managers of Box 3.14 discovered when retailing in the United States. The most open international managers will be flexibly alert in cultures both strange and familiar.

Of course, it is necessary to learn about the specific context. Business practices, the nature of markets, the level of technical expertise of staff and so on, have to be studied. This knowledge then has to be blended with an understanding of the characteristic attitudes in a particular culture to authority, change, achievement, time - in fact, everything with which this book is concerned. As previous chapters show, there is a great deal to be learned.

Box 10.11 The Hong Kong and Shanghai Bank International Training Programme

Graduate trainees in the international stream of the Hong Kong and Shanghai Bank have opted to be available for posting to any of the bank's operations worldwide. They undertake a six-month executive development programme which draws participants from all over the world. As many as ten nationalities will be working together on a programme which develops technical and managerial skills and gives a range of opportunities to develop cultural sensitivity and build cultural synergy.

There are four stages in the programme. The first is an initial orientation and team-building seminar to develop cultural awareness. The second stage is a ten-day outdoor personal development course, conducted in multi-cultural teams. It provides participants with experience of such overt cultural differences as cleanliness, dress, eating habits and attitudes towards privacy. It also requires coming to terms with implicit cultural differences in trust, participation and interpersonal relations.

The third stage is a week-long interpersonal skills course, and in the fourth stage participants have to undertake an international assignment, working in a culture different from their own. Attachments after the programme may not be to the initial posting because the aim is to develop general cultural sensitivity, not simply specific knowledge of another culture.

(summarized from Hawthorne *et al.*)

Box 10.12 lists some key aspects which returning expatriates regularly identify as causing difficulties and misunderstandings. These are in addition to the usual stresses that working in any new situation cause, such as anxiety about the unfamiliar, feelings of lack of belonging, and confrontation with one's own prejudices.

One training method designed to encourage early cross-cultural preparation by working through a series of short case-studies is the

Box 10.12 What to Know for Managing in a Different Culture

Some key topics that need to be considered when managing in any different culture are:

1. ways of working (such as the balance between concentrating on the work to be done and fostering good relationships) – see Boxes 3.2, 5.2, 8.12, 9.11.
2. notions of time and space (such as timekeeping for meetings, appropriate distance from colleagues when talking) – see Boxes 2.12, 3.8, 5.6
3. form of language and thought (such as high- or low-context speech) – see Boxes 2.8, 4.3.
4. proper managerial conduct (such as how far to be authoritarian) – see Boxes 7.11, 8.2, 11.10.
5. the balance between group demands and the individual's needs – see Boxes 7.27, 8.9.
6. rituals and beliefs – which are likely to be different and challenging, since few of us recognize our own culture's rituals. We tend to think we don't have any! See Boxes 2.1, 7.21, 8.20.
7. class and status (such as the marks of high and low status) – see Boxes 5.8, 8.17, 9.13.
8. values (such as concerning what is desirable in politics, economics, the environment) – see Boxes 7.14, 8.21.

(adapted from Brislin *et al.*)

'Cultural Assimilator'. The cases give critical incidents which introduce the manager to some of what will be required when working in a different culture. The large number of cases are intended to be comprehended gradually by repeated comparison with real-life situations Box 10.13 gives one of the case incidents.

Those who wrote the case argue that the correct choice of answer is option 4. While it is true that, in a highly 'masculine' culture such as Japan, a manager would be surprised that so much account is taken of a wife's opinion, Mr Tanaka noted that Mr Legrand himself did not wish to take up the position. So option 2 has less impact in confounding him than does option 4. As Chapter 7 shows, in Japanese as in other collectivist societies a person is defined much more as a member of a group (employee, parent) than by an individual identity. Fulfilling the group expectation to the best of one's ability is regarded as outweighing one's own personal inclinations. Indeed, one's own personal inclinations are likely to be to fulfil the expectation of the group. Thus Mr Tanaka would consider that Mr Legrand's responsibility as a company employee should lead him to accept the position whether or not he is happy about the idea. Mr Legrand's refusal is thus bewildering and makes him think that his belief in Mr Legrand's dedication has been completely misplaced. Mr Legrand, however, comes from a culture, described in Chapter 4, in which individual choice giving less regard to others is highly valued and so he exercises his right to refuse the new post with little compunction.

It is not only the Japanese who can be nonplussed by the French

---

Box 10.13 Engineering a Decision

Read the case incident, and answer the question.

Mr Legrand is a French engineer who works for a Japanese company in France. One day the general manager, Mr Tanaka, calls him into his office to discuss a new project in the Middle East. He tells Mr Legrand that the company is very pleased with his dedicated work and would like him to act as chief engineer for the project. It will mean two to three years away from home, but his family will be able to accompany him and there will be considerable financial benefits to the position – and, of course, he will be performing a valuable service for the company. Mr Legrand thanks Mr Tanaka for the confidence he has in him but says he will have to discuss it with his wife before deciding. Two days later he returns and tells Mr Tanaka that both he and his wife do not like the thought of leaving France and so he does not want to accept the position. Mr Tanaka says nothing but is somewhat dumbfounded by his decision.

Why is Mr Tanaka so bewildered by Mr Legrand's decision?

CHOOSE ONE OPTION
1. He believes it is foolish of Mr Legrand to refuse all the financial benefits that go with the position.
2. He cannot accept that Mr Legrand should take any notice of his wife's opinion in the matter.
3. He believes that Mr Legrand is possibly trying to force him into offering greater incentives to accept the offer.
4. He feels it is not appropriate for Mr Legrand to place his personal inclinations above those of his role as an employee of the company.

(adapted from Brislin *et al.*)

concept of individual freedom. Box 10.14 shows how one of the most successful cross-cultural managers of the post-war era still managed to startle his American colleagues at one point in his career.

Equipped with some sensitivity to cultural differences and some knowledge of the host culture, a manager will be in a better position to cope effectively with an expatriate assignment. When it is over, the manager will be returning home – only to discover that another set of cultural adjustments is required.

The culture shock of the returning manager is very strong with stages analogous to those in Box 10.5 that are liable to occur when going to a strange country. This time the country is thought to be familiar. Yet managers change during their overseas assignments, often developing unrealistic, even idealistic, views of what it is like back home. So the returning 'spectator phase' does not last very long before the battle for adjustment begins. There are two basic sets of reasons for the onset of discouragement on returning home: economic differences and managerial ones.

Box 10.14 Come and Join the Board

When Jacques Maisonrouge, the head of IBM Europe, based in Paris, was first asked to join the IBM Corporation main board and thus move to the USA, he refused. Although during his long career with the company he had spent several periods in America, at the time of asking a change did not suit him for personal reasons (aged parents, children at school) – and anyway, he and his wife had very close friends in Paris and loved living in France. The board was disappointed and bewildered that such a magnificent promotion opportunity was not taken, and Maisonrouge's career was held back. Later he was invited again. Since his personal circumstances had changed, he now felt able to accept and thus became the first non-American to be an IBM main board director.

(from Maisonrouge)

The economic differences are concerned with such issues as salary differentials, housing and lifestyle standards, and educational arrangements for children. For example, it is difficult to adjust to the fact of not having a house servant if these had been customary abroad. Having to give up private schooling, or having to start it, can cause problems.

But the really major adjustment is the managerial one. Often higher management has not recognized that the manager has had different experiences and is thus now capable of a higher level of managerial responsibility. The expatriate manager will almost certainly have had to become more flexible, take a much wider range of decisions, hold responsibility for a broader range of work than is thought appropriate in the much larger, and more bureaucratic, parent company. But not enough thought is given to what job the returnee should take, and many feel that they are given non-jobs back at the head office.

It is important, therefore, to develop 'transition strategies' to help smooth the path. One such is the use of 'repatriation agreements', in which the firm agrees with their overseas managers how long the international assignment will last, and what type or level of job they will be given on return. Another strategy is to set up a 'mentoring system'. Mentors are senior managers at the head office whose task is to keep contact with the expatriate during the overseas assignment and to begin looking for appropriate jobs in the company six months to a year before the manager returns. Having a knowledge of their international experience and career aspirations, mentors can act as advocates for the expatriates in job allocation and promotion discussions. It is with strategies like these that cross-cultural managers can avoid the all-too-common feeling that the period spent overseas did nothing to enhance their careers.

So, by way of summary, the following twelve steps towards becoming a successful international manager may be suggested:

BEFOREHAND

1 You must want to become an international manager and find the challenge exciting.
2 Develop your global knowledge and thinking. Work to understand your own industry, including your organization's competitors, on a worldwide scale. Read appropriate international trade journals.
3 Gain a basic knowledge of the appropriate culture and management on which to build, by reading material such as this book.
4 Do all you can to ensure that any family who may accompany you also understand and accept the challenge of multi-cultural living.
5 Make an effort to learn the appropriate foreign language for a work context, not just a touristic one.

6 Obtain good preparatory training which focuses on cross-cultural inter-personal skills and managerial functioning.

WHEN YOU ARE THERE

7 Understand the adjustment process, including the inevitable culture shock, and manage yourself as you go through it.

8 Watch and listen very carefully, being continually prepared to up-date your views of particular individuals and situations.

9 Set yourself realistic objectives on the job, taking account of the new culture as well as of parent company standards.

10 Work to forge your own ethical position and understand its justification.

11 Develop and regularly use 'stability zones' to help in your adjustment. Create opportunities for 'letting go'.

ON RETURNING

12 Finally, be prepared for culture shock on returning to your own country and your own organization. This too must be understood and managed. The more successful you have been in adjusting to another culture, the greater it will be.

Further Reading

Adler, N. J. 1997. *International Dimensions of Organizational Behaviour* (3rd edn). South-Western College Publishing.

Bartlett, C. A. and S. Ghoshal. 1989. *Managing Across Borders: The Transnational Solution.* Harvard Business School Press, Boston MA, and Hutchinson Business Books.

Brislin, R. W., K. Cushner, C. Cherrie and M. Yong. 1986. *Intercultural Interactions: A Practical Guide.* Sage.

Torrington, D. 1994. *International Human Resource Management.* Prentice Hall (UK).

Other Sources

Gullick, C. J. M. R. 1990. 'Expatriate British Managers and Culture Shock', in *Studies in Third World Societies*, No. 42, Dept of Anthropology, College of William and Mary, Williamsburg VA, 173–206.

Hawthorne, P., S. Tang and P. Kirkbride. 1990. 'Creating the Culturally Sensitive Hong Kong Bank Manager'. *European Foundation for Management Development Journal*, No. 4, 14–17.

Maisonrouge, J. 1988. *Inside IBM: A European's Story*. Collins, London.

Newman, Karen L., and Stanley D. Nollen. 1996. 'Culture and Congruence: The Fit between Management Practices and National Culture'. *Journal of International Business Studies*, Fourth Quarter 1996, 753–79.

Perlmutter, H. V. 1969. 'The Tortuous Evolution of the Multinational Corporation'. *Columbia Journal of World Business*, 4, 9–18.

Ratiu, I. 1983. 'Thinking Internationally: A Comparison of How International Executives Learn'. *International Studies of Management and Organization*, 13, 139–50.

11 | Managing More and More Alike?

How much will the cross-cultural, international manager have to learn? Many different approaches to management in a large number of countries across the world have been described in earlier chapters. The strong influence of societal cultures in forming characteristic differences in attitudes and ways of working has been demonstrated. German, Nigerian, Polish, British and Chinese managements (for example) are certainly distinctively different from one another. So are there such wide discrepancies that managers will have to learn completely afresh if they work in a country different from their own? Will knowing how to be an efficient manager in one's own country give no clues at all to operating effectively in other countries?

Fortunately, the world is not as difficult a place as that. While there are vital – and fascinating – distinctions there are also key similarities across organizations in different cultures. As Box 11.1 illustrates, all organizations have recognizable hierarchies, even though there are subtle variations in how responsibilities are depicted. Box 11.2 describes an international study demonstrating this. There will be variations in the effects and use of hierarchy, but it appears everywhere.

There are also a number of factors other than culture which will influence the operation of organizations. Some particularly obvious ones have been pointed out in Chapter 2. They include the managerial need for success, the level of technological development, the type of ownership, the size of the organization and its own internal culture, and the different jobs that the managers do (e.g. in production or marketing or finance).

These influences will be apparent across all cultures. They underline the similarities in the tasks of management in all countries, as Box 11.3

Box 11.1 Please Look at This

Assume that you are visiting a firm in Japan but you do not read Japanese. At Reception your contact hands you a diagram. Would you have any clue as to what this section represented before it was explained and translated for you?

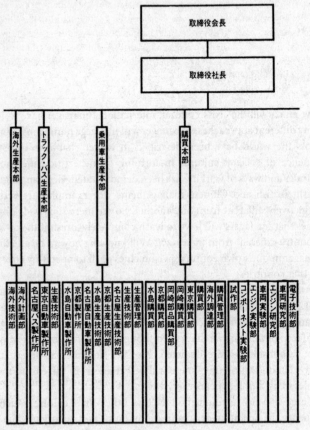

If you have any knowledge of organizations and their functioning, you will have spotted that it is part of an organization chart even before your contact started to speak. In fact, it is an extract from the organization chart of the Mitsubishi Motors Corporation, but most large firms in most countries in the world could produce a chart on similar lines.

Box 11.2 The Global Pervasiveness of Hierarchy

Tannenbaum and his colleagues have traced organizational hierarchies in numerous countries. They ask members of an organization: 'How much say or influence does each of the following groups have over what goes on in the organization?' The simplest groups to ask about are managers, supervisors and workers. Asking about the amount of influence of each of these on a 5-point scale from 'little or no influence' to 'a very great deal of influence' produces a diagram called a 'control graph'. This shows the average influence rating obtained by each level in the hierarchy. A hypothetical (but typical) example is shown below.

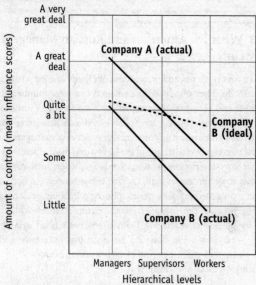

In the figure, the slope of the lines for Companies A and B (actual) shows the hierarchical distribution of influence and control as employees see it. It shows influence dropping from one level to the next down the hierarchy from managers to supervisors to workers. In all organizations, as seen by all employees, this slope is present. There is always hierarchy, everywhere. Even so, the steepness of the slope can differ. It is steeper in Italian manufacturing firms than in American ones, demonstrating that the relative influence of higher levels is greater in Italy. It is flatter, but still exists, even in Israeli *kibbutzim*. These differences in slope are what would be expected from the power distance scores for those three cultures. As Box 2.5 shows (in

Chapter 2) Italy has the highest power distance score, then the USA and finally Israel.

Organization members can also be asked what the relative amount of influence across the levels *should* be. This generates an 'ideal slope', as shown by the dotted line in the Figure for Company B. This is less steep than the actual slope, showing that many employees at lower levels feel that they themselves should have more say in what is going on. But the slope does not flatten completely, much less tip the other way. Few members of organizations in any culture suggest that lower levels should have more influence than higher ones. That is revolution!

(adapted from Tannenbaum)

Box 11.3 What Do American and Russian Managers Actually Do?

Luthans, an American researcher, and his colleagues studied what US managers actually do. They observed the managers in a large number of diverse organizations and classified their activities. Then in 1990 (just before the break-up of the Soviet Union) they collaborated with Russian colleagues to conduct precisely the same study on a smaller number of managers in a textile mill generally recognized to be one of the largest and most efficient in Russia.

There were 63 descriptions of what a manager does, such as: hires staff, decides what to do, processes mail, coaches subordinates. (In both America and Russia a proposed category of disciplining/punishing personnel had to be dropped because the managers were uncomfortable with this being observed by outside researchers.) Trained observers filled in a check list describing what was being done on 80 occasions over two weeks in a randomly chosen, 10-minute period in each working hour.

The results were classified into:

1. Traditional management activities: including planning, decision making, monitoring, controlling performance.
2. Communication activities: including exchanging routine information, processing paperwork.
3. Human resource management activities: including motivating, staffing, managing conflict.
4. Networking activities: including socializing, politicking, interacting with outsiders.

Which sort of activity did Russian and American managers do most? And least? The percentages were:

	Russians (66 managers)	*Americans* (248 managers)
Traditional management	43	32
Communication	34	29
Human resource management	15	20
Networking	9	19

The results demonstrate the differences which would be expected between the Russian system, still either centrally planned or with the lingering effects of central control, and the more open American system. Since for the Russian organization personnel were easy to recruit and had little or no choice of job, sales were fixed and internal departmental links were routinely directed, the Russian textile managers did not give the same attention to human resource management or to networking.

Despite this, the broad pattern of what each set of managers did is recognizably similar. More than that, in both countries networking worked. The more successful managers (those who had been promoted younger) spent more time networking among both Russians and Americans. Also among both, those who were seen by their subordinates as more effective gave more attention to communication.

Thus in two societies differing in economic systems and in cultures, the general pattern of what managers have to do and what better managers do best had a great deal that was in common.

(adapted from Luthans *et al.*)

illustrates. This shows that not only are the contents of middle managers' jobs comparable in two very different countries (USA and Russia), but the factors which contribute to success among these managers seem to be the same.

This chapter considers the argument that the non-cultural factors which act in the same direction upon managements of all cultures are getting stronger. As enterprises move more and more towards operating internationally, there is a convergence in management functioning which could mean that sooner or later there will be a common global 'management culture'. Thus organizations are heading for management globalization, when thinking is always in terms of global production, global markets and global communications. Box 11.4 gives a current instance of the consequences of instant information internationally.

From this point of view cultural differences in management would diminish. The convergence argument maintains that we are seeing a worldwide development of industrialization, common technology especially information technology, larger scale operation and growing interdependence of international multi-organization systems. To succeed and survive, organizations must use efficient management practices tailored to technical needs regardless of culture. What matters in understanding the management in a particular country is not primarily its distinctive culture, but first and foremost its level of economic development, foreign investment, technological sophistication and access to global communications and markets.

Box 11.4 Jobs for Automobile Workers

There are always continual pressures on organizations to change in order to improve performance. In 1994 the Volkswagen Motor Corporation in Germany was engaging in negotiations with the trade unions to develop a new package on wages and working hours. The basis of the deal was the need to avoid redundancy and unemployment with the high social costs that are then entailed. Workers would work shorter hours and the company would retain a larger workforce. The detailed working-out of the package shows the careful forward planning which was discussed in Chapter 5 as a characteristic aspect of German managerial culture.

But, of course, this exercise was being watched with intense interest by automobile manufacturers and unions all over Europe – and wherever else the possibility of redundancy for trained car workers exists. If VW showed that it is possible to retain a larger workforce with a shorter working week and still be efficient and profitable, how long would it be before French, Italian, US and British (even Japanese and Korean) automobile workers pressed for and obtained the same conditions? Thus the international motor industry cannot escape the worldwide pressures to converge towards common working practices which are efficient and profitable.

How strong is this convergence and will it continue to increase? It must be said at once that there is at present no clear-cut answer to this question. The 'convergence thesis' as against the 'culture-specific thesis' is one of the most debated issues in the study of international management. This chapter examines some of the evidence for it.

THE PRESSURES TOWARDS CONVERGENCE

The convergence argument can be put on a number of levels. At its strongest it has been suggested that whole societies are steadily moving together so that the similarities between all cultures will become much greater than their differences. The most obvious way in which we see this now is in the enormous global communications explosion. People are beginning to see immediately via satellite and cable television what is happening all over the world, and this is shaping their aspirations. How many male teenagers in the world, for example, would now prefer to wear some form of distinctive national dress rather than t-shirt, jeans and trainers? Pressures for convergence are set up as people everywhere, particularly the young, want the same clothes, pop stars, automobiles, sports, chance to vote in elections and everything else that is shown on television or networked electronically. The power of modern communications in upsetting controlled political systems is profound. For example, China needs fax and internet electronic-mail communication for business purposes. Official control of these media is very limited, so they will hasten the opening-up of that country, as they did in Eastern Europe.

A second level of the convergence argument is about economic systems. The most developed countries in the world, with the highest standards of living, are market economies. The market approach has been so successful relative to any other system (e.g. Marxist state control) that it is being adopted worldwide for the economic benefits that it brings. The collapse of the Eastern European communist regimes was primarily economic. They just could not deliver the Western and Japanese standards of living that were coming to be known about and expected. They were therefore replaced by freer market economies. Of course capitalist market economies are not completely free; they have to develop and operate within government-established, socio-legal frameworks as Box 11.5 shows. There are continuing arguments in market economies about what the precise degree of government regulation should be and what can be left to the market. However these are the sort of adjustments that can be hammered out as, for example, the European Union develops its common economic system with more and more countries across Europe joining.

Overall, it is argued, the convergence of economic systems is steadily taking place.

A third level of convergence is that of management functioning. Organizations all over the world need to be managed. If their managers aim for efficiency, growth and technological development then, it is argued, they will be driven to run organizations in ways which have been found to be the most effective elsewhere across the world. Add to this the transfer of technology from the most successful economies and the proselytizing activities of the multinational corporations, and there will be a steady global convergence of management.

Box 11.5 The Modern Industrial State

One of the best-known Western economic and political commentators, John Kenneth Galbraith, has argued that all states which wish to benefit from modern technology will have to develop a mixed system of private and state economic activity.

Conventionally, economic activity was thought of as the behaviour of buyers and sellers, regulated by the market through which the stimulus of competition was provided. Economic power is denied to any one person or firm because of price competition. But this system depends on the existence of a large number of producers of a good or service, none of whom is in a position to dominate the market; conversely it depends on a large number of buyers who individually are not large enough to affect the market.

As Galbraith forcefully points out, this is not the situation in Western industrial states. Instead, there is a process of mergers and takeovers by which the typical industry passes from a stage with many firms competing to a situation of a few large firms only – 'oligopoly' in economists' terms. As industrialization develops, bringing with it more and more sophisticated technology, the need for the large-scale corporations to control the market increases, since their investment is growing hugely and they want to protect it. Once time and money are invested (and products are taking longer to get to the market with greater technological sophistication – in the aviation industry, for example, decades rather than years) there is a great deal of inflexibility; it becomes very difficult to back out. Increasingly technology needs specialist experts who must be trained and managed. All of which underlines the need to reduce the uncertainties involved, which in turn, means planning to control the market and insulate the corporation from it. A monopoly supply situation or a guaranteed customer are aimed for. Both of these options bring increasing state intervention.

The management of demand for the products of high-technology industries is more and more a matter for the State, through its attempts to establish control of the wage–price spiral, its control of personal and corporate income tax, and its own role as a consumer. The net result is an increasing similarity between industrial societies in terms of the structure of capital, the elaborate organizations and the sophisticated technology which lead to the dominance of large corporations interdependent with the State. Only in this way can the planning required for modern technology take place. Originally this argument was applied to the developed West, but now this form of governmental intervention (not always officially admitted or even legal) takes place in all countries with large capital investment including, for example, Japan and Malaysia.

(adapted from Galbraith)

A major cause of this is industrialization. This is based on technology which speaks a universal language attractive to all, whatever the form of government or the culture of a people. Computers are basically the same everywhere, as are factory automatic machines. So is air freight and its handling. So are radios, televisions, CDs and videos. Technology spreads out so that the world is divided into countries which are industrialized and those which are becoming so. Few countries, the argument goes, will forgo the material benefits that industrialization brings. Of course, there is a growing realization that there are costs, too, in excessive urbanization and environmental pollution, for example. But, so far these concerns have made little headway against the trend.

Box 11.6 The Logic of Industrialism

The spread of industrial technology from the more advanced nations occurs in four main ways:

1. Through the normal channels of trade when developing countries buy products and manufacturing facilities.
2. Through imitation, e.g. when they set up technical schools and distance learning universities, and learn from expatriate managers and consultants.
3. Through the effects of economic aid, which usually involves the delivery of more advanced technology and manpower training.
4. Through military channels, since the global scope of defence industry competition has led to the training of workforces to build bases, maintain

vehicles and aircraft, etc. This yields skills necessary for wider industrialization.

The worldwide diffusion of this advanced technology creates a 'logic of
industrialism'. A similar range of tasks and problems come into being, and
the pressures towards efficient production will ensure that the most effective
ways of tackling these common tasks will become adopted worldwide. So
organizations tackling the same tasks, in whichever culture, will become
more and more alike.

(summarized from Kerr *et al.*)

The logic of industrialism (Box 11.6) has certain consequences. For
example, a decision anywhere in the world to produce automobiles as
cheaply as possible will require factories of considerable size (individual
craftsmen will not do), specialized machinery (hand tools or even general-
purpose presses will not be sufficient by themselves), and supplies of raw
materials and parts (provided through specialist technical processes).
Then trained people, expert in their particular tasks, would be needed
to contribute a wide range of specialist knowledge, skills and effort.
Professional managers, who can raise and use capital (individual, corporate, governmental) to bring all these factors together and to organize
putting them to work, will also be crucial. Hence the same basis for
vehicle manufacturing organizations everywhere.

So, with the spread of industrial technology goes a structure of industries. For vehicle manufacturing suppliers of steel, of tyres, of paint, of
upholstery would be necessary, each of which in turn will have its own
technology and experts. The industrial structure becomes transformed
from small craft units showing little technical specialization to a complex
structure of large, specialized units operating in an interdependent, multi-
organizational system. This system in turn leads to a particular division
of labour. There will be less use for someone who can make sheet steel
and rubber tyres *and* reinforced glass; firms concentrating on only one
of those tasks would be preferred. Production controllers, systems ana-
lysts, cost accountants and other staff specialists will be needed. So
training will be developed in both technical and managerial tasks, and
the candidate who by ability or training can fill the vacancy best –
regardless of colour, caste, tribe, religion, family or gender – will be
appointed.

As was pointed out at the beginning of this book, this growth of impersonal organization has been happening in the developed West for well over a century. That does not mean that the process is completed. It has been uneven. For example, few countries, if any, could claim that they have completely effective equal opportunities in employment and promotion for all their ethnic sub-groups, or for women. These limitations reflect the cultural assumptions regarding social status, race and gender which exist in all societies. But the changes are in this direction, and can be seen most notably now in the western Pacific Rim. Before the end of the 20th century, South Korea and Malaysia had established their own vehicle manufacturing industries and were treading this path, being pushed by the need for efficiency into the same technology, expertise, training, organizational structure and so on, as the others.

Asian industrialization has been paralleled by de-industrialization in the West. 'De-manufacturing' would be a better term, for it has been offset by booming service industries. Banking, financial advisers, retailing, restaurants and leisure parks, tourism, broadcasting and the internet, and more. These services use common technologies which again spread worldwide, just as the technologies of manufacturing did and still do.

The convergence view does not mean that the traffic is necessarily all one way from the more developed to the less developed – although the main weight of transfer will clearly be in this direction. But contributions to effectiveness could come the other way too, and will be incorporated into the worldwide way of doing things. For example, Japan was a late developer into industrialization, but the values and culture of the country enabled it to take place relatively quickly. The Japanese put a greater priority on training workers, part of a general Japanese emphasis on education and training, as we saw in Chapter 7. In the Japanese motor industry, workers were trained to produce parts and vehicles to highly reliable quality standards (Box 11.7). This investment paid off, giving a considerable competitive edge in the market, together with low rates of scrap and lower costs of reworking during manufacture. When they were shown to give competitive advantage, the same ideas were taken seriously in America and the rest of the world. With the development of the Total Quality Management movement, they became part of the global management convergence.

Box 11.7 An American Professor Goes to Japan

The originator of current attempts to improve product quality through better techniques on the job was the American professor, W. Edwards Deming. He urged setting up 'quality control circles'. These are regular meetings in which workers are encouraged to suggest quality improvements from their own detailed working experience.

He could not interest American managements very much in this idea. In Japan, however, his proposals were adopted enthusiastically. They fit into the Japanese culture with its emphasis on collective discussion and decision-making.

So particular management innovations will be inaugurated in cultures in which they are most likely to flourish. But if they are successful, they will be adopted worldwide, even in less receptive cultures.

THE SHAPING OF ORGANIZATION STRUCTURES

As manufacturing and service industries continue to develop around the globe, two factors have emerged as being of especial importance in shaping the structural form of organizations. They have the same consequences everywhere. They are the *size* of an organization, and how it is interlocked with other organizations in such a way as to be *dependent* on them. Managements take decisions on how large an organization will become, and how it will be dependent on others for finance and supplies and orders, and in turn these constrain the form it is likely to take.

Everywhere bigger organizations are likely to have more kinds of specialists and departments, and more formalized procedures with greater amounts of paperwork and standard computer software. And this effect is increased if they are part of a larger owning group, which generates still more of these control systems. Everywhere organizations more dependent on owning groups or on the government for money and services, or more tied in to particular suppliers and customers, are also likely to lose autonomy and be more centralized within themselves. Box 11.8 describes the research which drew attention to this.

These research results form a framework for understanding how organizations develop worldwide. In all countries bigger organizations are more specialized and formalized in structure because everywhere growth means reaping economies of scale and expertise by dividing tasks further, and as specialists with their limited knowledge come to outnumber generalists, formalized methods are required to coordinate and control their work. Informal custom becomes inadequate to control large numbers of personnel. This process is accelerated where there is a large owning group, because the organization will develop local specialists as counterparts to head office specialisms, and head office will lay down procedures and documentation that all subsidiaries must use. Every executive of a subsidiary in any country, given half a chance, will complain of the amount and type of paperwork and irrelevant information that have to be supplied to the parent organization.

In all countries too, organizations which are more dependent on others in their environment are inclined to take decisions centrally and in addition lose autonomy to, say, a controlling board or to a government ministry above themselves. This is because ties of ownership or of contract with suppliers and customers are so important that the relevant decisions must be taken at the top. For example, if an enterprise purchases components from many different suppliers, decisions on each contract, including price, can be decentralized to the buying department. For some items even to junior buyers. But a long-term commitment to another firm, which itself invests in equipment so that it can supply the major raw material, is likely to require the chief executive's personal attention, thus leading to greater centralization.

Box 11.8 Two Main Pressures on Form of Organization

The Aston Research Programme was inaugurated at the University of Aston in Birmingham, England, by the present authors and their colleagues. It spanned several decades in the latter part of the twentieth century. A series of projects by the authors and collaborators elsewhere studied over 1000 organizations in fourteen countries to see what factors affected their management structures. The countries were Algeria, Canada, Egypt, France, Germany, India, Iran, Israel, Japan, Jordan, Poland, Sweden, UK, USA – at least one country from each of the slices of the world culture cake diagram at the end of Chapter 2.

The Aston studies measured features of organizations. For example, some organizations have many highly specialized jobs and departments; in others, personnel have broader jobs which cover several kinds of work. The extent of specialization was assessed in, say, marketing by asking whether there were specialists in market research, and in advertising and in public relations, in addition to the basic selling function. In finance, were there specialist wages clerks, accounts clerks, budgeting or financial data-processing specialists? The researchers were able to calculate a numerical score for each organization.

The results show the very strong effect of size of organization on this aspect of management structure. Larger organizations in all countries are likely to have more of these specialist jobs. They are also likely to have more formalized structures – measured by a count of the existence of documents and formal procedures on activities such as product inspection, stock control, staff recruitment and sales catalogues.

A second major influence, dependence, was shown to affect centralization (measured as described in Box 9.15). The most dependent organizations, such as small subsidiaries of large organizations or tightly regulated State-owned agencies have little autonomy left to them in making decisions (that is, decisions are centralized above them) and, in turn, centralize within themselves those few decisions that are allowed to them.

Summarizing the results:

1. The larger an organization, or any group which owns it (in number of employees), the greater the specialization and formalization are likely to be. This is a very strong effect.
2. The greater an organization's dependence on others, the greater its centralization is likely to be.

(from Pugh and Hickson; and Donaldson)

The prevalence of these processes in all countries studied is striking. Size and dependence become key elements in the explanation of the broad features of organizations worldwide (see Box 11.9). To understand the structure of an organization, it appears to be at least as important to know how large it is, who set it up and what its dependence on others is, as to know the country in which it is located. Certainly, the differences between organizations within one country can be greater than the average differences between countries.

Of course the pervasive effects of size and dependence do not mean that all organizations are becoming the same in structure. What this means is that organizations are influenced in the same ways by changes in these factors. For example, growth in size increases the likelihood of greater specialization of tasks. However, decline in size can eventually reduce it. So if organizations grow in one country but decline in another, they will become ever more different, not converging on an identical form of structure. Similarly for dependence and centralization: if dependence is increasing, so will centralization, but a reduction in dependence on others

---

Box 11.9 It's Not All Culture

It is unwise to jump to the conclusion that every difference found between organizations in different countries is due to culture. That is not the case. For example, the average specialization and formalization scores of the organizations studied by the Aston Programme in Jordan are less than half of those in the British organizations. Does this mean that Jordanian *culture* requires generalists who act informally? Perhaps. That is an Arab inclination.

But, before coming to this conclusion, the sizes of the organizations in the two samples must be taken into account. In Jordan, since it is a newly industrializing country, the organizations are much smaller (mean size 234, range 30–1,511 employees) than in the British sample (mean size 3,411, range 284–25,052 employees). Thus the low specialization and formalization may not be due to the particular Jordanian culture but to the smaller size of Jordanian organizations. This supposition can be tested quite directly because, if it were true, then *within Jordan*, although the overall level is less, the *relationship* between size and specialization would be the same as within Britain. Thus, larger Jordanian organizations would be more specialized and formalized than smaller ones. This was found to be the case.

As another example, the Aston research in Poland (as shown in Example 9.15) indicates that firms there were considerably more centralized than the British sample. Does this mean that there is something in the Polish culture which is conducive to centralized authority? Not necessarily. When this research was carried out, Poland was a communist, centrally planned economy; organizations there had a much higher degree of dependence on the State-prescribed system of finance, suppliers and 'buyers'. If this is the reason for the high centralization, then again we would find that within Poland at that time, although the overall level is higher, the relationship between dependence and centralization would be the same as within Britain. Thus more dependent Polish organizations will be more centralized than less dependent ones. This relationship was, indeed, found.

(adapted from Hickson and McMillan, and Pugh)

will lead to decentralization. So size and dependence are not in themselves convergence factors. Only if they change everywhere in the same direction will that be so.

They have actually been doing so, on the whole. Over the years, both have been increasing. Industrialization has produced larger organizations with, therefore, more specialization and formalization of their structures. It has tied more of them into more intricate dependence upon owning parent groups, the state, suppliers and customers or clients with consequent greater centralization. Hence the general push towards convergence in organizational form. Within that, of course, should there be a decline in organizational sizes due to economic recession, or the appearance of high-tech industries and services with small-scale units, or privatization out of state ownership, the trend would become more uneven, or perhaps be reversed.

Box 11.10 The Problem of the Deputy Manager

The American manager of a plant processing and packaging PVC in the USA had a Venezuelan deputy. The process required a high standard of quality control. The product had to be mixed in exactly the correct proportions or it was dangerous. Irregularity in mixing and blending had to be reported immediately it occurred and the line concerned closed down at once, or unsaleable product would accumulate. A decision to shut down was an expert one requiring detailed technical knowledge. Even a delay of minutes was extremely costly. It was better on the whole to shut down prematurely than to shut down too late.

The Venezuelan deputy knew very well when the product was satisfactory and when it was not. When his manager was away from the plant and he was in charge, he brought any line whose quality was failing to an immediate halt. His judgement was both fast and accurate. When the manager was on site, however, he would look for him, report what was happening and get a decision. In the time it took to do this, considerable product was wasted. However many times the deputy was told to act on his own, that his judgement was respected and that his decision would be upheld, he always reverted to checking first with his boss whenever he could.

The problem was a clash between two cultural attitudes. In a low power distance approach, like the American, it is less important who takes the decision than that it is the right one. Whether it is the boss or the deputy is determined by the needs of the technology and the task. In a high power distance culture, like the Venezuelan, a boss is like a father, and you do not usurp his authority and thereby show disrespect, when he is present. Personal feelings and relationships are more important than efficiency.

(adapted from Trompenaars)

CONVERGENCE

Increasing industrialization sustains the pressure for the managing of manufacturing organizations and of service organizations and, indeed of national and local government administration, to become more and more similar the world-over. More similarity in hierarchies (again see Box 11.1), more similarity in departments, similar decisions, similar means of internal communication via e-mail, and so on. This erodes culturally-based differences.

For example, the study of cultural differences by Hofstede described in Chapter 2 found that *power distance* was a key feature. In high power distance cultures it is expected both by those above and those below that most decisions will be taken by superiors. Inequality is accepted. In low power distance cultures the opposite applies. Subordinates more often want to decide for themselves. *Centralization* of authority to decide was found by the Aston studies described earlier in this chapter (Box 11.8) to be a key feature of any organization. Here the cultural feature, power distance and the organization feature, centralization, are directly linked.

Venezuelans are inclined to have high power distance values, Americans low power distance values (see Box 2.5). Venezuelans would more often be comfortable with a centralization of authority, Americans more often comfortable with decentralization. Therefore, we would expect that centralized firms in Venezuela would run more smoothly, since it would 'come naturally' to middle managers to refer decisions to ever higher authority. Decentralized firms would have more difficulty; middle managers would find it difficult to take responsibility for decisions, and by pushing them upwards to their bosses would themselves, in practice, be making the firm more centralized. In the USA it would be the other way round: centralized organizations would continually be pressed by lower levels to let them take decisions, or at least to participate, which would in practice be making the firm more decentralized. Box 11.10 gives a good example of what might occur when the two approaches mix. What is going to happen in this firm in the long term? Can the American PVC plant go on operating less efficiently than it might in order to accommodate the respectful, high power distance, Venezuelan deputy manager? As they are interested in efficiency, probably not – he will either have to change or go. But what about such a PVC plant in Venezuela? Can it survive if the high power distance attitudes there make it less efficient? In the short term, yes; for there will no doubt be other efficiencies, such as lower labour costs. But in the longer term, the convergence thesis would argue that the need to operate the costly high-technology plant to maximum efficiency will require a more decentralized approach in the deputy's job even there. Perhaps this could be achieved by appointing a Venezuelan with lower power distance attitudes. It is important to remember that there will be such managers. Hofstede's characterization of Venezuela is a blanket one and does not apply equally to 20 million people. If such a new deputy perseveres and succeeds, the management in the organization will have changed. It will have shifted in a decentralized direction as required to work the technology efficiently. The difference between Venezuelan and American management will have lessened.

Box 11.11 Selecting the International Manager

In a survey of the top managements of forty-eight British companies, Ashridge Management Research Group asked two questions:

1 What are the five most important characteristics of the international manager?

Characteristics chosen by more than 40% of firms:

Strategic awareness	71%
Adaptability to new situations	67%
Sensitivity to different cultures	60%
Ability to work in international teams	56%
Language skills	46%
Understanding international marketing	46%
Relationship skills	40%

2 What are the five most important criteria for *selecting* managers for international postings?

Criteria chosen by more than 40% of firms:

Technical skill/expertise for the job	85%
Potential of manager to develop in role	69%
Knowledge of company systems, procedures, etc.	63%
Understanding the market and customers	48%
Appropriate language skills	46%
Necessary component of career path	46%

(adapted from Barham and Oates)

These little-by-little changes of attitudes and behaviour in cultures, when they come into contact with other cultures, are characteristic of the way development takes place. Attempts at large-scale, quick changes – revolutions – do not appear to have a lasting impact. The wheel turns back virtually to where it started. As Chapter 7 describes, the Chinese 'Cultural Revolution' did not succeed in changing much when the dust had settled. Previous values reasserted themselves. Of course, since it devalued experience, education and training, all of which are necessary for efficient management, the 'revolution' was going against not only Confucian-saturated culture but the wider managerial convergence as well.

The technical and task basis of that convergence is shown again by the study in Box 11.11. This demonstrates the differences between what are supposed to be the key characteristics of an international manager (question 1) and the criteria actually used in firms (question 2) to select managers for international assignments. Even though human resource managers may realize the desirability of adaptability in new situations, sensitivity to different cultures, and the ability to work in international teams, and fear serious consequences if these qualities are lacking, technical and market demands come first. The needs of the organization to operate effectively worldwide ensure that it is technical skill, job expertise, managerial potential and knowledge of company systems and procedures which primarily determine who is actually selected to manage abroad. The universal task elements, which foster convergence, are put to the fore.

HOW FAR WHICH WAY?

The strength of the convergence case rests on the impact of industrialization, technological development and effective operation. According to this, management structure and methods derive from the tasks which need to be done efficiently. The same work must be done worldwide with the same management hierarchy, the same departmental specialization, the same financial and other controls and procedures, and this organizational framework gradually shapes those employed in it in the same way. The world is getting smaller, with easier and cheaper communications, travel and trade, and this encourages the cross-cultural learning which supports the case. Even American organizations (surely operating in a culture which is supremely economically viable) are being pressed to accept aspects of Japanese practice and attitudes which have been held to be more efficient.

The alternative case is that cultural differences in thinking, attitudes and values will always lead people to interpret technological changes, the very same technological changes, differently in different cultures, and to run the same systems in different ways.

One conclusion might be that both views are right. While the culture sets limits to what changes will be acceptable, it is the convergence pressures for efficiency which inaugurate those changes. Under some conditions (e.g. with rapidly developing technology) the pressures for convergence might gather enough momentum to win out completely; but more often quite significant differences persist to generate different but also viable ways of managing and organizing. Indeed the ability of cultures to accept outside technology, knowledge and skills but re-interpret them to fit sets limits on any convergent tendencies that there might be.

Box 11.12 What is a Considerate Supervisor?

Smith and his colleagues studied supervisory behaviour in electronics assembly plants in the USA, Hong Kong, Japan and Britain. In all the plants studied, supervisors who were 'considerate' towards the members of their work-teams were positively evaluated. So consideration appears to be a global value. But when workers were asked what their supervisors should do to be regarded as considerate, it was found that supervisors have to do rather different things to earn approval in the different countries.

For example, one question asked what a supervisor should do if a member of the team is experiencing personal difficulties. In Hong Kong and Japan, workers said that to discuss the problem with other members of the team in the worker's absence would be a considerate thing to do. In these Asian cultures problems can be shared, and what to do can be collectively discussed. But in the USA and Britain, on the contrary, any public discussion was regarded as a very inconsiderate thing to do. In these Anglo cultures, someone else's personal problems should not be aired in public, but kept private. So clearly, although to be considerate is a general virtue, how to be considerate may be very different.

(adapted from Smith *et al.*)

So, although there may be similarities across cultures in what managers do, there will also be clear differences – often within those similarities. Another good example is given in Box 11.12. This examines the way in which the same concept of 'a considerate supervisor' is interpreted very differently in different countries.

The differences in what is expected by workers from a considerate supervisor clearly fit well with the portrayals of the Asian and Anglo cultures in Chapters 7 and 3. In Hong Kong and Japan a considerate supervisor would discuss a worker's personal problems with other members of the group because they are collectivist cultures with high-context subtle speech. As the emphasis is on 'we', the group would want to help. Since they have high-context speech, the group members would want to know about the problems so that they may allude to them only by saying what is appropriate, thus avoiding any affront to or shame on the worker.

In the USA and Britain, on the other hand, a considerate supervisor would not discuss a worker's personal problems with other members of the group. Because they are individualist cultures with low-context more direct speech, identity is based on individuality and there is only limited commitment to the work organization through the specific job. The work group, as a group, would not regard it as proper to be concerned with personal non-work problems; this could be regarded as an unwelcome intrusion into privacy. Since the speech is low context, a worker who wants personal help can ask someone else directly. If so, that person, even if it is the supervisor, should not disclose to others what is said on a non-work personal issue. Such a basic difference as this is deeply set in the societal culture.

So whatever management techniques are used, they are likely to be adapted by each culture to the needs of that culture. The way in which one of the classic 'Anglo' techniques, Management by Objectives, has been interpreted in other cultures is shown in Box 11.13.

Box 11.13 Management by Objectives in Different Cultures

Management by Objectives (MbO) is an example of a management procedure which has had great textbook popularity in many countries. It means boss and subordinate sitting down together to frankly talk over how well the subordinate has done. They then agree what the subordinate will aim at in the months ahead, aims which ideally are proposed by the subordinate who is therefore personally committed to them. How well does this operate in different cultures? It started in the United States and was used there to spread a pragmatic results-orientation throughout all levels of an organization. It has had most success there, particularly in situations where results can be objectively measured rather than only subjectively judged. It has its limitations and has received much criticism, but it proved to be one of the most popular American management techniques in the twentieth century. It fits the American and, to a considerable extent, the Anglo cultures generally.

Why is this so? MbO requires that:

● Subordinates are sufficiently independent to negotiate meaningfully with the boss (that is, lower power distance).
● The subordinate is personally willing to 'have a go' and make a mark (that is, high individualism).
● Both are willing to take some risks – the boss in delegating power, the subordinate in accepting responsibility (that is, low uncertainty avoidance).
● Performance and results achieved are seen as important by both (that is, high masculinity).

This is the Anglo pattern.

How would MbO work out in other culture areas? In the northern European culture area as described in Chapter 5, for example, Germany has low power distance, which fits, as does the results-orientation of high masculinity. However, the Germanic group is high on uncertainty-avoidance, which would work against the risk-taking and ambiguity involved in the Anglo process. So whilst the idea of replacing the arbitrary personal authority of the boss with the impersonal authority of mutually agreed objectives fits very well with the low power distance of this culture, because of the greater German need to avoid uncertainty by orderly procedures, MbO has become 'Management by Joint Goal-Setting' and elaborate formal systems have been developed. There is also a greater stress on team objectives (as opposed to the individual emphasis in the Anglo culture) and this fits with the somewhat lower individualism of this culture area.

How would MbO work in France, from the Latin group of Chapter 4? Since this culture group has high power distance and high uncertainty avoidance – completely opposite to the Anglo group – difficulties would be expected. MbO had been introduced to France in the 1960s, and it gained popularity for a time as a new technique which would lead to the *long-overdue democratization of French organizations*. The French name for MbO became 'Participative Management by Objectives' – yet in practice the title never became more than a vain slogan.

The problem was that, from the French point of view, a hierarchical structure protects against anxiety, whereas MbO generates anxiety. In a high power distance culture, attempting to substitute the personal authority of the boss by self-monitored objectives is bound to generate anxiety, since the boss does not delegate easily and will not stop overruling the supposedly delegated authority – and the subordinate will expect this to happen and to be told what to do. In such a culture, anxiety will be alleviated by sticking to the old ways.

(adapted from Hofstede)

Cultural differences, therefore, have a major impact on how organizations function. From this point of view, manufacturing consumer products or treating the sick in France, as distinct from Japan or Britain, calls for structures and processes that have 'Frenchness'. Since national cultures change slowly, new technology, knowledge and skills will always be interpreted by each culture in its own way, and this will set firm limits on the tendencies to managerial convergence.

So is it to be convergence so far but no further? In some features and not in others? More apparent than real because practices which look the same are actually subtly different? On the one hand, changes so far have been towards a convergence in management. On the other hand, the burden of this book has been that we are what we are, changing only gradually at heart in our cultural identity.

Further Reading

Barham, K. and D. Oates. 1991. *The International Manager*. London: Economist Books.

Galbraith, J. K. 1978. *The New Industrial State* (revised edn). Penguin Books.

Hickson, D. J., and C. J. McMillan 1981. *Organization and Nation: The Aston Programme IV*. Gower Publishing.

Hofstede, G. 1980. 'Motivation, Leadership and Organization: Do American Theories Apply Abroad?' *Organizational Dynamics* (Summer), 42–63; reprinted in D. S. Pugh (ed.), *Organization Theory*. Penguin Books, 1990.

Mueller, Frank. 1994. 'Societal Effect, Organizational Effect and Globalization', *Organisation Studies*, 15, 3, 407–29.

Pugh, D. S. and D. J. Hickson. 1976. *Organizational Structure in its Context: The Aston Programme I*. Gower Publishing.

Trompenaars, F. 1993. *Riding the Waves of Culture*. London: Economist Books.

Other Sources

Donaldson, L. 1986. 'Size and Bureaucracy in East and West: A Preliminary Meta Analysis', in S. R. Clegg, D. C. Dunphy and S. G. Redding (eds.), *The Enterprise and Management in East Asia*. Centre for Asian Studies, the University of Hong Kong.

Kerr, C., J. T. Dunlop, F. H. Harbison and C. A. Myers. 1960. *Industrialism and Industrial Man*. Harvard University Press.

Luthans, F., D. H. B. Welsh and S. A. Rosenkrantz, 1993. 'What do Russian Managers Really Do? An Observational Study with Comparisons to US Managers'. *Journal of International Business Studies*, 24, 4, 741–61.

Pugh, D. S. 1993. 'The Convergence of International Organizational Behaviour', in T. Weinshall (ed.), *Culture and Management*. Berlin. De Gruyter.

Pugh, Derek S. (ed.). 1998. *The Aston Programme: Vol. I Developments, Vol. II International Comparisons, Vol. III Extensions and Critiques*. Ashgate/Dartmoor

Redding, S. Gordon. 1994. 'Comparative Management Theory: Jungle, Zoo, or Fossil Bed', *Organization Studies*, 15, 3, 323–61.

Smith, P. B., J. Misumi, M. Tayeb, M. F. Peterson and M. H. Bond. 1989. 'On the Generality of Leadership Styles Across Cultures'. *Journal of Occupational Psychology*, 62, 97–100.

Tannenbaum, A. S. 1986. 'Controversies about Control and Democracy in Organizations', in R. N. Stern and S. McCarthy (eds.), *The International Yearbook of Organizational Democracy, Vol III*. Wiley.

Name Index

Subject Index

Chapter 5: The Northern Europeans, and Israel

Chapter 8: The Arabs of the Middle East

READ MORE IN PENGUIN

In every corner of the world, on every subject under the sun, Penguin represents quality and variety – the very best in publishing today.

For complete information about books available from Penguin – including Puffins, Penguin Classics and Arkana – and how to order them, write to us at the appropriate address below. Please note that for copyright reasons the selection of books varies from country to country.

In the United Kingdom: Please write to *Dept. EP, Penguin Books Ltd, Bath Road, Harmondsworth, West Drayton, Middlesex UB7 0DA*

In the United States: Please write to *Consumer Services, Penguin Putnam Inc., 405 Murray Hill Parkway, East Rutherford, New Jersey 07073-2136*. VISA and MasterCard holders call 1-800-631-8571 to order Penguin titles

In Canada: Please write to *Penguin Books Canada Ltd, 10 Alcorn Avenue, Suite 300, Toronto, Ontario M4V 3B2*

In Australia: Please write to *Penguin Books Australia Ltd, 487 Maroondah Highway, Ringwood, Victoria 3134*

In New Zealand: Please write to *Penguin Books (NZ) Ltd, Private Bag 102902, North Shore Mail Centre, Auckland 10*

In India: Please write to *Penguin Books India Pvt Ltd, 11 Community Centre, Panchsheel Park, New Delhi 110017*

In the Netherlands: Please write to *Penguin Books Netherlands bv, Postbus 3507, NL-1001 AH Amsterdam*

In Germany: Please write to *Penguin Books Deutschland GmbH, Metzlerstrasse 26, 60594 Frankfurt am Main*

In Spain: Please write to *Penguin Books S. A., Bravo Murillo 19, 1°B, 28015 Madrid*

In Italy: Please write to *Penguin Italia s.r.l., Via Vittorio Emanuele 45/a, 20094 Corsico, Milano*

In France: Please write to *Penguin France, 12, Rue Prosper Ferradou, 31700 Blagnac*

In Japan: Please write to *Penguin Books Japan Ltd, Iidabashi KM-Bldg, 2-23-9 Koraku, Bunkyo-Ku, Tokyo 112-0004*

In South Africa: Please write to *Penguin Books South Africa (Pty) Ltd, P.O. Box 751093, Gardenview, 2047 Johannesburg*

READ MORE IN PENGUIN

BUSINESS AND ECONOMICS

Webonomics   Evan I. Schwartz

In *Webonomics*, Evan I. Schwartz defines nine essential principles for growing your business on the Web. Using case studies of corporations such as IBM and Volvo, as well as smaller companies and web-based start-ups, Schwartz documents both the tremendous failures and the successes on the Web in a multitude of industries.

Inside Organizations   Charles B. Handy

Whatever we do, whatever our profession, organizing is a part of our lives. This book brings together twenty-one ideas which show you how to work with and through other people. There are also questions at the end of each chapter to get you thinking on your own and in a group.

Lloyds Bank Small Business Guide   Sara Williams

This long-running guide to making a success of your small business deals with real issues in a practical way. 'As comprehensive an introduction to setting up a business as anyone could need' *Daily Telegraph*

Teach Yourself to Think   Edward de Bono

Edward de Bono's masterly book offers a structure that broadens our ability to respond to and cope with a vast range of situations. *Teach Yourself to Think* is software for the brain, turning it into a successful thinking mechanism, and, as such, will prove of immense value to us all.

The Road Ahead   Bill Gates

Bill Gates – the man who built Microsoft – takes us back to when he dropped out of Harvard to start his own software company and discusses how we stand on the brink of a new technology revolution that will for ever change and enhance the way we buy, work, learn and communicate with each other.

BY THE SAME AUTHORS

Writers on Organizations

Who has said what about organizations and their management?

This handy compendium gives easy access to the principal ideas of the leading authorities, while brief, clear resumés bring out the main thrust of their thinking.

This fifth edition of an evergreen resource for student and manager alike adds Charles Handy, Andrew Pettigrew, Gareth Morgan, Karl E. Weick, Peter Senge, Paul J. DiMaggio and Walter W. Powell, and Christopher Bartlett and Sumantra Ghoshal to the wide range of experts whose work is summarized.

The authors cover a range of topics from the structure and national and international environments of organizations to management problems, and from managerial decision-making and influence to people problems and organizational change and learning. Derek S. Pugh and David J. Hickson have created a classic work that accompanies executives on management courses and helps management students in writing essays and exams. It has been translated into numerous languages worldwide. A companion volume, *Organization Theory*, edited by Derek S. Pugh, is also published by Penguin.

FIFTH EDITION